Designing for Playful Engagement in Museums

Designing for Playful Engagement in Museums is filled with creative fodder for practitioners who wish to make more memorable and engaging experiences that promote a sense of presence, effectively evoke emotions, tell stories that transport them, and harness visitors' innate playfulness.

Providing readers with a framework for understanding playful engagement, Rodley details four concepts that, when used effectively, can create a new generation of compelling visitor experiences. This book combines research and examples from the cultural and for-profit sectors with new insights from current research in psychology, neuroscience, and human-computer interaction to explore why these concepts are valuable to designers. Reflections from leading practitioners from around the globe and across the experience design spectrum provide unique insights into the current state of practice. This is augmented by examples from the author's 30-plus years of experience developing visitor experiences in a variety of science, art, and history museums.

Designing for Playful Engagement in Museums provides practitioners with a concrete way of thinking about engagement that centers on visitors. This book will be of particular interest to professionals in museums, libraries, and archives, but will also be essential reading for academics and students engaged in the study of museums, heritage, digital humanities, and experience design.

Ed Rodley is an award-winning experience designer and a Co-Founder and Principal at The Experience Alchemists (TEA), an experience design firm serving the cultural sector and beyond. Before starting TEA, Ed was Associate Director of Integrated Media at Peabody Essex Museum (PEM) in Salem, Massachusetts, USA.

Routledge Guides to Practice in Museums, Galleries and Heritage

This series provides essential practical guides for those working in museums, galleries, and a variety of other heritage professions around the globe.

Including authored and edited volumes, the series will help to enhance practitioners' and students' professional knowledge and will also encourage sharing of best practices between different countries, as well as between different types and sizes of organisations.

Titles published in the series include:

Practitioner Perspectives on Intangible Cultural Heritage
Joanne Orr

An Introductory Guide to Qualitative Research in Art Museums
Edited by Ann Rowson Love and Deborah Randolph

Institutional Change for Museums
A Practical Guide to Creating Polyvocal Spaces
Edited by Marianna Pegno and Kantara Souffrant

Ethics of Contemporary Collecting
Edited by Jen Kavanagh, Ellie Miles and Rosamund Lily
West with Susanna Cordner

Cultivating Futures Thinking in Museums
Edited by Dr Kristin Alford

Leadership of Inclusive and Sustainable Cultural Organisations
A Practical Guide
Piotr Bienkowski And Hilary Mcgowan

For more information about this series, please visit: https://www.routledge.com/Routledge-Guides-to-Practice-in-Museums-Galleries-and-Heritage/book-series/RGPMGH

Designing for Playful Engagement in Museums

Immersion, Emotion, Narrative, and Gameplay

Ed Rodley

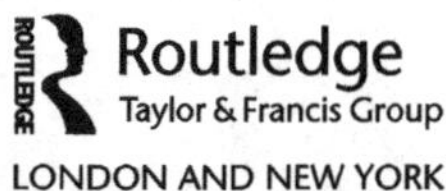

Routledge
Taylor & Francis Group

LONDON AND NEW YORK

Designed cover image: Photo by the author, Ed Rodley

First published 2025
by Routledge
4 Park Square, Milton Park, Abingdon, Oxon OX14 4RN

and by Routledge
605 Third Avenue, New York, NY 10158

Routledge is an imprint of the Taylor & Francis Group, an informa business

British Library Cataloguing-in-Publication Data
A catalogue record for this book is available from the British Library

ISBN: 9781032638683 (hbk)
ISBN: 9781032638676 (pbk)
ISBN: 9781032638690 (ebk)

DOI: 10.4324/9781032638690

Typeset in Times New Roman
by codeMantra

To Jennifer, who makes everything possible.
And to my children; Phoebe, Rhys, Connor, and Conor

Contents

Foreword

Sebastian Chan
CEO, ACMI the Australian Centre for the Moving Image

A quarter of the way into the 21st century, collectively, people have much to seize their attention spans, their mental focus, and to be 'engaged' with or 'immersed' in. We are chided if we are not 'engaged' productively—in politics, in leisure, in our communities. It is no wonder that in the early 2020s, there have been rolling moral panics about 'quiet quitting' in the US (Newport, 2022) and the Tang Ping ('lie flat') movement in China (Wikipedia n.d.).

Even though the phrase 'experience economy' was originally coined in 1998 by economists B. Joseph Pine II and James Gilmore, in which 'guests' sought the novel 'sensations' of 'memorable' 'experiences' (Pine and Gilmore 1998), the phrase took two decades to reach common parlance in museum discourse in the Global North.

In this heavily media-saturated and 'mediated' period of history, museums have responded by spending a lot of effort, and money, to redesign their exhibitions, their galleries, their buildings, and sometimes even their operational structures, to be 'more engaging' and 'more immersive.' Inspired and informed by the poorly understood logics of the Web and online 'digital culture,' museums have been drawn, unwittingly, into a framing which places them in competition with every other form of entertainment and for-profit media organization (e.g., Barber and Szántó 2024). This negative framing does little to allow museums to make a persistent case for what is uniquely theirs. The failure of the non-profit sector to find a common language for measuring impacts and outcomes, or even a theory of change approach, has exacerbated this drift toward the logics of an advertising and transactional model of culture.

Complicating matters further, the early 2020s, riven with sociopolitical tensions, war, and two years of the COVID-19 global pandemic, museums and their workers are now more on edge. If museums are seen to need to 'compete' with other forms of leisure and entertainment, then this competition is occurring in a time of decreased consumer spending, decreased philanthropic and governmental support, too.

In the more optimistic times of 2011 and 2012, Ed Rodley, Suse Anderson, Nancy Proctor, and I began an online discussion about Punchdrunk theater's *Sleep*

No More, a blockbuster 'immersive theater' production from the UK that had just begun its more-than-decade long run in New York (see Chan 2012, Anderson 2012; Rodley 2013). The four of us and then many more in the exhibition and design-related fields of the museum sector were excited by what this form of high production, high capital, immersive theater might mean for museum design. The multisensorial immersion—the 'sensation'—of *Sleep No More* with its embrace of smell and sound—two underutilized senses in traditional museum design—was exciting and novel, and challenged many of us.

At the same point in time, smartphone adoption had transformed how museum visitors came to museums. In the early years of the 2010s, the affordances of smartphones were championed by museum designers for enabling visitors to engage with exhibitions in new ways with location-aware audio tours, augmented reality, and just the simple ability for visitors to fact check whatever they were interested in. At the same time, they were also challenged by museums who also realized that they also interrupted the focus and 'flow' that exhibition designers, educators, and curators sought from visitors.

This was also the decade in which 'experience design' became a widely used phrase in museums as museums across the world went through a boom of major capital redevelopments during the 2010s (e.g., Kafka 2023). This coincided with the rise of 'user experience' or 'UX design' morphing from a narrow sub-category of digital product design into a plethora of short training courses run by educational startups like General Assembly and online trainers Skillshare. (Ironically, the tipping point for this moment might have been my appointment by the Australian Centre for the Moving Image as the first 'Chief Experience Officer' (Grey 2015) in the museum sector—a title that subsequently proliferated—but has now been retired by the institution.)

Once the preserve of exhibition design companies who were contracted by museums, the language of 'immersion' and 'engagement' has now become diffused across the inner workings of the museum itself. For-profit companies now mirror the platform logics of the 2020s-era services in order to find the necessary scale to please investors and shareholders, whilst the not-for-profit sector struggles with clarity of purpose and definition.

Fortunately, Ed Rodley's book charts a path for museums to better understand just what 'engagement' might mean, and what is required to deliver its promise effectively.

References

Anderson, Suse 2012. *Behavioural Priming and Museum Visitation*. https://museumgeek. xyz/2012/11/18/behavioural-priming-and-museum-visitation/

Barber, Felix & Szántó, András 2024. *Immersive Art Is Exploding, and Museums Have a Choice to Make.* Artnews.com, 24 Aug 2024 - https://www.artnews.com/art-news/ opinion/immersive-art-industry-and-museums-1234715051/

Chan, Seb 2012. *On Sleep No More, Magic and Immersive Storytelling.* https://www. freshandnew.org/2012/05/sleep-more-magic-immersive-storytelling/

Grey, Tim 2015. *What's a 'Chief Experience Officer'?*. Broadsheet, 9 Nov 2015, - https://www.broadsheet.com.au/melbourne/entertainment/article/engineering-better-experiences

Kafka, George 2023. *Follow the Money: Building the Museum.* The Architectural Review - https://www.architectural-review.com/essays/keynote/follow-the-money-building-the-museum

Newport, Cal 2022. *The Year in Quiet Quitting.* New Yorker, 29 Dec 2022 - https://www.newyorker.com/culture/2022-in-review/the-year-in-quiet-quitting

Pine II, B. Joseph, and Gilmore, James H. 1998. *Welcome to the Experience Economy.* Harvard Business Review, Jul-Aug 1998.

Rodley, Ed 2013. *On Immersion, Theatre, and Museums.* https://thinkingaboutmuseums.com/2013/01/14/on-immersion-theatre-and-museums/

Tang Ping in Wikipedia. n.d. - https://en.wikipedia.org/wiki/Tang_ping

Preface

Where This Book Came From

This book is about connecting with people and what happens to them when you're successful, in other words, "engagement." The bulk of this book is devoted to exploring four ways to enhance engagement: emotion, immersion, storytelling, and gameplay, but it begins, as all good stories do, with an origin story. In late 2018, I was stuck in an aisle seat on a nine-hour long redeye flight from Athens to Boston on my way back from a workshop on emotional storytelling in museums. As I started sketching out a blog post on the topic of emotion, I started listing other events I'd been to over the previous couple of years and realized that the same concepts kept popping up, namely the four concepts in the subtitle of this book. One blog post turned into four. As I sleepily started unpacking memories of those events, each of those four blog posts turned into a series of blog posts. One post became 4 became 16. But these concepts didn't usually travel alone, as the workshop combining emotion and storytelling exemplified. And where you'd meet one concept, there'd be at least one other and often more. It was at that point I realized that what I had sketched out was a book.

This book is not intended to establish the borders of museum experience design or describe a comprehensive list of tools and techniques needed to create playful engagement. These four concepts are by no means the sum total of all the things that can make something playfully engaging. They are, however, ones that come up frequently in research around engaging visitors in museum contexts, and usually in association with each other.

Museum experience design is a messy business, despite the polished appearance of its products. As a designer, I spend most of my life in that mess, so I wanted to make some sense of it and expose an order that seemed to be revealing itself to me. Teasing out the intersections and interactions between these concepts might help me better deploy them in my work and create products that had what ubiquitous computing pioneer Mark Weiser called "beautiful seams" so that others could see how a thing was built and recognize the constituent elements (Weiser 1994). Writing this book is part of that process, a way to deepen my own understanding and open up the ideas for constructive criticism and useful dialogue that hopefully gives us a way of talking about what happens to people in museum settings when they engage with the products of our labor.

Who Should Read This Book

This book is geared to people who are involved or want to be involved in making museum experiences, be they digital, analogue, or hybrid. It assumes you already know something about how to make programs, exhibitions, websites, or things-without-easy-to-remember-names, and want to do more, and do it better. It is meant for the boundary pushers, those practitioners who want to try different approaches and want theoretical support, research data, and examples to help them evolve their practice and that of the institutions they work with and for.

If you are a student or emerging professional, this book is meant to give you a solid theoretical framework for building your own practice and a lens through which to critique the field you are going to be tasked with evolving. If you are already an experience designer, this book is meant to provide you with an array of examples and research findings to allow you to explore new modes of museum experience making. If you are a senior executive, this book is meant to give you the tools to go deeper than the shallow "We need to do VR!" or "If we make a game, it'll appeal to the kids!" responses to new technologies that are costly, untried, and outside your experience, and channel that pressure into productive conversations about outcomes, impact, and most of all; the people we serve.

This book is *not* a how-to guide for making apps or exhibitions. Those books already exist and McLean (1993), Lord and Piacente (2014), and Walhimer (2021) are just a few of the ones you should check out if you're new to museums. More can be found in the References section in each chapter of this book and on the website.

How This Book Is Organized

Though this book started life as a series of blogposts about four concepts, the final product has evolved into a decidedly different form. As I looked for commonalities between immersion, emotion, storytelling, and games, I realized that a larger question about engagement loomed over all of them. I naively assumed I'd find a definition of visitor engagement that suited my needs and use that to tie my four concepts together. What I found was more complicated, many descriptions and "definitions" of engagement, none of which described what I wanted to know, namely what is happening in the mind and body of a visitor in the act of being engaged by something in a museum. So, I had to make my own. Chapter 1 retraces that journey and does a lot of introducing and defining the terms and ideas that have had profound impact on my work. It touches on the nature of experience, experience design, and engagement and proposes a particular kind of engagement that I call "playful engagement" as a way of describing the magic that happens when people encounter our work and are moved by it.

The next four chapters each focus on one of the four concepts and explores how and why it is useful to us in our quest to engage visitors. The chapters survey the scientific literature to unpack what research says about how that element affects the human body and brain, and how people can and do explicitly design experiences based on this knowledge. Along the way, each chapter includes sidebars that present additional content. There are two to three additional examples of places you can go to explore each element "in the wild," and brief reflections from museum leaders and experts from outside the field to provide more depth on specific topics.

My Background and Professional Journey

When I was a kid, the Museum of Science, Boston was the center of my world. I volunteered there from ages 11 to 16, and later worked a wide variety of front of house, entry-level jobs. The ways it shaped me are manifold. It was there that I made my first friends who didn't live in my neighborhood. It was there that I was introduced to the wonders of Dungeons and Dragons and all its lessons in participatory storytelling. It was there I learned the joy of sharing things I knew with people who didn't yet know them. It was there I learned what it meant to be part of a team. And though it was a workplace, it was never just a workplace. I met my first girlfriend there, and later met my future wife while we were working as guards. I also learned how to drink, smoke, goof off, and many other things. The point is this: the museum was not just a workplace, it was my world. I literally grew up in museums.

It is deeply important to me therefore that museums evolve and slough off their shameful inheritances of colonialism, racism, sexism, and all the other forms of oppression we need to interrogate in the 21st century. American curator Helen Molesworth (2018) mirrored a lot of my doubts when she wrote,

> The museum, the Western institution I have dedicated my life to, with its familiar humanist offerings of knowledge and patrimony in the name of empathy and education, is one of the greatest holdouts of the colonialist enterprise. Its fantasies of possession and edification grow more and more wearisome as the years go by … I confess that more days than not I find myself wondering whether the whole damn project of collecting, displaying, and interpreting culture might just be unredeemable.

Unlike Molesworth—who I believe was engaging in the "art museums=all museums" framing that is so common in the art museum world—I don't think the entire enterprise is unredeemable…yet. Different parts of the sector struggle and strive in different ways, and successes in one area don't easily map onto another.[1] There are successes, though. Look at the evolving conversations on decolonization, restitution, pay equity, unionization, and transparency. Endemic, longstanding problems with our sector are suddenly being surfaced, talked about, argued over, and problematized in ways that would have been unimaginable to my circa 1990 self or even my 2010 self. People out there are working on improving our cultural heritage institutions, making them better, holding them to account to uphold their missions to be of use to society, as John Dewey argued over a century ago. The paradigmatic crisis the sector finds itself in is dire, but I am also heartened by all the people out there trying to find new ways to help our communities. And if we adopt the mindset that our work should be viewed cyclically that Puawai Cairns (NDF 2023) has proposed, then that work is never finished, just like a garden is never "finished," only tended or abandoned. I am often reminded of a quote from Voltaire, who famously ends "Candide" with his hero saying, "Allons mes amis, il faut cultiver nos jardins." "Come friends, we must tend to our gardens." That always lifts my spirits. So, how do *we* tend to *our* gardens? Hopefully, this book will provide you with food for thought and things to try.

Acknowledgments

It seems only appropriate to acknowledge the many privileges I've benefited from, the biases I try to overcome, and some of the many debts I owe. This is not meant to be performative, but to give you, the reader, an idea of what experiences have led me to write the book you're about to read. I hope that you'll read it therefore as a critical friend. If you come across something later on that doesn't ring true to your experience, it's worth asking yourself, "is it me, or are his biases showing?" because they're in here. No amount of revising or editing can catch every slip or misstep. It's also worth asking me. My goal in writing this book is to spark dialogue, so find me online and ask!

My Privileges

I've had the privilege of working at large, well-funded museums for the first 30 years of my career. The benefits of that are numerous. I had large budgets to work with, large teams of collaborators inside and outside of museums, and most importantly, I think, the opportunity to travel widely. My museum work has taken me all over the world, to all kinds of cultural organizations, and my practice has been nurtured by that exposure. I also realize the extent to which I've benefited from the invisible privileges of being a straight white man. My way has been considerably easier than that of many of my colleagues and I acknowledge that. I am committed to do my part to make sure that *all* our successors are free from the indignities and inequities of the current museum field.

My Biases (At Least the Ones I'm Aware of…)

As an American who has worked mainly with American museums, my default viewpoint is therefore attuned to the idiosyncrasies of the U.S. cultural scene. America's conflicted relationship with the very idea of "culture" colors everything in my daily work, though I try to notice and rise above it.

My academic background is in anthropology and archaeology, and, despite my father's skepticism about its utility, I use that body of theory every day. Trying to understand the locals and their ways has become a second nature to me, regardless of where I go. I also came up in the field as a self-identified educator. At my core, I am interested in making experiences that teach as well as entertain.

The bulk of my experience has been working for private institutions. I'm less aware of the realities faced by many of my colleagues who work at national museums and have the complication of being organs of the state as well as cultural institutions. I understand it intellectually, but it's harder to really get it without living it.

I spent much of my career bristling at people who said "museums" when they clearly meant "art museums" and felt that erasure keenly. I amazed myself by making the same slip once I started working in an art museum and I apologize. This book is meant to be broadly applicable to museums of every stripe. When I say "museums" I mean "all museums."

My Debts

Nobody gets far in this field alone. The work is too complex, and the landscape doesn't tend to be well-marked, so guides are essential. I have gotten where I am today only with the help of many, many colleagues and friends. I can't hope to list all my debts, but I want to acknowledge some of the most important ones.

Jan Crocker gave me my start as a museum professional. Her mentorship, passion for the work, and friendship have been a constant blessing. She taught me what it meant to be a professional and the difference between taking the work seriously and taking oneself seriously. She also made clear to me that part of my job was to leave the field better than I found it for the next generation. She demonstrated what speaking truth to power looked like in the workplace and taught me that lifelong learning should be a constant feature of one's work life. Thanks, boss!

The fact that I'm able to write anything sensibly owes everything to Judy Rand. I thought I knew how to be a writer, until I had Judy as an editor. I can't think of a better boot camp for a young exhibit developer than working under her benevolent, ruthless oversight. I have never been as productive as when I had a document full of her insightful comments, and an intricate, interlocking cascade of looming deadlines. That alone would be enough to earn her a place in my heart, but her work as an interpretive planner and developer has been something I constantly return to. Go read her 2001 article, *The 227-Mile Museum, or, Why We Need a Visitors' Bill of Rights*. Her emphasis on the importance of knowing who you're serving and articulating ideas clearly, before *anything* else can happen, has been utterly transformative to my practice. And her friendship has been priceless.

I wouldn't be where I am today without Mike Alexander, who inherited the department I was in after a painful layoff and reorganization. Suddenly faced with a bunch of new direct reports who did something completely different than the rest of his staff and outside his own expertise, he did the best he could to not just manage us, but to mentor us just like the rest of his people. We had many fraught talks about jobs and careers at a time when I was stuck in my own. Mike embodied how a compassionate leader acts in tough times. His willingness to have the difficult conversations as well as the pleasant ones is something I will always be grateful for and have tried to carry with me. In no small measure, this book is one of the fruits of those conversations.

The year 2020 was miserable for me, like so many others. In my case, it started off with caring for my dying mother, and segued straight into getting laid off at the height of the pandemic. What made up for that were Annie Lundsten and Jim Olson. Our many, many Zoom conversations that year morphed into us deciding to start a company during a global pandemic, and I cannot imagine better partners and friends with which to take that terrible plunge. Their deep belief in the value of the work and complete unwillingness to go along with a status quo that none of us liked have been the bedrock upon which The Experience Alchemists has been built, from its public benefit corporation structure to its circle of creative partners. I am grateful for them every day I go to work and continually honored that they asked me to come along with them.

Some of the Communities and People Who Helped Build This Book

- Alibis for Interaction
    Sebastian Deterding, Johanna Koljonen, Bjarke Peterson
- Immersive Design Summit
    Ida Benedetto, Noah Nelson, Sean Stewart, Jenny Weinbloom
- EMOTIVE-EU
    Maria Economou, Conny Graft, Sara Perry, Maria Roussou, Alyson Webb
- Digital Storytelling in Museums project #DSMuse
    Kate Haley-Goldman, Annie Polland, Amelia Wong
- Clash of Realities conference
    Eric Zimmerman
- Connected Culture and Natural Heritage in a Northern Environment (CINE)-EU
    Skuli Bjorn Gunnarson, Lemke Meijer
- National Digital Forum (NDF)
    Puawai Cairns, Lucie Paterson, Frith Williams
- International Council of Museums (ICOM) International Committee for Exhibitions (ICEE)
    Maggie Greyson, Linda Norris, Hillary Spencer

References

Lord, Barry, & Piacente, Maria 2014. *Manual of Museum Exhibitions*. Rowman & Littlefield Publishers.

McLean, Kathleen & Association of Science-Technology Centers. 1993. Planning for People in Museum Exhibitions. Association of Science-Technology Centers.

Molesworth, Helen. 2018. "Art is Medicine." Artforum. 2018. https://www.artforum.com/print/201803/helen-molesworth-on-the-work-of-simone-leigh-74304.

NDF—National Digital Forum (Director). 2023, November 19. Puawai Cairns—Live Keynote at NDF23 [Video recording]. https://www.youtube.com/watch?v=5TiUh8VNd9w

Rand, Judy 2001. The 227-Mile Museum, or Why We Need a Visitors' Bill of Rights. *Curator: The Museum Journal*, vol. 44, no. 1, 2001, pp. 7–14.
Walhimer, Mark 2021. *Designing Museum Experiences*. Rowman & Littlefield Publishers.
Weiser, Mark 1994. Creating the Invisible Interface. *Proceedings of the 7th Annual ACM Symposium on User Interface Software and Technology*, UIST '94, 1.

Note

1 The 2019 debacle at the International Council of Museums (ICOM) about updating the definition of the word "museum" gave an indication of how fraught things are.

1 The Magic Circle of the Visitor Experience

There is a certain magic in reading a book. You enter a text, and you enter a new world where you have powers you don't have in the real world. Sometimes, you're omniscient and know what the characters in the story are thinking and feeling. You experience time in multiple ways. You inhabit the minds and lives of others. You learn things and feel things you might never learn or feel in your ordinary life. And then when you stop, you re-enter your everyday, default world. You're still you. The events in the book didn't actually happen to you. And yet, sometimes, you are changed by the experience. Magic.

The same magic happens to people when they enter a museum building or heritage site. Whatever they were before, they become someone new when they cross that threshold. They become a "visitor" and a seeker of ... something. It might be learning, it might be contemplation, it might just be a couple hours respite from their routine, or a chance to socialize. They come to engage with art, history, science, the natural world, and whatever that museum offers. Often, they don't really have a specific goal for their visit, but they come hoping that *something* will engage their attention and speak to their condition. They come looking for that magic.

This is where you come in.

In this chapter, I will introduce a way of thinking about museum experiences that's drawn from sociology and play theory; that of "the magic circle," a designed space where participants interact with things and each other with the support of explicit guidelines that allow them to take on new roles and personae and emerge hopefully having had a meaningful, satisfying time. I'll then introduce and describe key terms that will occur throughout the book: experience, experience design, and engagement. I will define a particular variety of engagement I call *playful engagement* and advocate for an experience design approach to making playful museum experiences as a more holistic alternative to the traditional silos of content and design. I will end the chapter by introducing four crucial concepts for creating playful engagement: sensory immersion, emotional evocation, narrative transportation, and gameful participation.

The heart of this book (Chapters 2–5) presents a discussion of each of these four concepts that strives to avoid the hype-based commentary that surrounds all four. As Brett Davidson said about narrative, "there is always a danger when a term becomes a trend, because it starts to become a short-cut for thinking – a term

DOI: 10.4324/9781032638690-1

without precision – where everybody thinks they know what it means, but nobody really does for sure" (Davidson 2016, p. 2). This is my attempt to know what they mean to me. These concepts are entangled in complex ways, but I think it is useful to explore them first individually, noting the overlaps, before trying to see them holistically. The concluding chapter ties these all together and advocates for museum practitioners to seize the opportunities of the post-pandemic era to experiment and create new museum models that are fit for the 21st century and beyond.

Throughout this book, I'll ask you to do something museums ask of their visitors all the time: to roleplay. I want you to take on a persona that may be unfamiliar to you; that of an "experience designer," and imagine yourself as a person responsible for designing and creating all the sights, sounds, and scenes that those visitors will encounter and hopefully engage with, regardless of whether or not you have a job with the words "experience" or "designer" in the title. From this new vantage point as an experience designer, you can stand to the side of the current orthodoxies of the museum organizational charts and see whether designing for playful engagement makes new things possible. It's a lot of ground to cover, but you've expressed enough interest to pick up this book, so I trust you'll be willing to see it through to the end in the hopes of learning something new and hopefully useful. In this respect, I'm asking you to do exactly what museums ask of their visitors. "Trust us with your time, even if you don't know what to expect, and we'll make it worth your while."

The Magic Circle of the Museum: The Visitor, the Object, and the Alibi

I owe a lot to two books for reframing how I viewed my work and started me on my journey from being an exhibit developer to being an experience designer: Johan Huizinga's *Homo Ludens: A Study of the Play-Element in Culture* (1938), and Katie Salen Tekinbaş and Eric Zimmerman's *Rules of Play* (2003). Huizinga argued that our desire and aptitude for play is a defining characteristic of the species, hence "Homo Ludens" rather than "Homo Sapiens."[1] Using a variety of historical examples, he constructed a theory of play that placed it at the heart of human endeavors like religion, law, war, philosophy, and the arts. For Huizinga, play had three characteristics: it is *voluntary*, it is *not ordinary* or real, and it is *distinct* from "ordinary" life in both location and duration (p. 9). In describing where play happens, he wrote,

> All play moves and has its being within a playground marked off beforehand either materially or ideally, deliberately or as a matter of course. Just as there is no formal difference between play and ritual, so the "consecrated spot" cannot be formally distinguished from the play-ground. The arena, the card-table, the magic circle, the temple, the stage, the screen, the tennis court, the court of justice, etc., are all in form and function play-grounds, i.e. forbidden spots, isolated, hedged round, hallowed, within which special rules obtain. All are temporary worlds within the ordinary world, dedicated to the performance of an act apart.

(p. 10)

Museums, though not in Huizinga's list, certainly fit right in with theaters and temples as places where people perform "an act apart"; in the case of museums, the act performed is that of consuming (and maybe creating or participating in) culture. When I started my career in science museums, "play" was a loaded term, freighted with connotations of un-seriousness and childishness. I was an informal science educator—a serious professional—and play was not something I considered in my exhibit development work. Huizinga allowed me to realize how narrow my view of play had been, and how central the players were to the whole endeavor.

Katie Salen Tekinbaş and Eric Zimmerman plucked the words "magic circle" out of Huizinga's list and used them to stand in for "the idea of a special place in time and space created by a game" in their foundational book *Rules of Play* (2003).[2] They wrote, "To play a game means entering into a magic circle, or perhaps creating one as a game begins" (p. 95). I immediately recognized the museum visit as a kind of magic circle and was particularly interested in how Tekinbaş and Zimmerman's "magic circle" is *both* a boundary and a container. On the outside is the default world, and inside the magic circle is the play space. When people cross the circle's threshold, the rules change, norms change, and people's roles and behaviors change. What is discouraged in the default world can become acceptable inside the magic circle. The quiet, meek person who turns into a cutthroat poker player is just one example of how play redefines the rules, or at least establishes a different set while the play is occurring. In the same way, people entering a museum take on a new identity, that of "visitor" or "guest." They have the possibility of entering a world with very different rules and norms, and encouraged and discouraged behaviors, to the extent we are willing to design them. In this book, I adopt Jaakko Stenros' (2015) definition of the magic circle, "The idea of a magic circle of play is that as playing begins, a special space with a porous boundary is created though social negotiation" (p 12).

The idea of the magic circle spoke to me on many levels. As an exhibit developer, the parallel between the gallery entrance and the boundary of the circle was clear, and the idea that you could construct a temporary world for the people in that space was a holistic contrast to the more narrowly defined roles of developer, designer, curator, etc., each focused on their own smaller domain. And to be honest, the fact that the word "magic" was part of it spoke to me, because I'd seen that magic at work countless times over the years on visitors' faces. Magic captured both the elusiveness and ephemerality of success and also the lack of control one had over it as a designer. We can never directly design the behavior of visitors. Engagement is an emergent phenomenon; it is not always possible to anticipate how the thing you've designed will function once visitors begin using it. In this respect, museum experience design is a second-order design problem, much like game design. We can design the circumstances that allow the magic of "engagement" to happen, but we can't do that directly because it only comes about as a result of people volunteering their time and attention to engage with our creations. We create experience, but only indirectly.

Conceiving of the museum experience as a magic circle neatly encompassed all the theoretical advances that I'd lived through, like Stephen Weil's articulation of the shift from museums being about objects to being for people (Weil 1999), the visitor-centered approaches articulated by Falk and Dierking (2012), Samis and Michaelson (2016) and Wood and Latham's (2013) Object Knowledge Framework approach to reconciling museums' object-centric focus with the new audience-centric reality. But what the magic circle made clear to me was the third factor: Huizinga's "special rules" and their importance in constructively structuring the social negotiation that occurs.

So, what is in this magic circle? The magic circle of the museum experience for me comprises three elements. First and foremost, there is *the visitor*: the person who favors us with their time and attention. Next, *the object* or objects—which I construe very broadly to include the entire physical experience (artworks, artifacts, labels, media, environments, architecture)—that we design and build. Lastly, there is *the alibi*, the rules and social contract of a play space which give people a pretext to interact and feel safe doing so (Deterding 2017). We'll get deeper into each of the three in a bit more detail in the next section. The magic circle is similar to Falk and Dierking's conception of the three contexts of the museum experience: the personal, the social, and the physical (Falk and Dierking 2012). The distinction, for me, is that contexts felt like factors beyond my control, things to be aware of. As a designer, the components of the magic circle feel more concrete. I can design these rules and give that permission to engage.

Visitors are People

The vital part of the magic circle is *people*. It should go without saying that without people, all you have are empty buildings and unvisited websites. These people have traditionally been referred to as visitors, though the term has become a bit unfashionable in some quarters and is often replaced with terms usually lifted from other industries like "audience" or "guest." Often, what we want them to be is participants, active. A former director I worked for disliked the word "visitor" but also disliked all the synonyms and would refer to our audiences as "the people we serve." It doesn't trip off the tongue, but described what he wanted us to keep in mind; that visitors are first and foremost people. "Visitor" is a temporary role people take on when they interact with museums, in the same way that you become a "player" only as long as you are playing. "Visitor" also puts the agency where it belongs because a visitor has chosen to visit. Like "guest," it also hints at our responsibility to be hospitable hosts. For the sake of parsimony, I will use "visitor" throughout this book because it's already widely used and captures something of the transient and ephemeral nature of our relationship with our audiences.

Peoples' lives are much bigger than the time they spend with us. People dip into and out of relationship with a museum, be that online or in person. Though they may take on the persona of a visitor once they arrive, they don't leave everything else at the front door. Falk and Dierking's Museum Experience Model describes three contexts that profoundly shape the museum experience: the personal, the sociocultural, and the physical (Falk and Dierking 2016, p. 26). That personal context, their lived experience, prior knowledge, interests, and expectations all lie outside our ability to influence, but that does not mean they are not important to understand and factor into our designs. The Finnish experience designer Johanna Koljonen's description of the participant journey through an experience is powerful to me because it makes clear how much bigger their experience is than the thing they are experiencing.

Dan Hill in *Dark Matter and Trojan Horses* (2012), his brilliant book on strategic design, quotes the Finnish-American architect Eliel Saarinen as saying, "Always design a thing by considering it in its next larger context—a chair in a room, a room in a house, a house in an environment, an environment in a city plan." The museum experience is no different. In the same way that visitors are situated in all these larger contexts, the thing you're making is also occurring within the larger context of "the visit" which also includes getting there, getting home, finding the bathrooms, wandering around, eating, and a host of other activities that often do not receive the level of design attention that galleries and grand entrance spaces do. Koljonen's diagram (Figure 1.1) neatly captures the reality of that larger context and just how much of it is outside of our sphere of influence in the center.

If you only pay attention to the thing you're designing, you place yourself at a disadvantage, because so much is happening before the visitor even gets to your product, be it a website, program, or exhibition. Equally important, the process of an experience turning into a durable memory largely occurs after the event. It is critical to try to understand what visitors bring with them to the experience, but it is even more important to give thought to what visitors will take with them from the experience because the thing we're after as designers—the transformation that can happen as a result of a meaningful experience—doesn't occur in the

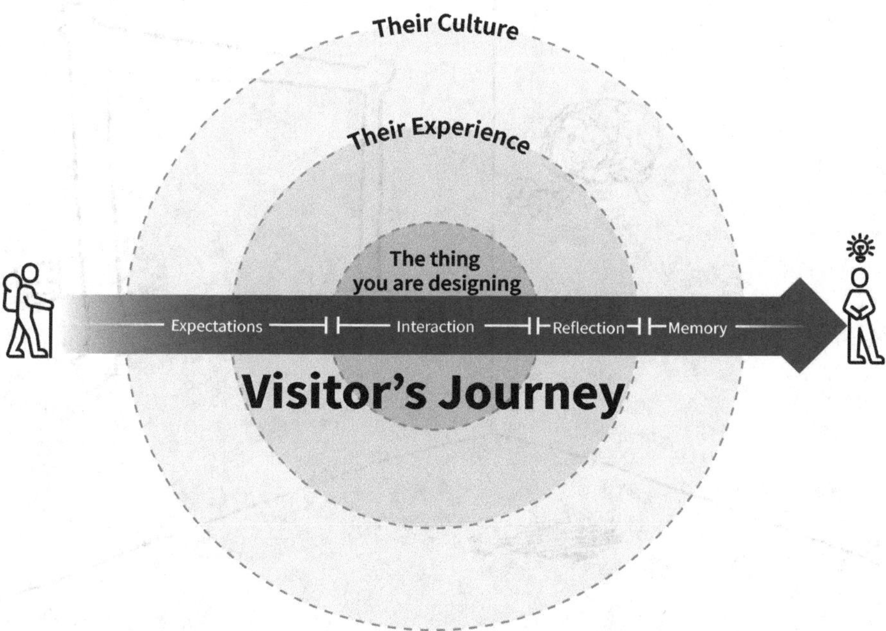

Figure 1.1 Koljonen's participant journey diagram

moment. To paraphrase John Dewey, "We do not learn from experience. We learn from reflecting on experience."[3] The memorability of a meaningful experience is, to me, one of the distinctions between museum experiences and the growing field of location-based entertainment and immersive art venues, and possibly the superpower that competing kinds of experiences can't provide.

Visitors are More than just a Brain and Eyes

For much of my career, I was an informal science educator and thus spent a lot of effort on visitor learning and cognitive goals. Almost all of that work resulted in things for visitors to look at: labels, exhibits, media. Traditional approaches to museum experience design often seemed to treat visitors as though they were disembodied brains with eyes, floating at adult head height with no regard for the environment around them or needs other than good sight lines (Figure 1.2).

The reality is that the people and objects and ideas in the magic circle are all parts of a dynamic system where each influences and is influenced by the others that produce engagement. Brendan Keogh (2018) articulates a phenomenology of video games that centers the cybernetic[4] circuit of a person both engaging with a

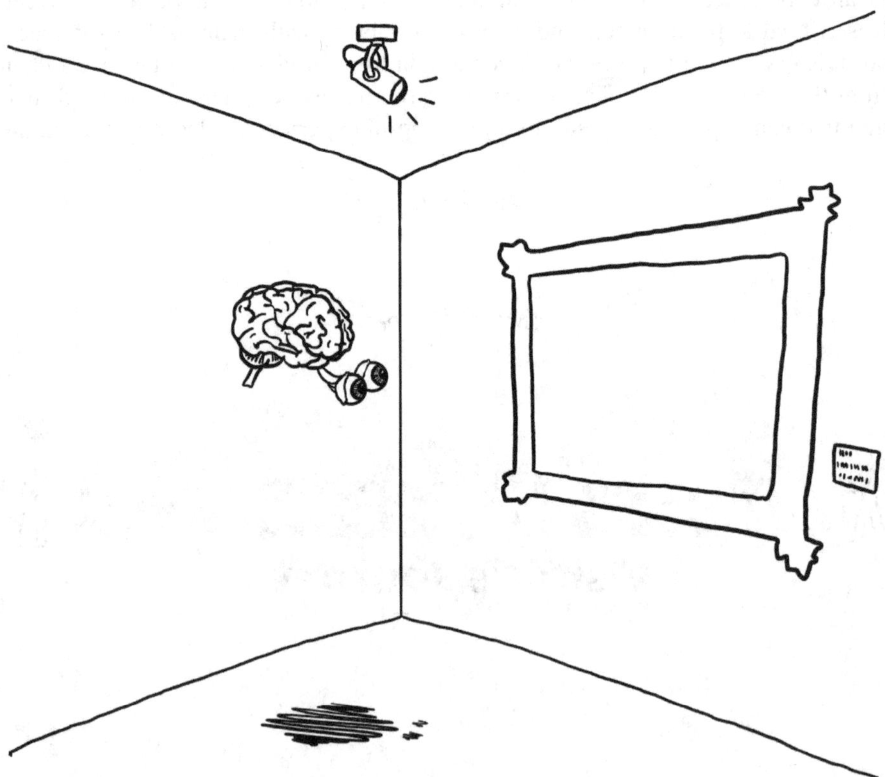

Figure 1.2 The Perfect Visitor? Image by Phoebe Rogue.

videogame and being physically impacted by that experience, and I would argue that museum interactions function in a similar way. As an experience designer, I want to constantly remember that the complex entanglement of a visitor being engaged in an experience is always happening in a fully embodied way, even if that engagement is mediated through a digital device. The U.K. artist collective Marshmallow Laser Feast, creators of immersive VR and digital artworks, emphasize embodiment as part of their core philosophy, which they describe as:

> the sense of experiencing ourselves and the world through our bodies, not just our brains. In neuroscience, cognitive science and psychology, researchers have found that accessing the emotions in our body - in essence, being actively attuned to our senses - has a discernible impact on our well-being, and strengthens our connection to other people and the world around us.[5]

Even though we all do this every day as an aspect of being human, we tend not to be very aware of our embodiment.

This resonates strongly with Kristina Höök's articulation of an embodied design stance, "Embodiment speaks of how we are always in the world, with our bodies, sociality, and practices – that we are inseparable from the world. The way our perception and knowing works is entangled deeply, inseparably with our surroundings" (Höök 2019, p. xxi). We see and hear and smell and touch, and our bodies respond to the experience in every moment, swiping across screens, manipulating objects, moving our bodies in space. And though we may think with our brains, we do not think only with our brains, as Paul and other proponents of embodied cognition argue (Paul 2021).

We need to understand the dynamics of that system and explicitly take them into account in our experience design if we want to maximize the chances that the magic we seek to create actually occurs. This is true in the physical, but especially in the digital realm, where embodiment is largely ignored. As Noah Shusterman observed "[N]o technological invention of virtual reality will negate the body's centrality as the focus of affective, perceptual experience through which we experience and engage the world" (quoted in Höök 2019, p. 181).

The Object

While visitors are essential to the magic circle, they need something to encounter. They need objects. Collecting, caring for, and displaying objects are core to museums' reason for existing, and sharing the knowledge, expertise, and stories embodied in them and associated with them has been museums' *raison d'etre* for centuries. Over time, though, the variety of objects that museums have used to engage visitors has increased dramatically. As an experience designer, I am interested in all them, not just the ones with accession numbers painted on them in discreet locations. Throughout this book, I use the word "object" to mean anything we deliberately place in the visitors' physical or digital path with the expectation that encountering it should be part of their journey. An object can be an artwork hung on the wall, the content on a computer screen, a conveniently placed bench, a blog post, or interactive device purpose-built for the occasion. It can also be a moving image, a sound, or a smell. I use the word "object" very expansively and for reasons. Consider a social media post, a label, an artwork or artifact, an entrance ticket, an educator giving a talk, and an interactive exhibit. Each of these classes of objects has radically different production workflows and staff associated with them. They are as different as apples are to haiku, but to visitors, they are all "the museum" and all contribute to (or detract from) their experience.

The affordances of objects vary widely depending on their status as collections object or not, and their materiality as physical or digital. Let's briefly look at the major categories, starting with physical collection objects, the centerpieces of most museums.

Physical Collections Objects

First, a little disambiguation. What most museum professionals call an "object," I will refer to as a physical collections object, meaning an object that has been collected or is displayed like one. It may seem like a quibble, but I find that using the word "object" to mean "physical collections object" is an unhelpful obfuscation, just like using "museum" to mean "art museum." So, in the interest of clarity, I will make the distinction. Throughout the book, if you encounter the word "object" by itself, it will mean the entire universe of objects that we might use to engage visitors, and if I'm referring specifically to collections objects, I will describe them as such.

Physical collections objects are often imbued with power that has everything to do with the prior knowledge of the museum professionals dealing with them, knowledge that most visitors don't (yet) possess. As practitioners in the field, surrounded by these objects and deeply embedded in the systems that help people appreciate them, it is often easy for us to ascribe powers to collection objects that they do not, in fact, possess, like the ability to communicate like humans. As Elaine Gurian (1999, p. 181) diplomatically put it, "the notion that objects, per se, can communicate directly and meaningfully is under much scrutiny." Many times over the course of my career I've heard statements like, "Let the objects speak for themselves." or "We've put these two objects in conversation with each other." And while I understand the sentiment being expressed, it obscures what is really happening when visitors interact with collections objects in a museum. The expert looking at an object about which they know a great deal, and the novice visitor who may have no frame of reference for approaching a collections object will have drastically different experiences and that object will not "speak" to them the same way. Unless it has a speaker in it, text on it, or is capable of speech, most objects do not communicate, at least not in the general understanding of human communication as the process of sending, receiving, and interpreting messages.[6] The "aura" Walter Benjamin described in his oft-repeated 1935 essay *The Work of Art in the Age of Mechanical Reproduction* refers to the unique and supposedly irreplaceable presence that an original work of art or historical artifact possesses, presence which has everything to do with the historical and cultural context which gave rise to the object, and the object's authenticity and/or originality or uniqueness. As museum practitioners, this creates a tremendous challenge since museums are the great decontextualizers, displaying collections objects in a carefully neutral setting vastly different than their original one. The rich set of associations with the collections object which museum professionals carry around in their heads are largely inaccessible to the uninformed and exist largely outside the physicality of those objects. These metadata carry the stories that make collections objects so meaningful. Nothing on the *Mona Lisa* tells us who made it, it is unsigned. We call Leonardo da Vinci its creator because the painting's provenance has been carefully preserved from Leonardo's time up to the present.

This is not to say that collections objects aren't central to our work. Paris' *Perspectives on Object-Centered Learning in Museums* (2002), Dudley's *Museum Object: Experiencing the Properties of Things* (2012) or more recently Wood and Latham's *The Objects of Experience* (2018), and Wood, Tisdale, and Jones' *Active Collections* (2018) all provide multiple lenses through which to approach working with collections objects in ways that neither denigrate nor fetishize them. Helping people get the most out of their limited time with these mute objects requires us to pay careful attention to interpretation.

Digital Objects

The 20th century, in addition to the shifting understandings of the role of objects in museums, brought with it both the complication of mechanical reproduction that Walter Benjamin famously problematized, and then toward the end of the century, the digital object. In the wild, you are most apt to run into digital objects in the form of digital surrogates of physical collections objects and also as born-digital collections objects valued in their own right, and not for their reproduction of some physical original.

One of the biggest differences about objects in the digital realm occurs where they run into the traditional museum values attached to "authenticity" and "originality." Hazan (2002), Geismar (2018), Hindmarch, Terras, and Robson (2019), and Meehan (2023) have all wrestled with the question of whether digital objects possess the aura a physical collections object might.[7] In a world where a limitless number of copies can be made of any digital object, each identical to the first, how does a museum value any of them? A discussion of digital materiality, a topic beyond the scope of this book, is ably summarized by Park and Samms (2019) in their exploration of how the Victoria and Albert Museum might collect digital objects in a way that acknowledges the ways that digital objects challenge current understandings of object-based work that privilege tangible materialities.

As experience designers, the most challenging aspect of digital objects of any kind is their immateriality. All our ability to sense digital objects is mediated through how they get physically expressed.

The "Other Stuff" aka "Everything Else"

This discussion thus far has focused on the objects that collecting museums are organized around, and has hopefully given you a sense of the possibilities and challenges around physical and digital collections objects. But these are numerically speaking, the smallest category of things we might place in a given digital or physical space. Our training as museum professionals tends to make us focus on objects, but most visitors do not experience our spaces the same way. The architecture, the furnishings, the interpretive devices, the light and soundscape of the space (planned and accidental), and even the flooring all directly impact how visitors feel and therefore how they learn or appreciate their time with us. They are all also amenable to being designed. The power of an experience design approach to museum experiences is that when you recognize that "*everything* is a designable surface," as Johanna Koljonen likes to say, you are likely to want to design more of them. That will, I hope, lead to more diverse, more interesting, and more impactful museum experiences, which is why I've written this book.

So now that we've covered the two parts of the magic circle you're likely familiar with, let's turn our attention to the third, the interaction alibi.

The Interaction Alibi: Permission to Play

The third element of our magic circle is the *interaction alibi*, what participation designer, larp theorist, and media analyst Johanna Koljonen describes as "an explicit framework that gives people permission to behave differently than they might in their everyday lives. It can be a rule, object, or change of state that allows someone to interact" (Koljonen 2016). An interaction alibi helps you understand what you're expected to do, feel safe trying something new, and trust that the outcome will be worth your time. An alibi is an excuse to perform an act of some kind without fear of the consequences or social embarrassment. If you as an experience designer want somebody to try something new, or do something scary like interacting with people they don't know, giving them an alibi is an explicit way of giving them permission to be someone else.

Interaction alibis are a way of overcoming the fear of embarrassment that keeps people from acting in ways that might draw unwanted attention to themselves. Oftentimes, these are implicit or understood. Screaming is generally frowned upon public behavior, but if you're at a music festival or sporting event, it's understood to be acceptable, and you can scream till you're hoarse. The game Twister is a great example of the power of a good explicit alibi. Getting your limbs tangled up with other people's is usually frowned upon, but if you're playing Twister, the transgression of invading someone else's personal space is forgiven because it's part of the game.

In the immersive theater production *Sleep No More*, the audience were allowed to roam freely through the multistory building in which the play occurs. This could've created a problem for guests and cast alike; how to tell who's in the audience and who's an actor? Their solution was to give every visitor a white mask that the audience is expected to wear at all times. It has eyeholes, but is designed so that your mouth is not visible, reinforcing the instructions that you receive when you enter that you shouldn't speak. It's simple, elegant, and its design signals to the audience that they are a kind of ghostly presence. The minute people put them on, you can see them start to act differently. Wearing a costume as an alibi, according to Murray, allows people to "mark themselves as participants and signals our role as role players, not ourselves" (Murray 2019, p. 140). By the same token, once you remove the mask, you step out of the role of audience member and return to your default identity.

Alibis are not just an important tool to overcome fear of embarrassment. They provoke playfulness and are especially useful with adults, who have by and large been socialized out of playing. Sebastian Deterding explains in *Alibis for Adult Play* (2018)

> ...the most obvious motivation for play—autotelic enjoyment[8]— also sits in most direct tension with adult identity. To account for their play, adults therefore regularly resort to alibis, motivational accounts that deflect negative inference from their play behavior to their character. Adults account for play as serving their adult responsibilities.
>
> (p. 15)

I've seen this countless times, particularly at science centers, where adults will excuse their interacting with the exhibits as something they did to help the children they were with.

The social negotiation at the heart of museum-going is largely unwritten and received by new generations of museum goers mainly through observation and mimicry. You just follow along and watch other visitors and infer what's acceptable and what's not. This has been known for a long time. Falk and Dierking devote part of the final section of *The Museum Experience* (2012) to exploring why visitors mimic other, more confident-seeming museumgoers. This lack of explicit permission or alibi is part of the reason adults who are newer to museum-going are so inhibited; nobody wants to be seen to be "doing it wrong" and avoiding that embarrassment is a powerful force we have to overcome in our work.

Other Key Terms

I have found the magic circle to be an enormously useful framework for thinking about the museum experience as it is experienced by visitors. The path to playful engagement leads into and out of that circle. So let's next talk about some key terms.

Experience

Pine and Gilmore's supremely influential 1999 book *The Experience Economy* is responsible for the current vogue for the idea of "experience." In it, they posited that the service economy was being replaced by a new model, an experience economy where companies offering compelling experiences for their customers, would see not only increased customer allegiance but also more profits. Since then, experience is everything and everywhere. The experience economy is our real competition, as witnessed by the proliferation of companies and venues that offer varying kinds of "experiences" that promise to let customers encounter culture and spectacle in new and engaging ways.

"Experience" is a *very* overused word. What is an experience? How does the noun "experience" relate to the verb "experience" and what does it mean for someone to experience an experience? In its simplest sense an experience is something that has happened to us that we have noticed. Important here is the element of conscious effort or attention. If you were unconscious, the event may have happened to you, but you haven't experienced it. Experience requires mental effort; it requires us to pay attention. It is important to remember that this change of awareness, this transformation, is internal. What is changing is the mind of the person. So, an "experience" is a transformative phenomenon that occurs within the mind of the person who has lived through it. Trying to describe what happens in our heads when something happens to us has been a problem scientists have been trying to understand for a long time.

Neuroscience, psychology, and philosophy have all attempted to describe the nature of experience from their different viewpoints, though there is still a lot of room for researchers to try to bridge these disciplines and integrate these learnings into one cohesive idea of "experience." We all swim in the sea of our experiences and their all-encompassing nature makes them hard to pin down. For our very specific purposes that's not necessary, thankfully. To do our work effectively, it is enough to remember that we come by all our knowledge as a result of experience, as Merleau-Ponty is quoted as saying, "We know not through our intellect but through our experience."[9] In a museum context, Tiina Roppola (2013) argues, "Experience speaks to the processes that characterize the embodied act of being in a museum" (p. 30). So, though the museum environment can often be decontextualizing, it can excel at creating environments for experience.

In their excellent overview of the emergent field of experience design, Rossman and Duerden (2019) argue that one of the hallmarks of experiences is that they require more from the people who partake of them.

> An experience differs in that it requires the customer to be consciously engaged and the engagement is sustained through volitional actions of the participant. Consider the monikers used to describe the recipients of each. Service organizations think of their customers as guests, clients, patients, etc., all implying that something needs to be done for them. Experience-producing organizations think of their customers as participants…. Experience demands conscious attention, engagement, and action—in a word, participation.
>
> (p. 6)

They later propose a framework or continuum that consists of five experience types and their associated key characteristics: prosaic (autopilot), mindful (effortful mental engagement), memorable (emotion), meaningful (discovery), and transformational (change) (p. 39). The idea of participation leading to transformation resonates strongly with museums' institutional missions. It also challenges us to design for visitors to be active participants, which is very different than being a passive audience. Clay Shirky describes it thus, "To participate is to act as if your presence matters, as if, when you see something or hear something, your response is part of the event" (2011, p. 21).

Attention

An essential part of an experience involves participants deciding to focus on it, so let's talk a little about attention. We are constantly besieged by sense data, and our brains select a subset of that torrent to focus on. William James (1950) said,

> Millions of items of the outward order are present to my senses which never properly enter into my experience. Why? Because they have no interest for me. My experience is what I agree to attend to. Only those items which I notice shape my mind — without selective interest, experience is an utter chaos.
>
> (p. 380)

Alexandra Horowitz, in her marvelous inquiry into the blinders we wear in our everyday lives, observes, "Attention is an intentional, unapologetic discriminator. It asks what is relevant right now, and gears us up to notice only that" (2013, p. 12). We all have limited capacity to attend to something, so attention is a process of deciding what to attend to *at the expense of everything else*. Even the way we talk about attention in English hints at its finite capacity. We "pay" attention to something, as though we have a pot of attention, and we can parcel it out in bits until it's empty. Csikszentmihaly and Hermanson (1995) say, "Attention is a scarce resource – perhaps the most precious scarce resource there is" (p. 67).

The psychologist Daniel Kahneman has devoted a whole career to trying to understand attention and how humans do (and don't) attend to the world around them. Like many other authors, he uses the metaphor of attention being like a searchlight. Things in its beam are attended to and everything else is ignored. In *Thinking, Fast and Slow* (2011), Kahneman also introduces the idea that we possess two different attention systems that govern the way we think: System 1 is the fast, subconscious, and intuitive system that allows us to breathe and maintain balance. System 2 is the slow and deliberate system we apply when we have understood something that is happening to us. If you've ever walked into a door you thought pushed open only to find it pulls open, that's an example of System 1 and System 2. You're operating on System 1 until the moment you crash into the door and then System 2 takes over and you examine your surroundings and figure out how to open the door. Kahneman argues that the constant interaction of these systems determines how our brains process information.

> The division of labor between System 1 and System 2 is highly efficient: it minimizes effort and optimizes performance. The arrangement works well

most of the time because System 1 is generally very good at what it does: its models of familiar situations are accurate, its short-term predictions are usually accurate as well, and its initial reactions to challenges are swift and generally appropriate.

(p. 22)

As experience designers, we are in the business of asking visitors to give us some of that scarce resource, a resource can never be paid back. I particularly like the way Simone Weil described attention, "Attention is the rarest and purest form of generosity" (Pétrement and Rosenthal, 1976, p. 462) because it challenges me to be mindful of how we ask visitors to spend it.

Experience Design

The California Association of Museums set out to explore what experience design means to museums. They offer the following definition which I quite like. It says,

> Experience design is a broadly applied term that refers to a transdisci-plinary field that combines service design, usability studies, interaction design, information architecture, engineering and a wide range of other sub-disciplines. It applies to both digital media and traditional, established, and other diverse disciplines such as theater, graphic design, storytelling, exhibit design, theme-park design, online design, game design, interior design, and architecture.

(California Association of Museums 2012)

It's a bit of a laundry list, but it clearly establishes the breadth of utility of what we do. Experience design (often shortened to XD) describes an inherently holistic mindset that focuses on embodied, immersive, environmental design in both the physical and digital realms. Braden, Rosenthal, and Spock (2005) trace experience design's intellectual pedigree back much further to four scholars who have profoundly affected our understanding of human behavior.

The first is the 19th-century American psychologist William James. James was an early advocate of the idea that human consciousness is active, not passive. Humans are not vessels to be filled, but intellects actively seeking out and making meaning as they make their way through life. James also rejected the traditional Western dialectic between thinking and feeling. "Forthrightly engaging the realm of emotion is not sensationalism. Indeed, it is integral to cognition and should be embraced wholeheartedly" (quoted in Braden et al. 2005, p. 14). Though he was writing this more than a century ago, it's clear where he would stand on the "education versus entertainment" debates that gripped the museum field in the 1980s and 1990s.

Second is the American philosopher and educator John Dewey (and author of *Art as Experience*), who, amongst his myriad other interests, explored the connection between experience and learning. For him, experiential meaning making is intrinsic to human biology. We are hard-wired to take in sensory information and turn it into meaning, in a process of "active intelligence in continuous transaction with its environment" (quoted in Braden et al. 2005, p. 14).

Third is the Swiss psychologist Jean Piaget, who has had tremendous influence on our understanding of how children learn and develop as they grow.

> [A] key component of any experience design should be the opportunity to play. Jean Piaget defined play as an activity one engages with for its own sake. In other words, play is intrinsically motivated, voluntary in nature. This harmonizes so strongly with Falk and Dierking's definition of free-choice learning that one can easily see museum-going and museum learning as variants of play.
>
> (Braden et al. 2005, p. 15)

The fourth and final eminence in their museum experience design pedigree is the 20th-century Dutch sociologist Johan Huizinga who we met at the beginning of this chapter. Like Piaget, Huizinga rejects the idea that play is the opposite of seriousness and positions play as a central element of human society.

Braden et al. go on to list a number of other ways that an experience design mindset differs from more traditional approaches to design. For them, experience design should:

- understand how interaction with an environment, physical or virtual, can enhance or impede active learning and strive to provide conditions that facilitate it;
- privilege social interactions, both between visitors and the museum, and more importantly, between visitors and other visitors;
- encourage "playful interaction of people with each other, the content of the museum, and the museum environment taken as a whole;"
- convey and elicit passions; and
- engage the whole person and engage all the senses (Braden et al. 2005, p. 16).

For Braden et al., a museum experience design mindset therefore encompasses understandings of human behavior that position learning as an active, self-directed, continuous process, undertaken by people whose whole selves are both emotional as well as rational. These people, when they enter the "temporary world" of the museum, perform "an act apart" from their daily life; that of museum "visitor." While we may want visitors to have a specific experience, our ability to determine what they take away is limited. Patrick Newbury (2013) described the problem thus,

> How can you design an experience? After all, experience is a subjective phenomenon that occurs within the mind of the individual. The best one can do is to influence what someone experiences (such as a sense of value, utility, usability, etc.) through design.

In terms of designing museum experiences, it means that visitors make meaning of your experience based on their own experiences and all their interactions with the museum. How easy it was to get there, whether the place felt welcoming, sensibly organized, well-equipped for their bodily and mental needs; all these factors go into their mental arithmetic when they're watching your program, using your website, or moving through your exhibition. By the time they arrive at what you may think of as the beginning of your experience, they're already well on the way toward making sense of their experience, and if your design process only begins at that point, you've lost a substantial opportunity to engage with people. This is why designers often create introductory experiences that aim to "reset" visitor attitudes, of "disorient to reorient."

As an emerging discipline, there is still a lot of discussion around what the boundaries and contents of experience design are. So, I offer up my own definition of experience design, which is heavily inspired by Braden, Rosenthal, and Spock (2005), Wood (2018), and many others:

> Experience Design is a cross-disciplinary design perspective centered on human outcomes, particularly the level of engagement and satisfaction that people derive from an experience, and the relevance of that experience to their needs. Experience Design sees learning as an ongoing, lifelong process of evolving iteration and reiteration of knowledge, stimulated by participation in an experience.

I encourage you to try on the title "experience designer" if you make programs, interpretations, exhibitions, or anything that involves actual living breathing people to make use of it.

Engagement

The goal of this book is to provide experience designers with tools to engage visitors. The magic circle of the museum visit provides a framework for creating engaging experience, and an experience design mindset positions you to understand how to design for engagement. Before we delve further into ways to design for playful engagement, we should first have a shared understanding of what we mean by engagement.

SIDEBAR: Labels

I went to the Museum of Old and New Art in Hobart, Tasmania, not long after their opening. There were several controversies swirling around the museum's approach. Visitors were prompted to vote on whether they "love" or "hate" the artworks. There were no printed labels. None. Anywhere. All the interpretation was carried on a mobile device. The museum's founder and owner liked to display deliberately provocative artworks with a generous helping of sex and

Engagement is easy enough to see when you look for it. When I ask colleagues and peers to describe what engagement looks like, they can usually give me a list of similar observations that signal engagement is happening. When I ask them to define engagement, it gets a lot harder. I'll share some of the ways museum practitioners talk about engagement and finally offer my definition of what I call playful engagement. I'll throw a bunch of definitions at you because I had to make my through then all to arrive at the idea of playful engagement as necessary concept.

When I started working on this book, I realized that, like "experience," the word "engagement" gets used in a lot of different ways, and that most often it's a term of convenience. We use it as shorthand to convey a range of ideas and activities that make conversational sense, but when you try to define it, it gets complicated. Engagement is something educators, formal and informal, talk about a lot, but so do digital marketers and senior executives. And they all mean something slightly different, and they value engagement for different reasons. As Wood and Wolf (2008) note in their survey of museums' use of concepts of engagement, "individuals using the same word does not guarantee understanding." They went on to state, "With no field-based definition of engagement, educators are left to do the heavy lifting to examine the personal and institutional assumptions that stem from more individualized definitions" (p. 124). It's not just educators being left in the dark. Seph Rodney has pointed out that, "[e]ngagement is now widely considered

death. As an exhibit developer for whom label writing was a core job competency, I went, but with conflicting feelings. Part of me was predisposed to hate the place for having no labels, part of me was predisposed to hate the place because it was popular, and part of me was very excited to see and do something different. And I had a deeply transformative experience there. As an aside, note that even as a professional going on a fact-finding mission, every term I used at the time to describe my motivation was emotional.

When I went to MONA in 2012, you got handed a mobile device (in 2012 it was an iPod) with headphones and directions on how to use it. The museum is, in fact, full of information on the artworks on display, it's just all in the device. If you want to know something, you have to look for it. Rather than "pushing" it at visitors with printed labels, the visitors have to "pull" it out of the device because they want to know something. This simple shift of agency is profound. The example that did it for me was looking at a vaguely Modernist painting and thinking, "This looks like a crappy Picasso. I don't much like it." When I looked it up on my device, what was it? A Picasso (Figure 1.3).

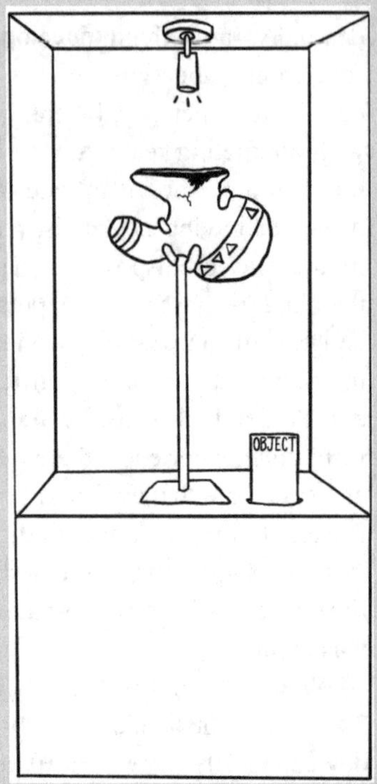

Figure 1.3 Tombstone label, n. Brief label providing a tiny subset of information about an object. Called such because it's where a visitor's interest in an object goes to die. Image by Phoebe Rogue

And I realized in that moment, that if I'd encountered the work with a label reading "Pablo Picasso (1881–1973), Spanish, active in France," I probably wouldn't have been able to dislike it as much as I did, if at all, because Picasso is a central figure in the Western art canon. I grew as a museum visitor and became a more confident art appreciator and carry that confidence with me to this day, all because a museum *didn't* put a label on a painting for a very specific reason. To be clear, I'm not advocating for getting rid of labels. The transformation occurred precisely because there were labels, they were just sequenced differently so that I looked at the object first, and then chose to look up the information. The design of the experience gave me a kind of agency I rarely have in museums, especially art museums.

in museological discourse to be one component of a triad of key responsibilities that encompass and describe museum practice" along with preservation, and curation/interpretation (Rodney 2019, p. 126). I especially appreciated his description of Peter Welsh's description of engagement for its ability to embrace the diversity of audiences that museums engage with:

> One researcher, Peter Welsh (2005), describes engagement as encompassing the ways in which "museums seek to establish relationships with a wide variety of people, [...] and reciprocally, the ways that people establish relationships with the museum.
>
> (pp.105–106)

Rodney also articulates how much of the museum's operation are engagement-based,

> viewing engagement as the forming of a relationship places education, programming, and exhibitions, but also marketing, publicity, and donor development, all on similar footing.
>
> (p. 129)

Taking engagement as a given is so ingrained in the profession that Graham Black, in his excellent book "The Engaging Museum: Developing Museums for Visitor Involvement" (2005), doesn't even define engagement beyond providing a dictionary definition of "engage," and then only in the final chapter (p. 266).

So, let's look at engagement and the different ways it gets talked about.

Learning itself is seen as a form of engagement. The U.K. Museums, Libraries, and Archives Council published an influential paper about the importance of "learning" as opposed to "education" which stated, "Learning is a process of active engagement with experience… Effective learning leads to change, development and the desire to learn more" (Hooper-Greenhill et al. 2003). Skinner and Belmont (1993) define engagement in educational settings as, "The intensity and emotional quality of a user's involvement in initiating and carrying out activities. Engaged users show sustained behavioral and cognitive involvement in activities accompanied by positive emotional tone." Looking more broadly at digital interventions of all kinds, psychologists have proposed that engagement is, "a state of energy investment involving physical, affective, and cognitive energies directed toward a focal stimulus or task" (Nahum-Shani et al. 2022, p. 837). O'Brien and Toms (2008) surveyed aesthetic, flow, play, and information interaction theories to synthesize a definition that, "Engagement is a category of user experience characterized by attributes of challenge, positive affect, endurability, aesthetic and sensory appeal, attention, feedback, variety/novelty, interactivity, and perceived user control" (p. 941). They also found several attributes that accompanied engaging experiences that are common including attention, emotion, embodiment, and intrinsic motivation and agency,

> Central to this research was identifying the attributes of engagement. Interwoven throughout the engagement process were a variety of attributes: attention, novelty, interest, control, feedback, and challenge. In addition, we found evidence for emotional (affect and motivation), sensory (aesthetics and interactivity), and spatiotemporal (perception of time, and self- and external awareness) threads of experience.
>
> (p. 950)

Coming from a human-computer interaction (HCI) perspective, Dalsgaard (2008) wrote,

> [E]ngagement can be understood as a focused form of interaction in which the user enters into a reciprocal relationship which potentially effects changes

in both the user and the situation. Engagement relies on a certain mode of experiencing the world, namely inquiry.

(pp. 88–89)

Hookham and Nesbitt (2019) conducted a survey of over a thousand articles on engagement in serious play. Of those articles surveyed, only 26 of them offered any definition of what they meant by engagement (p. 2). In reviewing the varying definitions, they distilled some common themes,

> This review found three primary uses of engagement: engagement referring to use, the player is 'engaging' in or with an activity or game; engagement referring to a player state, the player is 'engaged'; and engagement referring to the property of a game or object to be 'engaging'.

(p. 8)

Engagement in the Digital Realm

"Engagement" is a term commonly used in digital professions to describe the relationship between "users" and "content" produced by an organization or brand. In the digital realm, this is fraught because engagement happens between the digital actions of a physical entity engaging with users who are never encountered in the flesh and whose engagement can only be measured by looking at traces of their activity. It's a largely forensic endeavor, measuring past actions of people to measure success and plan future actions of the organization. Working in the digital realm made me appreciate what a gift it was to get out on the museum floor and watch visitors whenever I wanted to. Digital marketers can do incredibly detailed investigations of engagement based on page views, open rates, conversions, clicks, likes, shares, retweets, and comments. Likewise, any kind of computer-mediated interaction is inherently amenable to all kinds of data collection. Electrons are cheap, after all. Total numbers of button pushes, heat maps of which parts of the screen visitors tapped most, and how many times this sensor triggered, all these traces of activity can build an intricate picture of the behaviors in which people engage. But they can't tell us why. This kind of engagement requires tremendous amounts of data to use as fodder for analysis upon which to base future decision-making. Being "data driven" is an admirable quality, though like anything, it can be carried to extremes. Digital marketers know their users in ways that most museum professionals never will, and that practice of launching, analyzing, and iterating is a mindset that is good to cultivate.

Though this book is focused on engagement as a personal experience—a thing that happens to people when they decide to pay attention to something—the more common usage in the cultural and business sectors is to talk about engagement as a relationship between "visitors" or "users" and organizations. Practitioners like Seema Rao and Adam Rozan speak about engagement as being a reciprocal relationship between the museum and the visitor (Rao 2019; Rozan 2016).

Chad Weinard (2019) sees this kind of engagement as including notions of commitment, duration, transformation, and, perhaps most importantly, mutuality.

> It's not just visitors engaged to the museum, it's the museum engaged to visitors. It's not just about how visitors are changed by going to an exhibition, it's about how are the museum is changed by having visitors at the exhibition.

This version of engagement is very much in keeping with the recent trend toward viewing visitor experience as holistically as possible. Witness the emergence of Chief Experience Officers (CXOs) as a sign of this desire on the part of institutions eager to more effectively engage with their audiences. And this is the crux of my entanglement; this distinction between being engaged by something, versus being engaged with someone.

This idea of an organization being able to have a "relationship" with individuals is the kind of useful fiction that I am always leery of accepting too readily, though I do it myself all the time. It's the same tendency that makes us talk about companies like they're people, or talk about objects "being in conversation with each other" because they're placed adjacent to one another. They may be useful fictions, but fictions they are. No matter how much I love a particular museum, it's never going to love me back. So that kind of relationship is different, and I will leave it to others to further explore.

Playful Engagement

My initial interest in defining engagement was to understand and define what is happening to the visitor who is engaged. As a practitioner, I want to define terms, particularly complicated ones, so that I can use them. I'm not a theorist or scientist trying to articulate the truth of something. For a designer, truth is in utility. So, for me, definitions are always about whatever they're helping you to solve; in this case, whether people are getting out of an experience what you've put into it.

As you can see from the multiple engagements listed above, a large part of the challenge for the experience designer is being consistent and explicit about which kind of "engagement" we are seeking to create. The "engagement" I'm interested in having us better understand is what visitor engagement comprises physiologically, neurologically, intellectually, and emotionally. As an experience designer, that is paramount in my very instrumental desire to use that engagement to advance the institutions' goals for whatever I'm designing, be it a label, an interpretive device, an exhibition, or a building. So here are the building blocks of what I will call "playful engagement" throughout this book.

Playful Engagement Is Emotional and Active

The Merriam Webster dictionary defines engagement in the sense I'm talking about as "emotional involvement or commitment." This is why we describe people who have decided to get married as "engaged" to each other. There is an emotional commitment that underlies their attachment. You can't be engaged and emotionally detached. So far, so good, but there is more to engagement in this context. The Oxford English dictionary defines "engage" as "to attract and hold fast (attention, interest)." So engagement is an active, emotional process, one of being attracted and held by something or someone of interest. Chapter 3 addresses this in detail.

Playful Engagement Is Self-Directed

Psychologist Mihaly Csikszentmihalyi has spent a career looking at how people learn and what motivates them. His work in this area is supremely relevant to everything I will discuss later on, so I hope you will consider reading more of his work if you haven't already. Probably the most fundamental finding of his research is that true engagement is voluntary, it's intrinsically motivated. You can't *make* someone be engaged. It has to come from within. Museums have long played a part in encouraging intrinsic motivation. Csikszentmihalyi and educator Kim Hermanson (1995) examined the phenomenon of intrinsic motivation in museum learning and found that "what information we select to attend to, and how intently, is still the most important question about learning" (pp. 67–68). So calling what happens in a museum or cultural institution what Falk and Dierking (2000) call "free-choice learning" seems more accurate than "informal" education to me.

Playful Engagement Is Satisfying

Can you imagine an activity that you would find both engaging and unsatisfying? They're out there. Realizing you've spent an hour doomscrolling social media, most gambling, doing your taxes, all of these can be deeply absorbing, but they're not what I'm after in our experiences. I think most practitioners would argue that learning about the natural world, art, science, and history should be enjoyable and satisfy visitors. If we continue with the idea that engagement and flow are similar, then we can take Csikszentmihalyi's (1991) assertion that their primary purpose is enjoyment,

> Such flow activities have as their primary function the provision of enjoyable experiences. Play, art, pageantry; ritual, and sports are some examples. Because of the way they are constructed, they help participants and spectators achieve an ordered state of mind that is highly enjoyable.
>
> (p. 72)

Sarah Brin will problematize this in her reflection in Chapter 5.

This is not to say that engagement necessarily means fun. Museum educator Rebecca Herz makes the point that engagement is not synonymous with fun.

> True engagement is defined by an individual's choice to take on a difficult (but not too difficult) task that has relevance for him or her, whether

it be physical (playing a sport or a musical instrument) or purely cognitive (making sense of competing ideas).

(Herz 2017)

Adam Rozan, former Director of Audience Engagement at the Worcester Art Museum, described audience engagement as an active process. For him, engagement "works to create a range of positive, stimulating experiences for audiences throughout their visit" (Rozan 2016).

Csikszentmihalyi describes a flow experience as one where

> …concentration is so intense that there is no attention left over to think about anything irrelevant, or to worry about problems. Self consciousness disappears and the sense of time become distorted. An activity that produces such experiences is so gratifying that people are willing to do it for its own sake, with little concern for what they will get out of it, even when it is difficult, or dangerous.

(p. 71)

Csikszentmihalyi calls this autotelic experience, meaning one that is *"a self-contained activity, one that is done not with the expectation of some future benefit, but simply because the doing itself is the reward"* (p. 67). The experience is satisfying in its own right, not because of external factors.

Playful Engagement Requires Conscious Effort

British educator and innovator Valerie Hannon argues that engagement in learning can be observed:

- When the student cares, not just about the tangible outcome of their learning (usually their test scores), but also the development of their learning.
- When they take responsibility for their own learning.
- When they bring discretionary energy to the learning task.
- When they can locate the value of their learning beyond school and wish to prolong learning beyond school hours (Hannon 2009).

Several of these categories overlap with ones we've already discussed, the emotional attachment, the sense of self-direction, the deployment of effort, and the autotelic nature of learning. Hannon's focus on effort or attention as a measurable sign that engagement is occurring applies equally to the free-choice learning environment.

I think it's safe to say that it's impossible to be engaged with an experience without paying attention, and attention—what the brain focuses on and how—is an area of deep interest to me. My former colleague Tedi Asher explores how neuroscience can inform the work art museums do to engage visitors. Underpinning that work is a focus on what visitors attend to when they're in the museum. For Asher, engagement occurs when one's attention is captured in a way that generates an emotional response and leads to the formation of a memory (Asher 2019).

Playful Engagement Changes You

Perhaps the most elusive part of the engagement puzzle is understanding why it's so desirable. And I think the reason why is the *outcome* of all that conscious effort, self-motivation, attention, and emotional attachment: change or transformation. The result of engagement is that you are changed as a result of it and behave differently. Consumer neuroscientist Carl Marci defines engagement as attention to something that elicits an emotional response, triggers a new (or reinforces an existing) memory, and influences your future behavior (Marci 2017). Seema Rao, former Chief Experience Officer at Akron Museum of Art, links it to transformation, "What does audience engagement mean? To me, it means transformation…People are at the definition of engagement to me. It's a word that stands in for all the efforts we make to connect people to collections" (Rao 2019). Seema's statement about transformation and connecting people to collections is an essential part of the equation. People engage *with something*, and in this context, that would be not just the collections of a museum (assuming they are a collecting museum, which not all are), but also the other products the museum creates and certainly the staff of that museum. And most importantly, they come away transformed as a result (Figure 1.4).

By now, you've hopefully seen some substantial overlap between the various ways other authors talk about engagement. It is something controlled by the visitor,

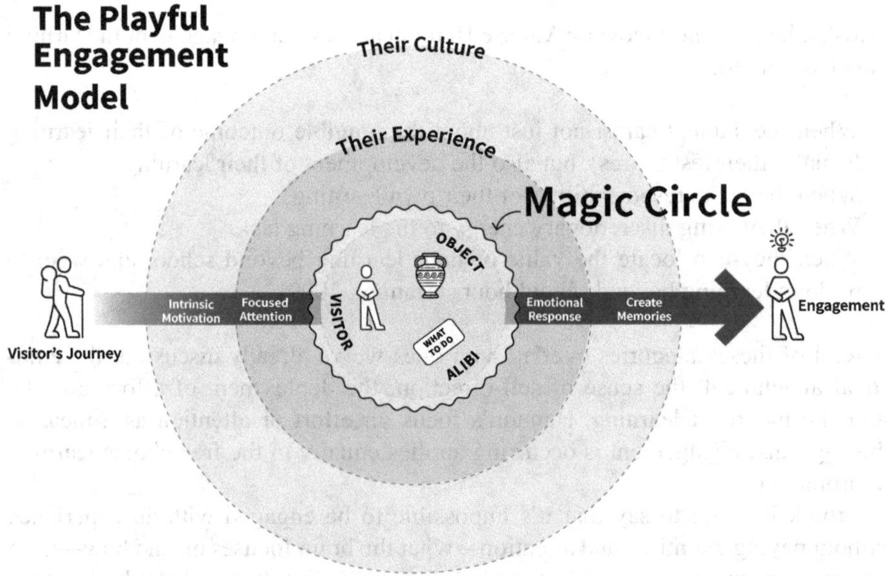

Figure 1.4 Playful Engagement model. Image by Colorbox Industries

not by the experience designer. Visitors choose to attend to something, not for some external reward, but because they find it rewarding or satisfying to do so. As part of that process, they have an emotional reaction to the experience. If they aren't moved by it, they're not engaged. This emotional response facilitates them remembering the experience, and once the experience becomes part of their memory, they behave differently as a result. For the rest of the book, I am going to use the following definition for playful engagement:

> Playful engagement is an intrinsically motivated process where a person directs their conscious, focused attention to a satisfying experience which triggers an emotional response, leads to the creation or reinforcement of a memory, and influences their behavior afterward.

It's a tall order, which may be part of the reason so few people try to define engagement. To hit all those conditions requires considerable effort and different ways of thinking about the design of museum experiences. Modern experience designers need to know how to attract and hold visitors' attention, provide relevant, satisfying experiences that explicitly aim for emotional affect. And how to evaluate the extent of behavioral change will be a critical measure of success.

That said, I don't think playful engagement is an "all or nothing" occurrence, where you've failed if your experience doesn't hit all these criteria. The magic for the experience designer lies in combining the different ingredients so that the overall experience is as engaging as possible. There's more of a spectrum of possibilities, where one end is unengaging, and the other end is maximally engaging. My hope in writing this book is to push the average a little further toward being more engaging.

Designing for Playful Engagement

So now, armed with a definition of engagement, how can an experience designer attempt to create the conditions where engagement happens and deepens? I will argue in the following chapters that there are (at least) four elements that underlie engaging museum experiences which can be employed to maximize the chance that audiences will find the experience satisfying and meaningful. These elements are:

1 *Sensory Immersion*: providing rich multisensory environments to focus visitors' attention.
2 *Emotional Evocation*: increasing the memorability or "stickiness" of experiences by building emotional triggers into experiences.

3 *Narrative Transportation*: taking advantage of narrative transportation to increase memorability of experience.
4 *Gameful Participation*: leveraging visitors' intrinsic motivation to have experiences where they can feel satisfaction, mastery, and autonomy.

These elements are not specific to museums by any means. These elements are perennial topics of interest in the cultural heritage sector and increasingly in for-profit sectors like theme parks and consumer research, and between them offer avenues to create more impactful and successful museum experiences (Figure 1.5).

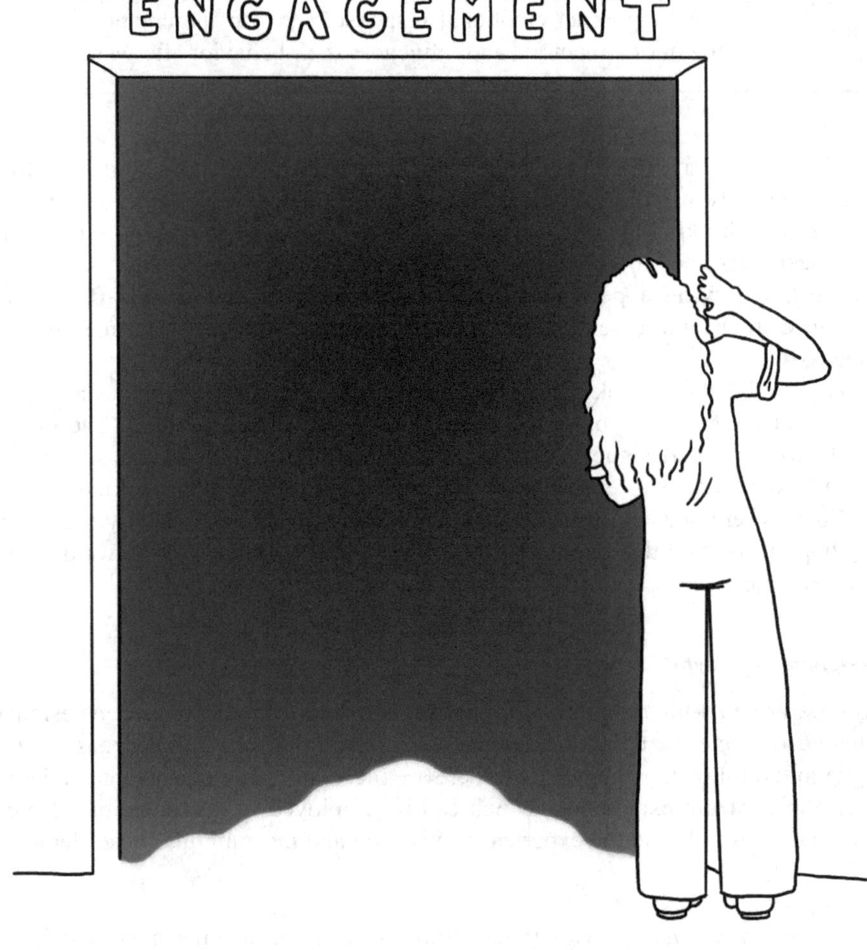

Figure 1.5 What Lies Beyond? Image by Phoebe Rogue

Emotion, intrinsic motivation, attention, satisfaction, memory, and behavioral change are central to what is observable and measurable about engagement, but at the heart of it is the "something" that starts the whole process. What is that something? If everything beyond the doorway above is exciting and meaningful and beautiful, how do we convince the visitor to take the plunge and overcome the "threshold anxiety" that is an inevitable part of a new and unknown experience? That is the challenge of experience design.

Reflection
Facing the Mona Lisa

By Johanna Koljonen

Facing the *Mona Lisa*, I felt like a freak. A lifetime of museums, an excellent humanities education, and a deep background in helping cultural institutions understand how the physical and social layers of the audience experience interact had not prepared me for this moment. I stood at the barrier, facing the painting like an idiot, when literally everyone else turned their back on her to document the moment in a selfie.

In some Paris churches, people line up to kneel and kiss fragments of the holy cross; in this secular temple, the appropriate posture was a slight backbend, leaning into a photograph. My declining to do so suggested I had lost either my phone or my mind—curious and mildly annoying. If I wasn't going to do this right, I might as well get out of the way.

Everywhere else in the museum, we had all acted the same, looking at pictures, listening to guides, and standing in lines. If someone didn't know what to do, mimicking everyone else was easy enough. Experience designer Teresa Axner calls this *herd competence* (Stenros and Montola 2019, p. 21), and it is how we commonly pick up the usual way of acting in a specific kind of space. That the behavior around the *Mona Lisa* was different does not indicate a failure of visitor competence, but that other norms had emerged to govern that space.

The magic circle of the museum contains smaller, nested magic circles, with different meanings and rules. The moment you step inside the room with the *Mona Lisa*, you will notice that people are moving differently, standing closer to each other, with their attention directed not toward works on the walls but at each other or their phones, as we are habituated to do when standing in line.

The front of the queue delivers visitors to an even smaller magic circle, physically represented by the barriers around the painting. Encountering the *Mona Lisa* only really entails being offered a sight line, and most people arrive at that point with their phone already in hand. Not being physically allowed to approach the painting, raising the device is a natural way to extend ourselves toward it. A logical behavior in a culture where capturing an image of every interesting or meaningful moment has become a reflex.

Not for me, but then the motivation of my visit was specifically to experience what reproductions hadn't told me. I also live in Europe and expect to return, while for most visitors, the moment is once-in-a-lifetime. Having traversed continents to experience art history, most perfectly represented by the presence of the actual *Mona*

Lisa, why wouldn't you perform the social ritual to prove you had? Especially when that is what everyone else is doing.

How visitors experience objects depends on interpersonal dynamics and on social norms, both inside and outside the museum, which is why designing the interaction alibis is just as important as creating the spaces. Alibi design involves considering what the physical and social environment is *encouraging* people to do, what they will feel *safe* and *confident* doing, and what they will calculate as the *cost* of doing it.

In the case of norms, that cost is social, the risk of losing face weighed against the opportunity for a communal experience, the value of a moment of respite, or the potential for some personal transformation. To you this equation may sound trivial, but the weight of uncertainty, embarrassment, and shame differs greatly depending on who we are. It is easy to set up a dance floor where beautiful people feel comfortable dancing, but you're not hosting a great party unless all your guests can dance like no-one is watching.

This is particularly challenging, because we who work in museums or with museums move through such spaces with the confidence of catwalk models. We know too much and worry too little about whether we are doing the right thing, understanding enough, or having the correct experience. In front of the *Mona Lisa*, even as I smarted slightly from the sting of being perceived as odd, I admittedly also felt slightly superior. My subjective expertise—in this room I had never visited before—allowed me to confidently act counter to de facto prevailing norms.

On one level, I could therefore permit myself a genuinely reverent moment with La Gioconda. On another, I was playing the gentle game of challenging group behavior, at zero social risk. As a white, middle-class woman, I felt comfortable looking at that painting from my first-row spot for rather too long and could have acted far more playfully without attracting censure. Even at the Louvre, which does not invite fun.

At the same time, engaging playfully at museums is also something we professionals find disproportionally difficult, and it's telling I did it through reverting to traditional behavior. For all my playful thoughts, I was very serious about "properly" experiencing the painting. Then I wasted the rest of my visit, absently preoccupied with the challenge of "solving" the selfies—with how to change the only place in the entire museum where visitors were beamingly, jubilantly engaged.

The opposite of design is tradition. When you don't actively design behavioral structures, visitors will do what they know. At traditional institutions with diverse audiences, this creates tension. If the traditional behaviors are unfamiliar, or even undermined by the physical and social experience, audiences bring in habits and norms from the outside instead. A familiar act like taking a selfie can make a new situation feel safe, and if enough people repeat it, herd competence makes it self-perpetuating.

I don't actually hate the *Mona Lisa* selfie. Embracing emergent behaviors can be a kind of inclusion, very valuable, if it's intentional. The problem here is that many visitors might also be yearning for a more focused and unmediated experience. Currently this is physically possible, but socially expensive, and therefore not available to everyone. The Louvre is unlikely to address this, as we tourists will show up regardless, but there are easy brute-force fixes combining spatial design with new house rules. There could be two lines, in one of which phones are forbidden. Or no photos of the painting permitted at all, but glorious, celebratory selfie stations in an adjoining space.

Enabling people to truly see the *Mona Lisa* if they so choose, to experience it with their bodies without being judged or jostled, is a way of respecting the visitors and the work. Honestly, I suspect most professionals respect neither. La Gioconda's status as probably the world's most reproduced painting can make it seem banal to be interested in her at all. And it's easy to dismiss as superficial anyone rushing past hundreds of masterpieces in the museum on the way to this one, only to turn their backs to produce a mechanical reproduction of their own.

Or, you could say this makes it the most interesting painting of all time. If *Mona Lisa's* visual impact has been diluted through centuries of reproduction, its social meaning has increased proportionally, the aura of familiarity so strong that she is now socially alive. No wonder she is treated like an actual person, a celebrity encounter.

It seems wasteful not to leverage that aura toward the original purpose of all those reproductions—to popularize art history as well as to challenge and play with its norms and historical hierarchies. Seeing the world's most famous painting for yourself is cool, but shouldn't we aim for it being transformative?

We could encourage and enable visitors to reflect on what it means that an artwork is original; on who the woman in the painting was and has become; on the craft, mastery, and coincidence involved in creating something immortal; on images of the *Mona Lisa* in our own lives, and on what seeing that serene smile in some future will make us recall of this day.

This is where experience design becomes thrilling. Our canvas is never just objects in spaces: everything is a designable surface. For every visitor to participate in the meaningful museum experience, we must design for their sense of agency, curating a physical and social environment where they can feel confident that their curiosity and individual perspectives will be welcomed.

Even if, like in this case, the exhibition has a star, the museum experience consists of everything that prepares us to meet her and her peers at eye level, everything that shapes who we get to be inside that building, and all the design choices determining whether we will arrive at that painting frustrated, hungry, and overwhelmed—or comfortable, curious, and engaged.

In the Louvre of my dreams, tours wouldn't end at the best-known work but get there fast and use its familiarity as an invitation, an emotional rabbit hole into the wider collections. The experience design question here is not how to make people stop taking selfies at the Mona Lisa, but how to make the rest of the objects matter even a fraction as much to the visitors. The answer must begin with making the visitors matter to the museum.

Notes

1 Since then, scientists have discovered that play is practiced by a number of species, as is detailed in Chapter 5.
2 The magic circle has since become a foundational concept of game design and has its own sub-literature devoted to critiquing (Taylor 2006; Juul 2008 among others) or defending the idea (Stenros 2015).

3 I have frequently encountered this "quotation", but could not find it anywhere in Dewey's published writings. Robert Lagueux (2014) did a lengthy literature review of Dewey's corpus and did not find this quote either. He suggests it is a paraphrase, possibly from "Democracy and Education", p.173, and attributes the statement's wide spread to the way "it concisely encapsulates Dewey's approach to reflective practice and its relationship to learning" (p. 1).

4 Cybernetic, not in the sense of computer-related, but in the sense of a self-regulating system where each of the parts of the system acts upon and responds to each other.

5 Label in "Marshmallow Laser Feast: Works of Nature" at the Australian Centre for the Moving Image. Consulted Now 26 2023.

6 I acknowledge my Western bias here. My colleagues in Aotearoa New Zealand use the Maori word *taonga* (treasure) to describe physical collections objects. It is a given to them that taonga are alive and possess the ability to communicate. And they are not unique in that. I was working with an American museum on a gallery that would feature portraits of people. A Native American colleague wanted to include a non-figurative stone object, and when I pressed them that we wanted to only display objects representing people, said, "Rocks are people too" in complete seriousness.

7 Whether this question matters to visitors is another question.

8 Something that is autotelic contains its own purpose. Autotelic enjoyment is its own reward.

9 Widely cited as being from the *Phenomenology of Perception* (London & New York: Routledge Classics, 2002). I was unable to find it in any of his published works and believe it to be another convenient paraphrase, like the Dewey quote earlier in this chapter.

References

Asher, Tedi. 2019. Visitor Engagement. https://www.pem.org/neuroscience-initiative/visitor-engagement

Black, Graham. 2005. *The Engaging Museum: Developing Museums for Visitor Involvement.* Routledge, p. 266.

Braden, Donna, Rosenthal, Ellen, & Spock, Daniel. 2005. What the Heck Is Experience Design? Exhibitionist, 24(2), 14–20.

California Association of Museums. 2012. Museums and Experience Design. California Association of Museums. p. 4.

Csikszentmihalyi, Mihaly, and Hermanson, Kim. "Intrinsic motivation in museums: Why does one want to learn?" In John Falk and Lynn Dierking, (Eds.), *Public Institutions for Personal Learning*, 67–78. Washington, DC: American Association of Museums, pp. 67–68.

Csikszentmihalyi, Mihaly. 1991. *Flow: The Psychology of Optimal Experience.* HarperCollins.

Dalsgaard, Peter. 2008. Experiential Design: Findings from Designing Engaging Interactive Environments. In Shane Pinder (Ed.), *Advances in Human Computer Interaction.* InTech, pp. 89–90.

Davidson, Brett. 2016. *Narrative Change and the Open Society Public Health Program.* Open Society Foundations, p. 22.

Deterding, Sebastian. 2017. Alibis for Adult Play: A Goffmanian Account of Escaping Embarrassment in Adult Play. *Games and Culture*, *13*(3), p. 263.

Dudley, Sandra H. (Ed.), 2012. *Museum Object: Experiencing the Properties of Things.* Routledge.

Falk, John H., and Dierking, Lynn D. 2000. *Learning from Museums.* Rowman & Littlefield, p. 9.

Falk, John H., and Dierking, Lynn D. 2012. *The Museum Experience Revisited*, 1st edition. Routledge.

Falk, John H., and Dierking, Lynn D. 2016. *The Museum Experience Revisited (eBook.)*. Routledge, p. 26.

Geismar, Haidy. 2018. *Museum Object Lessons for the Digital Age*. UCL Press.

Gurian, Elaine Heumann, 1999. What Is the Object of This Exercise? A Meandering Exploration of the Many Meanings of Objects in Museums, *Daedalus*, Summer, 1999, Vol. 128, No. 3, America's Museums (Summer, 1999), pp. 163–183.

Hannon, Valerie. 2009. Learning Futures: A Contribution to the Innovative Learning Environments Project of OECD/CERI. https://www.oecd.org/content/dam/oecd/en/publications/reports/2013/09/innovative-learning-environments_g1g331b7/9789264203488-en.pdf

Hazan, Susan. 2002. *The Virtual Aura - Is There Space For Enchantment in a Technological World?* In Museums and the Web 2001.

Herz, Rebecca. 2017. What Is Engagement, and When Is It Meaningful? | Museum Questions. Museum Questions. https://museumquestions.com/2014/08/20/what-is-engagement-and-when-is-it-meaningful/

Hill, Dan. 2012. *Dark Matter and Trojan Horses: A Strategic Design Vocabulary*. Strelka Press, p. xx.

Hindmarch, John, Terras, Melissa, and Robson, Stuart. 2019. On Virtual Auras: The Cultural Heritage Object in the Age of 3D Digital Reproduction. In In Hannah Lewi, Wally Smith, Dirk vom Lehn, & Steven Cooke (Eds.), *The Routledge International Handbook of New Digital Practices in Galleries, Libraries, Archives, Museums and Heritage Sites*. Routledge. pp. 243–256.

Höök, Kristina. 2019. *Designing with the Body - Somaesthetic Interaction Design*. p. xxi. MIT Press.

Hookham, Geoffrey, and Nesbitt, Keith. 2019. A Systematic Review of the Definition and Measurement of Engagement in Serious Games. *Proceedings of the Australasian Computer Science Week Multiconference*, ACM, p. 8.

Hooper-Greenhill, E., Dodd, J., Moussouri, T., Jones, C., Pickford, C., Herman, C., Morrison, M., Vincent, J., and Toon, R. (2003). Measuring the Outcomes and Impact of Learning in Museums, Archives and Libraries: The Learning Impact Research Project End of Project Paper.

Horowitz, Alexandra. 2013. *On Looking: Eleven Walks with Expert Eyes*. Scribner.

James, William. 1950. *The Principles of Psychology*. Dover Publications, Vol. 1, p. 380.

Juul, Jesper. 2008. The Magic Circle and the Puzzle Piece. *Conference Proceedings of the Philosophy of Computer Games 2008*.

Keogh, B. 2018. *A Play of Bodies: How We Perceive Videogames*. The MIT Press.

Koljonen, J. 2016. Experience Design to Use Today. *Alibis for Interaction* 2016. Mälmo, Sweden.

Lagueux, Robert C. 2014. A spurious John Dewey quotation on reflection. https://www.academia.edu/17358587/A_Spurious_John_Dewey_Quotation_on_Reflection

Marci, Carl. 2017. Content and Media Overload: Advertising to Distracted Consumers. https://www.marketingprofs.com/articles/2017/31999/advertising-in-the-age-of-distraction

Meehan, N. 2023. Digital Museum Objects and Transnational Histories. In Emma Bond, and Michael Morris (Eds.), *Scotland's Transnational Heritage: Legacies of Empire and Slavery*. Edinburgh University Press, p. 173.

Murray, Janet H. 2019. Hamlet on the holodeck: The future of narrative in cyberspace. MIT Press. https://mitpress.mit.edu/books/hamlet-holodeck-updated-edition

Nahum-Shani, Inbal, Shaw, Steven D., Carpenter, Stephanie M., Murphy, Susan A., Yoon, Carolyn. 2022. Engagement in Digital Interventions. *American Psychologist*, vol. 77, no. 7, Oct. 2022, p. 837.

Newbery, Patrick. 2013. Experience Design Is a Perspective, Not a Discipline | UX Magazine. *UX Magazine*. https://uxmag.com/articles/experience-design-is-a-perspective-not-a-discipline

O'Brien, Heather L., andToms, Elaine G. 2008. What Is User Engagement? A Conceptual Framework for Defining User Engagement with Technology. *Journal of the American Society for Information Science and Technology*, vol. 59, no. 6, Apr. 2008, p. 941.

Paris, S.G. (Ed.). 2002. *Perspectives on Object-Centered Learning in Museums*. Lawrence Erlbaum Associates.

Park, Juhee., and Samms, Anouska. 2019. *The Materiality of the Immaterial: Collecting Digital Objects at the Victoria and Albert Museum*. MW19, pp. 1–19.

Paul, Annie M. 2021. *The Extended Mind: The Power of Thinking Outside the Brain*. Mariner Books.

Pétrement, Simone and Rosenthal, Raymond 1976. Simone Weil. Mowbrays.

Pine, B. Joseph II, and Gilmore, James H. 1999. *The Experience Economy: Work Is Theater & Every Business a Stage*. Harvard Business School Press.

Rao, Seema. 2019. What Is Audience Engagement? Museum 2.0. https://museumtwo.blogspot.com/2019/10/what-is-audience-engagement.html

Rodney, Seph. 2019. *The Personalization of the Museum Visit: Art Museums, Discourse, and Visitors*. Routledge.

Roppola, Tiina. 2013. *Designing for the Museum Visitor Experience*. Routledge. p. 30.

Rossman, J. Robert, and Duerden, Mathew D. 2019. *Designing Experiences*. Columbia University Press, p. 39.

Rozan, Adam. 2016. Audience Engagement: How Museums Learned to Love Their Visitors. Museum ID. https://museum-id.com/audience-engagement-how-museums-learned-to-love-their-visitors-by-adam-rozan/

Samis, Peter. S., and Michaelson, Mimi. 2016. *Creating the Visitor-Centered Museum*. Routledge.

Shirky, Clay, 2011. *Cognitive Surplus: How Technology Makes Consumers into Collaborators*, Reprint edition. ed. Penguin Books, p. 21.

Skinner, Ellen A., and Belmont, Michael J. 1993. Motivation in the Classroom: Reciprocal Effects of Teacher Behavior and Student Engagement across the School Year. *Journal of Educational Psychology*, vol. 85, no. 4, 1993, p. 571.

Stenros, Jaakko 2015. *Playfulness, Play, and Games. A Constructionist Ludology Approach*. University of Tampere.

Stenros, Jaakko, and Montola, Markus. 2019. Basic Concepts in Larp Design. In J. Koljonen, J. Stenros, A.S. Grove, A.D. Skjønsfjell, and E. Nilsen (Eds.), Larp Design: Creating Role-Play Experiences. Landsforeningen Bifrost.

Taylor, T.L. 2006. *Play between Worlds*. MIT Press.

Weil, Stephen. E. 1999. From Being about Something to Being for Somebody: The Ongoing Transformation of the American Museum. *Daedalus*, vol. 128, no. 3, 1999, pp. 229–258.

Weinard, Chad. 2019. Comment on "Defining 'Engagement' – Thinking about Museums." Accessed March 1, 2020. https://thinkingaboutmuseums.com/2019/12/04/defining-engagement/

Welsh, P. 2005. Re-configuring museums. *Museum Management and Curatorship*, 20, 103–130.

Wood, Elizabeth E., and Latham, Kiersten Fourshé. 2013. *The Objects of Experience: Transforming Visitor-Object Encounters in Museums*. Routledge.

Wood, Elizabeth, Tisdale, Rainey, and Jones, Trevor. (Eds.). 2018. *Active Collections.* Routledge.

Wood, Elizabeth, and Wolf, Barbara. 2008. Between the Lines of Engagement in Museums: Indiana University and the Children's Museum of Indianapolis. *The Journal of Museum Education*, Vol. 33, No. 2, Summer, 2008, p. 127.

Wood, Tom 2018. Experience design: A definition. https://www.foolproof.co.uk/journal/experience-design-a-definition/

2 Sensory Immersion

The Sense of "Being There"

Imagine you're sitting on a bench in the lobby of a large national museum, one of those grand, imposing architectural spaces; made of polished stone with soaring ceilings, monumental doorways, and the reverberating noise of crowds of people. The air's a little cool and as close to 50% relative humidity as the museum can make it. You can feel the hardness and cool stone of the bench under you, and the air has that museum-y smell of unknown chemicals, old stuff, and other people. Look around the space. What do you notice? Is it the architecture? The objects on display? The other people? Can you feel yourself in that space? If you can, what you've done is take those sensory inputs from the environment and constructed an immersive environment in your head.

Now imagine you've put on a virtual reality (VR) headset and fired up a VR application like *Gaudí: Atelier of the Divine*, and you're going to visit his studio in 1920s Barcelona. What do you do? What attracts your interest? Move your head around to change the view. Listen to the sound change. Can you imagine yourself standing there? If so, you've taken those sensory inputs, decided to accept them as real, and constructed an immersive environment in your head.

You've likely encountered the term immersion a lot out in the world, where it is employed almost to the point of losing any meaning. In fact, "immersion" and "immersive" are so overused in the world of experience design that Walt Disney Imagineering bars use of the word "immersive" in their internal pitch decks (Elger and Brigante 2022). Be that as it may, our ability to create magic circles that engage visitors on many levels has expanded as new technologies have arrived that allow designers to create amazing all-encompassing sensory environments. In this chapter, I will explore the first of four concepts for creating playful engagement: sensory immersion—that feeling of "being there"—where "there" is some other interesting place. I will look at defining what immersion is, take a brief tour of the surprisingly long history of immersive experiences, different theories and models of immersion, explore the psychological impacts of presence and plausibility on our ability to create an immersive experience in our heads, and look at examples from around the world of physical, digital, and hybrid immersive experiences. Research into how we perceive digitally extended environments like augmented reality (AR), mixed reality (MR), and VR will be highlighted, not only for what it tells us about how these kinds of environments work, but what it also tells us about immersion in the

DOI: 10.4324/9781032638690-2

physical world. All along the way, you will see evidence for the deep entanglement of the four concepts I'm exploring in this book. Around the same time the idea of this book was forming, Jenny Kidd (2018) noted the rising interest in all four of these four concepts as part of her research into heritage experiences (pp. 1–2). Narrative, games and play, and emotional affect all make appearances in this chapter, just as immersion will continue to show up in the later chapters.

We will also engage with some of the critiques of immersion that go beyond the tired and unhelpful debates about whether immersive experiences are "authentic" or not. As Peter Tullin, Co-Founder of the REMIX Summits has said (2022),

> The immersive genie is well and truly out of the bottle. Whether it is the unrelenting pace of technological progress driving the creation of more and more realistic immersive environments (digital, physical and hybrid) or the changes in audience taste the trend appears set in stone.

Thinking about sensory immersion as a tool and, increasingly, as an audience expectation is part of the experience design landscape now, so what are we to make of it?

The History of Immersive Exhibits

Immersion is certainly having a moment in the 2020s. While the display technologies being deployed are new, the desire to be immersed in an "other" reality is not. Oliver Grau's *Virtual Art: From Illusion to Immersion* (2004) provides a useful antidote to the ahistorical narratives surrounding the current crop of digital immersives.

> The idea of virtual reality only appears to be without a history; in fact, it rests firmly on a history of art tradition, which belong to a discontinuous movement of seeking illusionary image spaces… the idea stretches back at least as far as classical antiquity and is alive again today in the immersive visualization strategies of virtual reality art.
>
> (p. 339)

A look at a few select early immersive experiences will demonstrate the strategies different generations of designers have employed to capture visitors' attention with immersion and demonstrate longstanding tension between "is it art?" and "immersive as spectacle/technical achievement."

Physical Immersion

Immersive experiences have a history that predates their adoption by museums. Dioramas[1] are probably the most commonly encountered kind of immersive experience in museums and have their own literature including Mortensen (2010), Bitgood (2011), and Kamcke and Hutterer (2015) as do their art museum cousins, the period room, with Murtha (2005) and Harris (2012). One thing dioramas and period rooms both have in common is their refusal of entry to visitors. You peer through glass or look over a railing into an environment you are unable to fully enter. As a visitor, you are aware of the barrier that keeps you out. For centuries, designers have explored ways to minimize or remove that barrier and create experiences that allow you to feel as though are really "in" that place.

Barker's Panorama, 1787

In 1787, Robert Barker coined the word "panorama" to describe a new display technology, a 21 meter-long, 180-degree painting of Edinburgh that was designed to fill the viewer's entire field of view. He later built the first purpose-built panorama building in 1793, a 360-degree view of London. Despite its commercial success, much of the public conversation alternated between appreciation for the technical achievement and debate about whether it was "real" art (Grau 2004, p. 58).

Robertson's Phantasmagoria *1799*

In France, Étienne-Gaspard Robert, who used the stage name "Robertson," employed image projectors, a real environment (an abandoned convent), and a mix of scientific demonstrations and literary allusions to toy with the idea of life and death and provoke horror in his audiences to the extent that one observer said,

> The illusion is certainly complete. The total darkness of the location of the scene, the choice of the figures, the astonishing magic of their truly terrifying gradation, the prestige that surrounds them, all come together to strike your imagination and to take over all your observational senses…
>
> (Harris, 2022)

When you consider that most of Robertson's adult audience had lived through both the French Revolution and the Reign of Terror that followed it, their experience of horror underlines the power of immersion.

Anton von Werner's Sedan Panorama, *1883*

Anton von Werner's panorama of the Battle of Sedan opened in Berlin on September 1, 1883, the anniversary of Prussia's victory over the French in 1870. It was in its day the largest (1,725 m^2) and most expensive painting in the world (Grau 2007). The environment blended real props with a painted background and was designed using state of the art research on sensory perception to create its illusion of completeness. It was lauded as much for its scale and technical accomplishments as for its artistic merits. The painting placed viewers in the middle of the battle at the moment of victory of the new German empire and was explicitly designed to instill a sense of martial pride in Germans. It stayed on view for 30 years and is conservatively estimated to have been seen by 10 million visitors.

Immersive Van Gogh and the current crop of projection-based digital immersive experiences sit squarely in this lineage of large-scale, public spectacles. The display technology has evolved, but the public appetite for spectacle is the same. The South Korean government's recent underwriting production of a series of immersive experiences "to allow its citizens to experience history and gain pride in its heritage" (Cureton 2021) would probably not surprise von Werner.

Virtual Immersion

The history of headset-based VR is also long. Wheatstone's exploration of binocular vision in the 1830s and his announcement in 1838 of the first 3D viewer, the stereoscope, predate Daguerre's first public announcement of photography (Mills 2018). By the 1860s, stereoscopes, essentially handheld VR headsets, were popular and (unlike today) inexpensive devices that allowed people to view distant sites and famous people, all from the comfort of their homes. In the 20th century, the inventions of motion pictures and then television all had corresponding dreamers attempting to make 3D versions of successful 2D display technologies. Then came computers and the race continued.

Ivan Sutherland's Sword of Damocles, 1968

Sutherland and his students created the first head-mounted computer 3D computer display in 1968 (Virtual Reality Society n.d.). Due to the size and weight of the equipment, it was ceiling mounted and hung over the head of the wearer, thus spawning its slightly threatening name.

VPL EyePhone, 1987

Jaron Lanier coined the term "virtual reality" in 1987 to describe the experience of using his company's first commercial head-mounted display (HMD). The system included not just the HMD, but a pair of glove-based input devices called DataGloves and a full-body outfit with sensors to track movement. Despite its initial popularity, the VPL was bankrupt by 1990 (Laplante 2017, pp. 1293–1297).

Oculus VR Oculus Rift, 2012

Palmer Luckey started his company in 2012 to produce VR headsets, and launched a crowdfunding campaign to underwrite the development of their first product, the Oculus Rift. Public and computer gaming industry interest in such a device was enormous and turned the Rift into an overnight sensation. The company was purchased by Facebook in 2014 for US$2 billion, beginning the current era of massive investment in VR by the largest digital technology companies like Meta (formerly Facebook), Google, and Apple.

VR has stubbornly hovered on the edge of becoming as popular as stereoscopes were in the 1860s for almost 30 years. The technology consulting firm Gartner

Associates created the Gartner Hype Cycle in 1995 to measure adoption of new technologies and the marketing excitement created around them. In 1995, VR was already categorized as being in the "trough of disillusionment" the point where "interest wanes as experiments and implementations fail to deliver" (Gartner n.d.). Fast forward 20 years and the New Media Consortium's Horizon Report 2016: Museum Edition, a publication dedicated to educational technology forecasting for museums, put VR in the "two to three years to public adoption" category (Freeman et al. 2016). Almost a decade later, despite a steady stream of new entries into the field, VR is still not quite ready for primetime, and remains a niche technology.

This is not to say that VR or its kin (AR/MR/XR) lack utility for museums. Quite the opposite. Museums have a long history of utilizing new technologies that the public does not have easy access to. The incredible intimacy of the medium and its all-encompassing control of the visitor's visual (and sometimes auditory) sense are powerful tools, as you'll see in some of the examples in this chapter. What it does mean for us as experience designers is that we need to be able to articulate the value of using VR over any other possible means of presenting content to visitors and be clear-eyed about the implications of employing "cutting edge" technologies and their potential pitfalls.

Despite Rose (2018) heralding "the immersive turn" in new media, we can see that the new interest in immersion is just the latest occurrence of an age-old human desire. Having put immersion back into its historical context, let's describe it more precisely.

The Hallmarks of Immersive Experiences

The Routledge Encyclopedia of Narrative Theory describes immersion as, "any state of absorption in some action, condition, or interest" (Schaeffer and Vultur, 2010). Immersion, for them, is a result absorption or focused attention.

> The term 'immersion' is most commonly encountered in theoretical contexts related to multimedia environments, * computer games, and other implementations of virtual reality. This leads sometimes to the erroneous belief that only modern technological devices have the capability to produce states or processes of immersion. In fact, immersion is central to mental simulation in general and to mimetic art in particular…

This is an important point. Despite its current connection to digital experiences, immersion is not a function of projectors or headsets, but a state of mind people have been wrestling with since at least Plato's time and probably longer. Janet Murray defined sensory immersion thus,

> Immersion is a metaphorical term derived from the physical experience of being submerged in water. We seek the same feeling from a psychologically immersive experience that we do from a plunge in the ocean or swimming pool: the sensation of being surrounded by a completely other reality, as

different as water is from air, that takes over all of our attention, our whole perceptual apparatus.

(Murray 2019, p. 124)

I will use this definition throughout this book for understanding the utility of sensory immersion.

One reason I think that we have such a hard time talking about immersion in the real world is that it is such a ubiquitous feature of waking life that it's hard to acknowledge. As the neuroscientist Banzai noted, "No matter where you go, there you are" (Richter 1984). We are continuously immersed in the world around us, and have evolved complex systems to interpret and act on the sensory data that we are being bombarded with. Isolating variables to understand how we experience environments can be extremely difficult. One (unintended) benefit of the current state of digital immersive technologies is that they offer a very limited set of variables to test; they're almost entirely visual with some auditory component. This is helpful because it allows researchers to focus on a subset of responses to what makes immersion happen. From that comes learnings that can be applied in physical environments. The common hallmarks of immersion I'll cite below come from a variety of disciplines and look at many different kinds of immersive experiences.

Intrinsic Motivation

The poet Samuel Coleridge coined the phrase "the active suspension of disbelief" to describe how readers can look past the fact that they are reading a story to project themselves into the story they're reading. Murray goes a step further than Coleridge, to center the intrinsic motivation people have to experience new things and names the same phenomenon "the active creation of belief." She writes,

> When we enter a fictional world, we do not merely "suspend" a critical faculty; we also actively create belief. Because of our desire to experience immersion, we focus our attention on the enveloping world and we use our intelligence to reinforce rather than question the reality of the experience.
>
> (Murray 2017, p. 136)

This explains how low-resolution virtual environments with their limited interactivity can seem so "immersive" to viewers. In actively creating belief in the fictive world of the immersive experience, we use our brains to fill in the details that aren't there. For some, like Pimentel and Texeira,

> The question isn't whether the created world is as real as the physical world, but whether the created world is real enough for you to suspend your disbelief for a period of time. This is the same mental shift that happens when you get wrapped up in a good novel or become absorbed in playing a computer game.
>
> (Quoted in Ryan 1999, p. 114)

The more details the designers add, the more raw material the viewer has to create the illusion of immersion.

> When an environment is very deep and detailed, we feel as if we are enclosed by it and it has a special holding power over us as an alternative to the disordered actual world of everyday experience. This is true of noninteractive environments, but it is especially powerful in environments we can navigate through with freedom of action.
>
> (Murray 2019, p. 211)

This intrinsic motivation can be seen in the rise in popularity of immersive experiences in the 21st century. We like exploring novel environments and seek them out.

Active Transition

One of the hallmarks of immersion is the apparent contradiction that your brain negotiates between knowing that your body is located in one environment, but processing information about an imagined environment as though it were real. Murray's "immersion" is an active, transitional process in which the person begins in one environment and enters another environment. Immersion requires two environments which are substantially, noticeably different. For the magic to happen, we have to be aware of the transition. This is important to remember because we are *always* immersed in whatever environment we are in. But just as its hard for fish to see the water they swim in, we take our default environment for granted once we understand the rules. When we leave our default environment, the one in which our Attention System 1 is comfortably taking care of things, and enter a different environment, our brains have to switch to Attention System 2 to try to understand what's going on. Immersion is, in one sense, the act of transitioning between environments and being aware of the transition. This distinction is critically important to us as experience designers. As Seb Chan has said, "immersion matters to create a distinction between the outside world and inside the exhibition, a magic circle where visitors gain superpowers" (Chan 2019). Whether visitors gain superpowers or not, the idea that the rules inside the magic circle might be different than those outside is essential. Immersion triggers a shift in how we attend to the environment. Provided with an interaction alibi that gives us guardrails to know what to do, all three parts of the magic circle are present, and we can fruitfully explore that environment and discover the superpowers the designer—you—have given them.

The challenge for many museums is that mainstream design in collecting museums has promoted minimalist environments which are purposely designed to recede so visitors can focus on the objects and exhibits. Writing in response to the crowded salon style installations of the 18th and 19th centuries, Benjamin Ives Gilman's primary concern at the beginning of the 20th century was in reducing what he called "museum fatigue" (Gilman 1918, p. 251). Given how much of Gilman's concern with museum fatigue had to do with human factors design, like viewing angles and seating, it is ironic that traditional museum practice has tended to ignore our embodied humanity in favor of intellectual and visual engagement. His aesthetic successors, the white cubes and black boxes have continued the trend of focusing attention exclusively on small numbers of discrete objects (Birkett 2012, p. 20). Designing an environment that is markedly different from its neighbors and designing an environment that is designed to be ignored are obvious anti-patterns. When we know where we are, we can operate on Kahneman's Attention System 1. It's only when we have to ask the question "Where am I?" that System 2 kicks in and we consciously perceive our surroundings in detail.

Agency

In the case of museum environments, the agency visitors possess to navigate around and interact with the environment is important. Since part of the immersive experience is the transition from the default environment to the new one, the metaphor of "visiting" with all its associations of self-directed travel and foreignness is ideal.

> For the purposes of experiencing multisensory immersion, one of the simplest ways to structure participation is to adopt the format of the visit. The visit metaphor is particularly appropriate for establishing a border between the virtual world and ordinary life because a visit involves explicit limits on both time and space.
>
> (Murray 2017, pp. 132–133)

Amusement parks have employed this for decades. Think of a fun house, or one of the rides that are designed to scare visitors, and they'll usually have a prominent portal that visitors must pass through but can't see beyond.

Agency—what Murray calls "the satisfying power to take meaningful action and see the results of our decisions and choices" (Murray 2019, p. 159)—becomes even more important in VR environments and other kinds of immersive experiences. It may seem counterintuitive but the idea that your digital avatar is engaged in activity that exceeds the actions your physical body is taking seems to be part of the appeal of virtual environments. This connection between agency and pleasure is essential. The exercise of that agency is both satisfying and self-reinforcing. Even acts as simple as navigation can be pleasant, regardless of the content of a physical or virtual landscape (Murray 2019, p. 162). Look at the current vogue for large, projection-based "immersive" art exhibitions, where the only interaction visitors have is looking, listening to ambient soundtracks, and moving around the space. The immersive nature of the space is highlighted and sustained by movement, and many visitors find this satisfying and sufficient (Capps 2021), to the chagrin of many in the cultural sector like Choi (2023) and Marsh (2023) who find these experiences underwhelming and lacking in intellectual and aesthetic depth.

Pine and Gilmore (1998) proposed four realms of a customer experience, namely, education, entertainment, escapism, and aesthetics. An obvious question to ask would be whether museum experiences are like other kinds of customer experiences. In one study (Radder and Han 2015), researchers found that visitors to three South African museums didn't distinguish much between education and entertainment. "Satisfaction" encompasses both. This seeming muddle can be clarified by applying Brian Lonsway's (2016) concept of "complicated agency" as a way to critically understand how an immersive experience can be both "empowering and disempowering, supportive and challenging of free will, educational and consumerist" all at once, and move beyond the reductionist debates that ceaselessly circle around the dialectic of experiences being "authentic" versus "fake." Lonsway's agency urges us to see the visitor to an immersive experience actively employing their agency to become a role-player (visitor) within the narrative (object) created by the designers of the experience, all the while understanding that they are playing a role (interaction alibi) and agreeing to play it as long as satisfies them.

Embodiment

One of the great advantages of employing immersion as a tool is how it naturally encourages us to design embodied experiences. Jenny Kidd underlines the potential of immersive museum experiences in their ability to engage all the senses in a fully embodied way.

> Traditionally museums have privileged visual and textual resources, but with immersive experiences we see a (potentially radical) realignment so that aural, haptic, olfactory and kinesthetic qualities are also explored. In the best of immersive scenarios, it is hoped that meaning-making becomes a whole-body endeavor.
>
> (Kidd 2018, p. 7)

Looking back on 30 years of creating museum experiences, I agree that acknowledging visitors' embodiment is essential, as interaction designer Kristina Höök says, "Embodiment speaks of how we are always in the world, with our bodies, sociality, and practices – that we are inseparable from the world. The way our perception and knowing works is entangled deeply, inseparably with our surrounding" (Höök 2019, p. xxi). For the experience designer, employing sensory immersion encourages us to design not only for the center of attention, but also the often-overlooked periphery of attention. Amber Case makes a strong case for utilizing the periphery as a way to preserve visitors' ability to focus.

> The periphery of our attention is important because we can't focus our attention on many different things at once. We have high-resolution perception in front of our faces, directly in line with our vision, and that resolution degrades as we move off to the sides. We can, however, hear sounds, see shapes, and feel objects without having to directly look at them.
>
> (Case 2016, p. 22)

This embodiment is with us, even in virtual settings. AR, MR, and VR are promoted to museums because they're *immersive*. Implicit in this framing is the assumption that museums *aren't* already immersive experiences, an assumption I think that is shared by many in the field. This framing is incorrect, obviously, and it displaces the locus of immersion from the person onto the technology. Digital technology is not what museums need to be immersive. "As a user experience, the feeling of 'being there,' or presence, is not intrinsically bound to any specific type of technology – it is a product of the mind" (IJsselsteijn and Riva 2003, p. 3). Sensory immersion is not merely a product of the mind, but is a system consisting of an experience and its contents and an embodied person moving within it according to the rules laid out by the designers. As Brendan Keogh (2018) points out exploration of embodiment in video games, "…immersion is often treated as an inherent attribute of the videogame form rather than a perceptual strategy performed by an actual player engaging with input devices, screen imagery, and digital sounds" (p. 33). The visitor exploring the novel environment and the things in it make another kind of magic circle.

Emotional Resonance

The neuroeconomist Paul Zak's book *Immersion* (2022) aims to help advertisers create more memorable commercials using immersion. As you'll see repeatedly, emotion, narrative, and emotion are deeply entwined. Like Murray and Ryan, he was looking at a stationary audience engaging with a linear narrative, in this case television ads. He was also interested in peoples' responses at a chemical level and how neurological signals could be measured to indicate immersion and predict behavior afterwards. Among Zak's key findings were that immersion and emotion are connected. For Zak, immersion requires both attention and emotional resonance, and it is that resonance that drives how immersed we feel. Experiences that succeed in holding our attention and resonate emotionally receive more processing in our brains and are therefore more likely to be remembered (p. 50).

Of interest to us as experience designers, Zak also noted the importance of feeling safe as a precondition

SIDEBAR: Is it immersive?

An example. I attended a workshop on immersion at the Detroit Institute for the Arts (American Alliance of Museums & Knight Foundation 2018). One of the speakers was the Vince Kadlubek, the CEO of Santa Fe-based art collective MeowWolf. MeowWolf creates enormous 30–90,000 ft²/3,000–9,000 m²) immersive environments. After his presentation on MeowWolf, there was the usual scrum of interested attendees eager to ask questions. One of them asked, "Do you think museums could be immersive spaces?" and Vince looked around the Crystal Court, where the workshop was being held and said, "Are you kidding me? Look around!" It was fascinating to watch how many museum people took in the space, with its food service tables, portable lectern and projection screen that all said, "meeting space" and didn't see the polished stone floors, gilded crystal chandeliers, giant torchiere lamps, velvet wrapped doors, and other stunning architectural features that Vince saw. They were in a "museum" and literally couldn't see how someone else might be an immersive setting. Part of the challenge of immersion is our need as practitioners to get out of our default ways of being and learn to see like visitors (Figures 2.1 and 2.2).

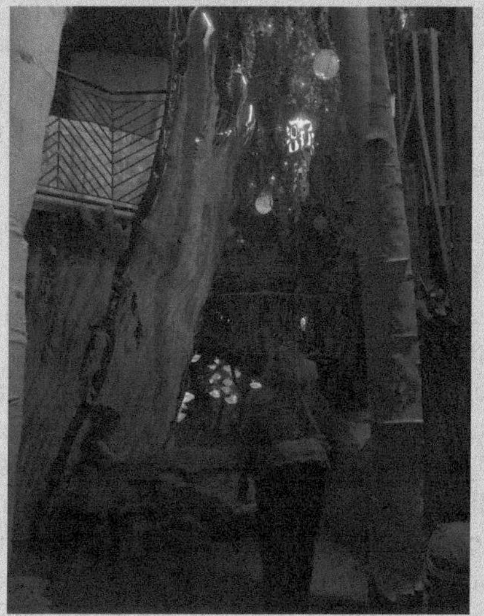

Figure 2.1 MeowWolf. Photo by author

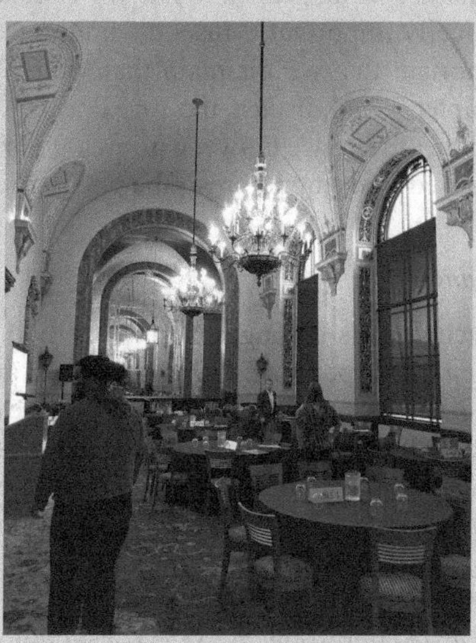

Figure 2.2 The Crystal Court, Detroit Institute for the Arts. Photo by author

of immersion. Regardless of the content of the commercial, people had to be in a mental state where they could relax enough to take in the sensory information.

> Psychological safety is the precursor to Immersion. If people are not relaxed, they do not have the metabolic energy to be immersed in an experience. Moreover, it is critical that diverse individuals feel comfortable in the physical space and social context of a learning experience.
>
> (p. 134)

This is the interaction alibi of the magic circle; the guardrails that allow visitors to let their guards down enough to engage deeply.

Zak also references another contribution of Kahneman to our understanding of how people process experiences. Barbara Fredrickson and he (1993) coined the term the "Peak-end rule" to describe the phenomenon that we tend to remember the emotional peaks and the end of an experience, especially a longer one, rather than the whole experience. This coupled with the brain's limited ability to maintain focused attention for longer than 30–40 seconds highlights the importance of emotional pacing. Identifying those emotional peaks will allow you to arrange them so that you can end on an emotionally resonant note. It should also encourage you to create the emotional "valleys" on either side where visitors can relax and recharge.

Zak's work is not without its critics, including me. It has a very strongly instrumentalist leaning to it. What we choose to do or not do with this information is critically important. Museums hold a tremendous amount of public trust, and it is important that we maintain that trust. We'll look at emotional evocation more in Chapter 3 and discuss the fine line between being evocative versus manipulative and the difference between allowing visitors to feel safe responding emotionally as opposed to trying to prescribe one particular emotional response.

"Being There"

Psychologists distinguish between two distinct illusions happening in our brains when we experience "immersion" in augmented or VR experiences. The first is a sense of "presence"—that our senses tell us we're *really* there. Lombard and Ditton describe presence as "the artificial sense that a user has in a virtual environment that the environment is unmediated" (Lombard et al. 2000). In other words, we decide to ignore the technological mediation of a screen or headset and speakers, and choose to pretend it's real. That technological intervention is another kind of magic circle in that it provides the boundaries within which that feeling can occur (Slater 2009, p. 3552). Psychologists like Slater call that sense of "being there" *the place illusion* (p. 3549). In digitally mediated environments it is generated by "synchronous correlations between the act of moving and concomitant changes in the images that form perception" (p. 3553). So when you do something with your body like changing the orientation of your viewpoint or turning in response to a sound, the virtual scene changes in response to that.

Interestingly, the idea of presence was closely tied to embodiment and originated in research of how people could view remote tools as extensions of their bodies. People in digital virtual environments, though, aren't disembodied. They're people with bodies, moving their heads to reorient the headset, waving controllers and pressing buttons, moving in real space to trigger a corresponding movement in the virtual one. Keogh (2018) emphasizes this embodiment and its incomplete nature: "Virtual worlds are partial worlds in need of the player's perceptual apparatus to bring it to life" (p. 55). Over time, the popular understanding of presence has shifted to a largely visual one because of the interest in virtual and augmented reality technologies (Slater 2009, p. 3551).

The second illusion is the *plausibility illusion*—that 'there' is *actually* happening, even though we know that we are *not* really there and that the events are *not* actually occurring. The plausibility illusion is also enhanced by the way environment operates. "Based on evidence over many experiments, it appears that a key component of [the plausibility illusion] is that events in the virtual environment over which you have no direct control refer directly to you" (Slater 2009, p. 3553). So the way that virtual light might reflect off a surface just like it would in the physical world would increase the plausibility of that environment. Interestingly, these two illusions are not tightly connected, and a virtual environment might do a great job at one illusion but not the other, and still produce a sense of "immersion" in the viewer.

Critiques of Immersion

Hopefully, you begin to see some of the ways that immersion can be a useful concept to employ in your work. An effective immersive experience contains many of the building blocks of playful engagement: it is intrinsically motivated and self-satisfying, it elicits emotional responses, and tends to enhance memorability. So far, so good. But immersion is not without its critics. As a tool to influence human behavior, immersion is value-neutral, it is neither good nor bad. How it gets employed is entirely up to the creators. As we saw in Zak's work on making more effective TV ads, the goal can be purely commercial, or even harmful. Likewise, for many of the commercial immersive experiences, their primary goal is get people to spend money to see them and success equals popularity which equals profit. In the case of museum experiences, which comprise a tiny percentage of the immersive experience sector, our concerns and ethical consideration do not get much space.

This led Alke Gröppel-Wegener and Jenny Kidd (2019), active creators and researchers in the field of cultural heritage and immersion, to devote an entire chapter of their book on immersive storytelling to critiques of immersion.

> [W]e (as authors) have both continued to find ourselves on occasion staggered by a lack of framing in (some) immersive experiences, or as confused and irritated by what those experiences were asking us to give, instances that required us to offer up our own stories and closely guarded secrets, our emotional responses, our empathy, our personal space, or our data, for what seemed inexplicable or indefensible ends. We have noted that much of the marketing literature about the creation of 'storyworlds' continues to advocate for the exploitation of emotion with little regard to the ethical dimensions of that practice... and we continue to find the technology being too regularly and simplistically conflated with immersion itself.
>
> (p. 87)

They go on to level four charges against the current discourse around immersion. First, they question the assertion often made that immersive experiences, which are often billed as more participatory and provide visitors with more agency, are therefore more empowering. Second, they contend that immersive experiences are being 'co-opted' by mainstream consumer culture, and are often understood only within the context of the experience economy. Third, they highlight how immersion particularly in video gaming can foster engagement and escapism to a degree that can become problematic and addictive. Last, they note that much of the discourse about immersion focuses on the digital technologies used in these experiences, even though nothing about immersion requires digitality. In short, immersion, as it's employed out in the world, is not without problems. As experience designers, we need to be intentional about how and why we employ it.

Models of Immersion

The phenomenon of immersion happens in many different contexts. You can be immersed in a book, a movie, a conversation, and a place, just to name a few. If you think of a museum exhibition (physical or digital) as "the medium of media" as Dan Spock defines it (quoted in Dillenburg 2011, p. 11), then it makes sense to look at how immersion is defined in a variety of media. The definition I quoted at the beginning of the chapter was written by a media theorist interested in interactive narrative. Literary scholar Marie-Laure Ryan distinguishes between three different types of immersion: spatial immersion (the response to setting), temporal immersion (the response to story), and emotional immersion (the response to character) (Bell and Ryan 2019, p. 27). Like Murray, she also believes that interactivity, especially in digital media, can either aid or hinder the feeling of immersion. She highlights the paradox of our already-immersive world being hardest to simulate. "Paradoxically, the reality of which we are native is the least amenable to immersive narration, and reports of real events are the least likely to produce a feeling of being on the scene" (Ryan 1999, p. 119). This may be one reason why virtual analogues of physical museum spaces aren't more compelling to more visitors, no matter how much museum professionals may want to recreate galleries in VR. The familiarity of the environment inhibits our ability to actively pretend what we're experiencing is as real as, say, a quasi-medieval wilderness full of dragons.

Hopefully you've noted that though I've been talking about immersion, the sources I've been relying on are studying emotion, narrative, and games. Immersion is a topic of interest to game theorists and designers, particularly since the rise of online computer games with persistent storyworlds and massive audiences of simultaneous players. Media theorist Jan-Noël Thon (2008) melds Murray's and Ryan's work (along with many others like Ermi and Mäyrä (2005), and Sweetser and Wyeth 2005) to propose a four part model of immersion that includes *spatial immersion*, which corresponds to the psychological concept of presence, that feeling of "being there"; *ludic immersion*, which corresponds to Mihály Csíkszentmihályi's concept of flow, where the brain is engaged in an all-consuming but pleasurable task; *narrative immersion*, which corresponds to Ryan's emotional immersion, or the ability to feel affected by events in the environment; and *social immersion*, which corresponds to the concept of social presence, where the presence of others and interaction with them are salient to your experience.

Stacey Mason uses frames of mind as the way to distinguish between two types of immersion: *mechanical immersion*, which corresponds closely to Csíkszentmihályi's concept of flow, and *narrative immersion*, which corresponds to both Murray's and Ryan's concepts of immersion (Mason 2013, p. 26). In one, the mind and body are engaged in an all-consuming task, and in the other, only the mind is engaged. The game scholar Mark Wolf, in his work on immersion, also makes the point of separating the physical from the mental. He distinguishes between three types of immersion: *physical immersion,* which corresponds to activities like theme park rides; perceptual *immersion,* which corresponds to activities like movies; and *conceptual immersion,* which corresponds to activities like literature (Wolf 2018, p. 204). If you imagine a modern museum experience, it might encompass all three of Wolf's types of immersion (Figure 2.3).

Immersion Frameworks

Murray	*Ryan*	*Thon*	*Mason*	*Wolf*
Immersion	• Spatial immersion • Emotional immersion • Temporal • Immersion	• Narrative immersion	• Narrative immersion	• Conceptual immersion
		• Ludic immersion • Spatial immersion • Social immersion	• Mechanical immersion	• Physical immersion • Perceptual immersion

Figure 2.3 Comparison of immersion schemes

Immersion as a Beginning, Not an End

Immersion can be, in and of itself, a satisfying experience. Just popping in for a visit to a new, interesting place is enjoyable. But as museum experience designers interested in deeply connecting people with our content, it can also be a first step to deeper engagement. One of the criticisms leveled at many of the current crop of commercial immersive experiences is that there's not a lot of substance to them aside from big images splashed on every surface of the venue. After the novelty of that effect wears off, there's nothing more to do. A lot of the criticism around immersive experiences has been whether they're legitimate or "authentic" art experiences. To me, as a designer and visitor to them, I see them more as missed opportunities for deeper engagement.

This is where Mark Wolf's work on immersion has been most impactful on my practice. Writing about computer games, Wolf proposes a continuum of player engagement where immersion is only the first level of potential engagement a person might have. In Wolf's model, *immersion* can lead to *absorption,* which corresponds to the process of learning the rules and structure of the experience; *saturation,* which corresponds to the feeling that one has taken in as much as one can, and finally, *overflow,* which corresponds to the satisfying realization that one can never hold the experience entirely in one's mind—the imaginary environment is just too big (Wolf 2018, pp. 205–212). This ladder of engagement, he argues is what makes large, persistent world computer games so absorbing to players. You can enter and re-enter the game and every time feel like you are having a new and engaging experience.

Wolf's model is compelling both in terms of its comprehensiveness, and in how its four-level structure maps onto the model of playful engagement I described in Chapter 1. Immersion requires intrinsic motivation and focused attention. Absorption is the satisfying experience of engaging with the experience, and saturation is the feeling of having mastered a new set of rules. If the experience is deep enough, one feels the sense of overflow, which means one could repeat the experience a second time and experience the same progression and satisfaction again.

Immersive Museum Experiences

Karim Ben Khelifa The Enemy *(2017)*

The Enemy (http://theenemyishere. org/) is a virtual-reality experience where visitors walk through a series of face-to-face encounters with combatants from opposing sides of the three conflicts. The physical space mirrors the layout of a digital space and the visitors steers by walking, avoiding the need for handheld controllers. This interplay between virtual and physical environments, not only create immersion in the act of entering the simulated environment, but make users more aware of the 'default' experience of the real world afterwards.

teamLab Borderless *(2021)*

The Tokyo-based art collective teamLab's *Borderless* in Tokyo, a 10,000 m² collection of 50 different immersive works—many, but not all projection based—each creating a different environment like a waterfall or a field of enormous digital flowers, is an example of the skillful use of place illusion to form the illusion of one borderless world. Interactive artworks intermingle with each other, and it is sometimes difficult to say where one ends and another begins.

Cleveland Museum of Art, Revealing Krishna *(2021)*

In *Revealing Krishna*, the Cleveland Museum of Art created a traditional museum exhibition combined with immersive video and headset-based mixed reality to explore a Cambodian statue of the god Krishna and give visitors a sense of its original home in the temple of Phnom Da. Rather than relying solely on immersion, the museum has carefully chosen to augment its modes of display. Visitors can dip in and out of different immersive moments while having a traditional object-focused experience.

Alejandro Iñárritu, Carne y Arena *(Virtually Present, Physically Invisible) (2017)*

"Carne E Arena (Virtually Present, Physically Invisible)," a hybrid physical/virtual immersive experience by movie director Alejandro Iñárritu, has been featured at multiple museums since its creation in 2017. An exploration of migration across the U.S. southern border, it creates its immersion by blending a VR narrative with a real physical environment that reinforces the feeling of being in the desert. Visitors walk through a large sandy area while viewing an encounter between migrants and law enforcement.

New York Hall of Science, Connected Worlds *(2015)*

Connected Worlds at the New York Hall of Science is a large-scale interactive ecosystem composed of six different habitats, connected by an interactive floor and a 45-foot-high digital waterfall. Visitors can not only inspect the space but also can reshape

into the stern cabin and out through the stern window. In the cabin were all the things that a painter needed to live on board, mattress, pots and pans, coffee grinder, as well as blank canvases, paints and brushes, and an easel. The view out the stern window was a large projection screen showing placid shots of local waterways. The canvas on the easel was a rear screen projection of a time-lapse animation of a painter painting the view out the window. Speakers embedded throughout the boat emitted sounds of water lapping against the hull, the noises of insects, frogs, and birds and the wind in the branches of the trees. Inside the cabin out of visitors' reach, we placed objects with strong odors like brushes soaked in turpentine and tarred marline twine.

The visitor experience of the studio boat was that once the threshold of the boat was crossed, the environment was very different. Nowhere else in the exhibition was there a fully recreated environment. Once they examined all the props in the cabin, the visuals of the water view and canvas tended to absorb visitors' attention as they looked back and forth between the two to see how the painting was developing in relation to the view out the window. The experience also takes advantage of the periphery of visitors' attention. The sound came from multiple locations. Water noises issued from speakers embedded in the hull and mounted under the environments through their actions. This exhibition immerses viewers in its world and allows them to interact with and change the world. Some seeds can be "caught" and planted, causing new plants to grow. Physical logs can be moved around the floor to divert projected water flow into the habitats, causing plants and animals to grow and thrive. The exhibition immerses and absorbs visitors as they experiment and discover the limits of their agency.

Conclusion

As museum experience designers, the kind of engagement we are seeking to create is deep and lasting. I would argue that the non-linear nature of museum going, particularly exhibition-going, where two visitors can pursue completely non-overlapping paths through a space and both say "I saw that exhibition" has much in common with the kind of gameplay Wolf describes. What kinds of experiences might we design if we took Wolf's model of immersion to heart? A large part of Wolf's research deals with the "storyworlds" of games; the universe of all the characters, objects, and plot lines of that world. We'll talk more about them in Chapter 4. Television series writers develop a "story bible" that details all the elements of that world. What would your next project look like if you conceived it as a storyworld within which visitors could climb the engagement ladder that begins with immersion? Where might you take visitors if immersion were only the first step of their journey rather than the end point? Part of the potential power of immersive experiences is their ability to ground visitors in a space—physical or virtual—with others, as Josephine Machon (2024) points out, "A unique charm of this work is that it can remind individuals of what it is to be present; alive and engaged in community and conviviality, reinvigorating social connection and exchange."

the seats, so visitors would feel the noise as well as hear it. The wildlife and wind sounds came from up higher and more from the direction of the open window, but also from the sides. If you stood close to rope separating visitors from the cabin, you could smell paint and wood and tar. All of this could be taken in without diverting one's gaze from the painting that was emerging and compare it to the video. The lack of explicit interpretation gave visitors the freedom to just sit and take in the sights and sounds, and many sat through multiple cycles of the nine-minute-long video. In the aggregate, the media took over visitors' attention and provided enough multisensory stimuli that many visitors reported feeling the boat move.

Note

1 Interestingly, the word "diorama," was coined and popularized by Daguerre, who had previously worked on panorama painting, before successfully creating a viable process for photography. He therefore sits squarely in the lineage of both physical and virtual immersives.

References

Alejandro Iñárritu. 2017. *CARNE y ARENA (Virtually Present, Physically Invisible)*. https://carne-y-arena.com/

American Alliance of Museums & Knight Foundation. 2018. *Immersion in Museums: AR, VR, or Just Plain R?* American Alliance of Museums.

Bell, Alice, and Ryan, Marie-Laure. 2019. Possible Worlds Theory Revisited. In Bell, Alice, and Marie-Laure Ryan, (Eds.) *Possible Worlds Theory and Contemporary Narratology*. University of Nebraska Press, p. 27.

Birkett, Whitney B. 2012. To Infinity and Beyond: A Critique of the Aesthetic White Cube. Theses. 209. https://scholarship.shu.edu/theses/209

Bitgood, Stephen, 2011. Immersion Experiences in Museums. In *Social Design in Museums: The Psychology of Visitor Studies: Collected Essays*, vol. 1, MuseumsEtc, pp. 272–282.

Capps, Kriston. 2021. The Explosion of Digital Vincent Van Gogh Exhibits - Bloomberg. Bloomberg CityLab+Pursuits, https://www.bloomberg.com/news/features/2021-09-14/the-explosion-of-digital-vincent-van-gogh-exhibits

Case, Amber. 2016. *Calm Technology Principles and Patterns for Non-Intrusive Design*. O'Reilly Media.

Chan, Seb. 2019. On Immersion & Interactivity via #MW2019 – Seb Chan – Medium. https://medium.com/@sebchan/on-immersion-interactivity-via-mw2019-ac72d9c700bd

Choi, Christy. 2023. Immersive Art Exhibitions: Spellbinding, or Forgettable? *The New York Times*.

Cureton, Demond. 2021. Seoul Taps AR/VR to Recreate Joseon Dynasty. *XR Today*. https://www.xrtoday.com/mixed-reality/seoul-taps-ar-vr-to-recreate-joseon-dynasty/ (accessed 3.1.23).

Dillenburg, Eugene. 2011. What, if Anything, Is a Museum? *Exhibitionist* Spring '11. National Association for Museum Exhibition (NAME).

Elger, Sarah A.S., and Brigante, Ricky. 2022. *Audience Advisory System Proposal: Immersive Arts and Entertainment Industry Mini Report*. Pseudonym Productions, p. 4.

Ermi, Laura, & Mäyrä, Frans. 2005. Fundamental Components of the Gameplay Experience: Analysing Immersion. *Changing Views: Worlds in Play - Selected Papers of the 2005 Digital Games Research Association's Second International Conference*. Digital Games Research Association & Simon Fraser University.

Fredrickson, Barbara L., and Kahneman, Daniel. 1993. Duration Neglect in Retrospective Evaluations of Affective Episodes. *Journal of Personality and Social Psychology*, vol. 65, 1993, pp. 45–55.

Freeman, Alex., Adams Becker, Samantha., Cummins, Michele., McKelroy, E., Giesinger, Courtney., and Yuhnke, Bryan. (Eds.). 2016. NMC Horizon Report. 2016 Museum Edition. New Media Consortium, Austin, TX.

Gartner Hype Cycle Research Methodology [WWW Document]. n.d. Gartner. https://www.gartner.com/en/research/methodologies/gartner-hype-cycle (accessed 3.3.24).

Gilman, Benjamin Ives. 1918. *Museum Ideals of Purpose and Method*. Riverside Press.

Grau, Oliver. 2004. *Virtual Art: From Illusion to Immersion*. MIT Press, p. 339.

Grau, Oliver. 2004. Immersion and Interaction. From circular frescoes to interactive image spaces. *Daniels, Dieter; Frieling, Rudolf (Hg.): Medien Kunst Netz/1. Medienkunst im Überblick*. Wien/New York: Springer.

Gröppel-Wegener, Alke., and Kidd, Jenny. 2019. *Critical Encounters with Immersive Storytelling*. Routledge, p. 87.

Harris, Mark. 2022. Phatasmagoria. *LinkedIn*, https://www.linkedin.com/pulse/phatasmagoria-mark-harris/

Harris, Neil. 2012. Period Rooms and the American Art Museum. *Winterthur Portfolio*, vol. 46, 2012, pp. 117–138.

Höök, Kristina. 2019. *Designing with the Body - Somaesthetic Interaction Design*. MIT Press.

IJsselsteijn, Wijnand, and Riva, Giuseppe. 2003. Being There: The Experience of Presence in Mediated Environments. In Giuseppi Riva, Fabrizio Davide, and Wijnand IJsselsteijn. (Eds.), *Being There: Concepts, Effects and Measurement of User Presence in Synthetic Environments*. Ios Press, pp. 1–14.

Kamcke, Claudia, and Hutterer, Rainer. 2015. History of Dioramas. In Sue Dale Tunnicliffe and Annette Scheersoi (Eds.), *Natural History Dioramas*. Springer Netherlands, pp. 7–21.

Keogh, Brendan. 2018. A Play of Bodies: How We Perceive Videogames *s*. The MIT Press. p. 33.

Kidd, Jenny. 2018. 'Immersive' Heritage Encounters. *The Museum Review*, vol. 3, no. 1. pp. 1–2.

Laplante, P.A. (Ed.). 2017. *Encyclopedia of Computer Science and Technology*, 2nd edition. CRC Press, Taylor & Francis Group.

Lombard et al. 2000. Measuring Presence: A Literature-Based Approach to the Development of a Standardized Paper-and-Pencil Instrument. *Project Abstract Submitted for Presentation at Presence 2000: The Third International Workshop on Presence*.

Lonsway, Brian. 2016. Complicated Agency. In S. Lukas (Ed.), *A Reader in Themed and Immersive Spaces*. ETC Press, pp. 239–247.

Machon, Josephine. 2024. What Is Immersive? Immersive Experience Network. https://immersiveexperience.network/articles/what-is-immersive/

Marsh, Geoff. 2023. Are Immersive Digital Experiences Even Better than the Real Thing? [WWW Document]. *Museums Association*. https://www.museumsassociation.org/museums-journal/features/2023/07/are-immersive-digital-experiences-even-better-than-the-real-thing/

Mason, Stacey. 2013. On Games and Links: Extending the Vocabulary of Agency and Immersion in Interactive Narratives. *Lecture Notes in Computer Science (Including Subseries Lecture Notes in Artificial Intelligence and Lecture Notes in Bioinformatics)*, vol. 8230 LNCS.

Mills, Virginia. 2018. 180 Years of 3D | Royal Society [WWW Document]. https://royalsociety.org/blog/2018/08/180-years-of-3d/ (accessed 10.7.22).

Mortensen, Marianne. F. 2010. Designing Immersion Exhibits as Border-Crossing Environments. *Museum Management and Curatorship*, vol. 25, 2010, pp. 323–336.

Murray, Janet H. 2019. *Hamlet on the Holodeck: The Future of Narrative in Cyberspace*. MIT Press.

Murtha, Hillary. 2005. The Reuben Bliss Bedchamber at the Brooklyn Museum of Art: A Case Study in the History of Museum Period Room Installations. *Winterthur Portfolio*, vol. 40, 2005, pp. 205–218.

New York Hall of Science. 2015. Connected Worlds. https://nysci.org/press-releases/connected-worlds-press-release

Pine II., B. Joseph, and Gilmore, James.H. 1998. Welcome to the Experience Economy. *Harvard Business Review*, vol. 76, 1998, pp. 97–105.

Radder, Letitia., and Han, Xiliang. 2015. An Examination of the Museum Experience Based on Pine and Gilmore's Experience Economy Realms. *JABR*, vol. 31, 2015, p. 455.

Richter, Walter Duch. 1984. *The Adventures of Buckaroo Banzai Across the Eighth Dimension!* 20th Century Fox.

Rose, Mandy. 2018. The Immersive Turn: Hype and Hope in the Emergence of Virtual Reality as a Nonfiction Platform. *Studies in Documentary Film*, vol. 12, no. 2, 2018, pp. 132–149.

Ryan, Marie-Laure. 1999. Immersion vs. Interactivity: Virtual Reality and Literary Theory. *SubStance*, vol. 28, no. 2, 1999. p. 114

Schaeffer, Jean-Marie, and Vultur, 2010. *Routledge Encyclopedia of Narrative Theory.* Routledge, Taylor & Francis Group.

Slater, Mel. 2009. Place Illusion and Plausibility Can Lead to Realistic Behaviour in Immersive Virtual Environments. *Philosophical Transactions of the Royal Society B: Biological Sciences*, vol. 364, no. 1535, p. 2009.

Sweetser, Penelope, and Wyeth, Peta. 2005. GameFlow: A Model for Evaluating Player Enjoyment in Games. *ACM Computers in Entertainment*, vol. 3, no. 3, 2005, pp. 1–24.

TeamLab. 2019. TeamLab Borderless Tokyo. https://borderless.teamlab.art/

Thon, Jan-Noël. 2008. Immersion Revisited: On the Value of a Contested Concept. In Amyris Fernandez, Olli Leino, and Hanna Wirman (Eds.), *Extending Experiences. Structure, Analysis and Design of Computer Game Player Experience*. Lapland University Press, 2008.

Tullin, Peter. 2022. What's Next for Immersive Experiences? [WWW Document]. REMIX Summits | Culture x Technology x Entrepreneurship. https://www.remixsummits.com/whats-next-for-immersive-experiences/ (accessed 2.26.24).

Virtual Reality Society. n.d. History of Virtual Reality. https://www.vrs.org.uk/virtual-reality/history.html (accessed 10.7.22).

Wolf, Mark J.P. 2018. Beyond Immersion. In Marta Boni (Ed.), *World Building:* Transmedia, Fans, Industries, p. 204.

Zak, Paul J. 2022. *Immersion: The Science of the Extraordinary and the Source of Happiness*. Lioncrest Publishing.

3 Emotional Evocation
The Importance of Feeling

Chances are, if you're reading this book, you've probably had some kind of impactful moment at a museum. It could be a connection to an object where the gulfs of time and space between you and it dissolve and you feel connected to the universe. It could be an artwork or installation which suddenly provokes unexpected tears for some reason. Or it could be a confrontation with history that leaves you viscerally, intimately connected to an event or time outside of your direct experience. I've had all three of those experiences, and countless others at different museums. The possibility of creating those kinds of moments is the thing that gets me out of bed and working every day. When you encounter people being deeply engaged in something you worked on, it feels great. Which is what this chapter is all about: feeling.

Take a minute and try to recall a museum experience when something resonated powerfully with you. What's the first thing you recall? Do you remember the content, or do you remember how it made you feel? One of my first transformative experiences was early in my career when I was a registrar. I was dusting a Roman bowl in a large case full of ceramics prior to mounting it; and when I turned it over, I saw there was a faint thumbprint in the base, where the potter's thumb had left a mark. Seeing that thumbprint, just like mine, put there by a person who had lived and died thousands of years before me literally stopped me in my tracks. I've forgotten most of what I did in that exhibition, but that terra sigillata bowl, its delicate lightness, the stamp with the mark the workshop of P. Clodius Proculus, and that thumbprint I gently pressed my gloved thumb into remains bright and clear in my mind decades later. That's an example of the potential of an emotional response to a museum experience.

In this chapter, I will explore the second of four techniques for creating playful engagement: emotional evocation. This chapter explores why emotional experiences have more lasting impact and are more memorable than purely intellectual ones and makes the argument that it is not enough to appeal to the rational, intellectual parts of the human brain. We need to take the whole person into consideration, and humans come with emotions.

The History of Museums and Emotion

Rene Descartes famously wrote in *Principia Philosophiae* (1644) "Cogito, ergo sum." "I think, therefore I am." Museums, as products of the Enlightenment and the

DOI: 10.4324/9781032638690-3

philosophies that arose in Europe in the 17th and 18th centuries, have traditionally been domains of the rational. This emphasis on rationality has influenced centuries of museum practice and encouraged until recently a practice that privileged the rational and argued that "encouraging emotional values is more pandering to the entertaining than the educational function of museums" (Gadsby 2011, p. 7). As a young exhibit developer, I can distinctly recall being told by an older colleague that we (a science museum) did not deal in feelings, we were in the business of facts. In fact, I would argue that the whole "education versus entertainment" dialectic is really about positioning the rational in opposition to the emotional. The reality is that museums exist in that contact zone between education, commemoration, and entertainment, all of which have emotional affect embedded in them (Dickinson et al. 2010). This entanglement also reflects the way our brains work.

While we may like to think of ourselves as rational creatures who also possess emotions, research in psychology and other disciplines suggests that the opposite is more accurate. Humans are not rational creatures who are also emotional, rather, we are emotional creatures who are also able to be rational, sometimes. But more than that, the relationship between emotion and cognition, Brosch et al. (2013) point out, is very complicated,

> ...[T]he duality of reason versus emotion that has been propagated for a long time is not reflected in the architecture of the brain and the functioning of the mind. Emotion and cognition are closely intertwined, complex human behaviour emerges from dynamic interactions between multiple processes and brain networks. Emotion determines how we perceive our world, how we remember it, and which decisions we take.

It's not an either-or proposition. Designing for emotional evocation as well as for intellectual stimulation is an acknowledgement of how we all experience the world, all the time.

For museums and similar cultural organizations, this historical tension between thinking and feeling presents a design challenge because emotion is a primary driver of visitation. Emotional stimulation has long been noted as one of the key values visitors seek from a museum experience (Gadsby 2011) and provides the vehicle for emotional and intellectual knowledge transfer between experiences and visitors (Hohenstein and Moussouri 2018, p. 24). In the UK, the Association of Independent Museums (AIM) and Art Fund issued a report

> to investigate which emotions drive public support for museums, why certain emotions are more powerful than others, and how museums might use these emotions to channel support amongst their communities as we emerge from the pandemic, but continue to face potentially challenging times.
>
> (Simmonds and Royal 2023, p. 5)

Through audience surveys, they identified three groups of emotions that drove visitors to support museums: pleasure, connection, and purpose. In the U.S. LaPlaca

Cohen's series of CultureTrack reports on Americans' relationship with arts and culture lay out just how important it is for museums to connect emotionally with their audiences. In their 2017 report, they listed 14 motivators for cultural participation and of those 14, "Having fun" was the top motivator and over half of the others were explicitly emotional like "Feeling inspired" (LaPlaca Cohen and Kelton Global 2017, p. 32). By 2020, "Play to Emotional Strengths" was a key recommendation for cultural institutions, as audiences increasingly look for fun, lighthearted, and beautiful experiences to help get them through the COVID-19 pandemic and beyond (LaPlaca Cohen and Slover Linett 2021, p. 23). Visitors arrive on our doorsteps and landing pages with the expectation, possibly subconscious, of having an emotionally rewarding experience.

Providing that emotional satisfaction is therefore essential in free choice learning environments because visitors are constantly deciding whether an experience is worth their time or not. As John Falk and Lynn Dierking point out in their foundational text, *Learning from Museums: Visitor Experiences and the Making of Meaning*, visitors engage with museum content because of their intrinsic motivations (Falk and Dierking 2000, p. 21). This choice

> ...plays a key role in all phases of the experience: visitors decide what to see, when to engage, and how long to stay. Emotions play a key role in each of these decisions, so the best activities tend to take emotional factors into consideration.
>
> (Lane 2015, pp. 435–436)

For social groups, who comprise a large segment of our audience, the least engaged person in the group is the one who often determines how long that group remains, since that motivation to have a good time out with friends and family is unmet if one member is obviously bored, uncomfortable, or unhappy.

Creating visitor experiences that acknowledge and attend to visitors' emotional state is an essential feature of the museum visitor experience and is therefore something we can and should design for (Roppola 2012). Margaret Wetherell et al. (2018) argue that "attention to emotion and affect allows us to deepen our understanding of how people develop attachments and commitments to the past, things, beliefs, places, traditions and institutions" (p. 6). As Alelis (2013) put it,

> designing for emotion is a valid form of learning; by integrating emotion with learning objectives, museums can create a more personal experience which can lead to repeat visits, donations in the form of time and money, and free advertising by content visitors.
>
> (p. 429)

The impact of emotion is hard to measure, but it is not impossible, as a growing body of research attests.

Despite all this evidence, designing for emotion remains what Smith and Campbell (2015) call "the elephant in the room" of heritage and museum studies: "the recognition, or rather lack of recognition, of affect and emotion as essential constitutive elements of heritage making" (p. 444). Despite this traditional neglect, emotion is central to museum going and designing for that reality should be at the core of our experience design mindset and practice. Let's look at what we've learned about emotion and how it works.

The Hallmarks of Emotion

Tremendous amounts of research have been published in both the psychological and neuroscience literature that demonstrate how scientists are beginning to unpack the complex relationship between the intertwined processes of cognition and emotion and the complex human behaviors which arise from that interplay. Interestingly, quite a few studies use museums as venues, and museum objects as examples precisely because researchers know that people go to museums to have emotionally satisfying experiences. It is not unusual now to find researchers deploying technologies like galvanic skin response (Cuseum 2020) and eye tracking monitors (Asher 2018) to record visitor's emotional responses in real time (Peng 2019) as they conduct their visit. As organizations interested not only in getting visitors to pay attention to their content, but also to feel that it is relevant to them, and be changed for the better by their museum experience, emotional evocation is an essential technique for us in our work. So, let's look at some current understandings of human emotion and its role in how we experience the world.

Definitions

First off, definitions. The Merriam-Webster dictionary (2021) defines emotion as "a conscious mental reaction (such as anger or fear) subjectively experienced as a strong feeling usually directed toward a specific object and typically accompanied by physiological and behavioral changes in the body." The English word "emotion" comes to us from the Latin *ex* (out) + *movere* (to move). Emotions are literally things that come out of us as a result of stimuli.

Two terms you will come across frequently in the scientific literature are *valence* and *arousal*. Valence describes how pleasurable an event is on a continuum from negative to positive. Arousal describes how intense that event is on a continuum from calm to excited. So, anger can be described as negative valence and high arousal, and bliss as positive valence and low arousal, etc… (Haviland-Jones et al. 2010). This essentialist model is not without its critics, who argue that while descriptive, these categories aren't very helpful in distinguishing between emotions. Anger is negative valence/high affect, but so is intense sorrow. For constructivists, emotion is a more situational and variable response to stimuli. For those interested, Lisa Barrett does an admirable job of summing up the last 2,000 years of scholarly writing on the nature of emotion in her essay, *Navigating the Science of Emotion* (Barrett 2016).

Though they tend to be used interchangeably in everyday discourse (and in this book), scientists make distinctions between affect, emotion, and mood. *Affect* is the larger category, and *emotions* and *moods* are particular states within this category, mainly distinguished by their duration, and by whether they are directed at a specific cause (Niven 2013, pp. 49–50). Emotions tend to be brief, intense experiences that are elicited in response to specific external stimuli. Moods tend to be longer lasting, less intense and lack a specific stimulus (Desmet et al. 2016). Since the experiences we create tend to be of relatively finite duration and focus on specific objects in the environment, I am most interested in emotions and how we can better design museums that offer visitors satisfyingly emotional experiences.

Emotion Comes First

One reason to keep emotion in mind in our designs is that emotional responses always come first; they occur within milliseconds in response to stimuli, whereas the more cognitively intensive responses take much, much longer to happen. In Kahneman's attention model, emotional responses are part of System 1, the automatic, near-instantaneous, instinctive system. It is only after that initial emotional response that our conscious, cognitive faculties kick in (Kahneman's System 2) to further process what's happening to us, if needed. In their study of how people engage with digital interactions, Nahum-Shani et al. (2022) have proposed a sequential framework that situates affective response at the very beginning of the engagement process (p. 828). As our brains further process that stimulus, that affective response will be added to other cognitive processing that combine to create our conscious "response" to that stimulus. This is an important point to remember. The process of engagement always starts with emotion, and that emotion has already happened by the time we consciously think about it.

Emotion is Integral to Learning

Csikszentmihalyi and Hermanson (1995) promote a view of museum learning where the visitor "develops and expands the self, allowing one to discover aspects of oneself that were previously unknown. Thus the learning experience involves the whole person, not only the intellectual but the sensory and emotional faculties as well" (p. 67). Falk and Dierking (2000) concur. "Though learning is usually framed as a cognitive activity, all learning has an emotional component, no matter what the subject" (p. 18). To facilitate the kind of personal meaning making that motivates visitors, they recommend that museums combine emotion with learning into all their experiences (p. 113). Falk's more recent work (2021) elaborates on that recommendation to propose that the relationship between emotions and visitor motivation is both cyclical and iterative. Visitors are emotion-driven before the visit, during the visit, and after the visit, or as Falk puts it, "Every facet of the museum experience begins, and ends, with emotions" (p. 60).

Emotion Aids Memory Creation

Try to remember the last time you were a little bit bored. What details can you recall? Probably not many, if any. Can you remember something that happened years ago, but not what you had for breakfast last Thursday? That's because our brains are built to remember emotional events. The psychologist William James rather floridly wrote that "an impression may be so exciting emotionally as almost to leave a scar upon the cerebral tissues" (quoted in Brosch et al. 2013, p. 2). McGaugh (2000) puts it more matter-of-factly; "humans remember more about an event when it is associated with an emotional story" (p. 249). It is usually dangerous to generalize about a group as heterogeneous as "museums," but I think it's safe to say that they all want visitors to remember what they did and saw and felt and learned during their museum experience. So, museum experience designers are really in the business of helping visitors create memories. Emotion is closely intertwined with memory, so let's take a moment to go over scientists' current understanding of how memory works. There's broad agreement that there are (at least) three main categories of memory: sensory memory, short-term memory and long-term memory.

Sensory memory, as the name implies, conveys a sense impression to the brain and lasts for a split second. They convey messages like, "You've just touched something hot," or "You smell food cooking." Unless we attend to them, they disappear immediately. Pay attention to them, and they transfer into your short-term or working memory. Short-term memory gets used all the time and can last from a few seconds to several minutes. Right now, you're using your short-term memory to recall the beginning of this sentence while you read to the end. Remembering a phone number you've just been told while you put it into your phone is another common example. If you've heard the story that humans can only remember about seven things, that is referring to short-term memory. The strategies you may have heard of to "improve your memory"—like chunking and rehearsing—all have to do with helping transfer memories from short-term to long-term memory, where we seem to have an infinite amount of storage.

When I was little, my mother made me memorize our address, our phone number, and my grandmother's phone number, in case of emergency. And though I haven't called it in decades, Nanny's phone number is still in there, alongside a host of associated memories, like how hard it was to turn the rotary dial on that phone, how long it took to dial a "0," standing on a chair to reach the phone, which was mounted to the wall in our kitchen, and so on. That's our goal, getting our experiences to resonate long enough to carry over from sensory and short-term memory into long-term memory, where they will join the multitudes of memories that form the building blocks of visitors' future selves.

The connection between emotion and memory is not a new discovery by any means. Francis Bacon asserted that "Memory is assisted by anything that makes an impression on a powerful passion, inspiring fear, for example, or wonder, shame or joy" (Bacon 1620). Modern cognitive science has confirmed that emotional arousal of any sort, be it positive or negative, tends to increase our attention to our surroundings (Sutherland and Mara 2017). We pay more attention to emotionally arousing events; thus, they are more richly experienced in our memory than others. That heightened attention endures even after the original stimulus is removed (Ochsner 2000, p. 242). Arousing someone's emotions, even mildly, causes them to create stronger memories of those stimuli (McGaugh 2013). And it's not just events that directly follow an emotional arousal. Scientists have conducted experiments where they induce emotional arousal *after* subjects learn material and found an enhanced recall of that material, even though it was not emotionally arousing in itself (McGaugh 2013, p. 10404). Brosch et al. (2013) found that the emotional relevance of a stimulus was an important feature influencing what we choose to attend to, and that once "attention has been drawn to and engaged by emotional stimuli, it may dwell longer at their location and facilitate the processing of subsequent non-emotional target stimuli appearing at the same location" (p. 2). Emotion is like a tide that lifts all boats.

We Remember Negative Emotions Better

Emotionally arousing events are remembered better, but there are differences based on the valence and arousal. Increases in either valence or arousal tend to enhance the accuracy of memory. Interestingly, though, we process positive and negative affective events differently, with negatively affective events tending to be better remembered than positive ones (Oschner 2000). During negatively affective events, our visual processing centers work harder to capture detail in ways they don't capture positively affective events (Kensinger et al. 2007). Cognitive scientists think this is an evolutionary adaptation, since it was important to our survival to remember negative situations accurately in order to avoid them in the future (Bohn and Berntsen 2007).

How this might work in a museum setting is demonstrated by research Falk and Gillespie (2009) did on visitors to a science center exhibition called *Goose Bumps: The Science of Fear*. Evaluators interviewed visitors who had been to the exhibition and a control group of visitors who had been to other parts of the museum. They then followed this with a post-visit interview four to six months after the visit. Their findings were significant.

> In the delayed post-visit interviews, Goose Bumps visitors were able to give significantly better descriptions of the exhibition of their choice than were visitors in the control group. Goose Bumps visitors had more salient memories of such things as exhibition colors and were also more able to describe details of an exhibition. Goose Bumps visitors were also able to list a significantly greater number of elements within an exhibition of their choice than were control group visitors. Goose Bumps visitors were able to talk in greater depth and breadth about an exhibition than were those in the control group.
>
> (p. 126)

Not only that, but they found that visitors to the emotionally charged experience reflected on it more compared to regular museum visitors (p. 127).

What This Means for Museums

Falk and Gillespie are very careful to qualify their findings as directional rather than definitive, and indeed there is so much more work that can and should be done to understand how emotion shapes museum visitors' experiences. But I think it is safe to say that taken as a whole, the literature is quite clear that emotion is an essential ingredient in memory-making, and therefore an essential tool for experience designers to factor into their work.

To answer why emotional evocation is important, I don't think anyone put it better than David Flemming, former Director of the National Museums Liverpool when he said,

> Museums are about people and emotions rather than about things. But the reality is that objects are terrifically important. What we have to do is achieve the right balance between objects and stories so that we are not obsessed with objects at the expense of communicating their power and meaning."
>
> (quoted in Gadsby 2011, p 9)

His "right balance" contains those elements that comprise the magic circle of the museum visit: visitors, objects, and interaction alibis. So, bearing in mind our concerns and larger contexts, what are some of the ways we can encourage visitors to bring their emotional selves to our experiences?

SIDEBAR: "Feeling Like Crying" in Museums

In general, emotion is hard to study unobtrusively. Most often, you have to ask visitors how an experience made them feel, with all the challenges that self-reporting bring. However, there is one kind of emotional response that is widely reported on, that feeling when something in a museum experience resonates powerfully with you and you feel like crying. I used it as one of my examples at the beginning of the chapter. I was thinking of a specific incident when I wrote that, so I found the journal entry I wrote after my first visit to Ragnar Kjartansson's video installation "The Visitors."

> "...'The Visitors' has stayed with me so powerfully, so unexpectedly, that I am in a bit of shock at how moving it was. Kate and I watched it twice through. I was on the verge of tears several times for reasons I don't really understand. There is something so true about it, though it is probably the most manipulated recording of a live performance I've ever seen..."

This kind of "feeling like crying" at art is similar to crying from sadness, but that doesn't mean the same thing is going on in our

Tools for Creating Emotionally Evocative Experiences

"Emotion and memory are linked in the human brain, and unless emotion is involved, our brains won't flag something as meaningful. Therefore, if we want visitors to have transformative and memorable aha moments, we must make space for emotion" (Norris and Tisdale 2017, p. 100).

Assuming you also want to create transformative, memorable "Aha!" moments, what are some of the ways designers have "made space" for emotion?

Begin with Emotion

For practitioners, Linda Norris and Rainey Tisdale's "Developing a Toolkit for Emotion in Museums" is a useful primer for how to think about incorporating emotional evocation in the development process from the very beginning. "By purposefully integrating ideas about emotions into the exhibition planning process, we can explore the full complexity of human emotion and create deeper, more varied, and more meaningful visitor responses to museum content" (Norris and Tisdale 2017, p. 103). Their toolkit lists nine practices to consider:

- Begin with the Team
  Introduce opportunities for team members to feel. By practicing observing and discussing emotion, the team can strengthen its ability to tease out content and design elements that have the greatest emotional potential.

brains. Writers as far back as John Dewey have hypothesized that this feeling represents a disruption in our model of interacting with art. He distinguished between facile "recognition," the successful matching of our expectations to what we see, and "meta-cognitive perception," a disparity between our expectation and observation that triggers a reorganization of our how view the world (Dewey 1980, quoted in Pelowski and Akiba 2011, p. 84). Pelowski (2015) later studied art museum visitors in the UK, Japan, and the US viewing paintings by Mark Rothko to try to understand what is happening in the brain when we feel like crying because of an aesthetic encounter. What they found across all three cultures was that feeling like crying coincided with a specific emotional progression, as viewers confronted an object, and felt confusion, self-awareness and epiphany: the hallmarks of an insightful experience (Pelowski 2015). Their results, across all three cultures, showed a strong relationship between feeling like crying and a complicated progression of emotions leading to a sense of personal epiphany. "Feeling like crying" is an indicator that a person has moved through these three outcomes. This is precisely

- Consider the Objects

  Add emotional potential to the criteria used in selecting objects for display, recognizing that objects can evoke different emotions in different people and different contexts.
- Make an Emotional Map

  Consider the exhibition as an emotional landscape that visitors will move through over time and map the emotional progression with its high and low points.
- Attend to the Physical Environment

  Plan the space, color, lighting, texture, smell, sound, and other design details that will further enhance the emotional map you create.
- Make Space for Human Voices

  Knowing that humans respond to the emotions expressed by other humans, seek out exhibition content—audio, video, quotations—that allows a variety of people to speak for themselves, with feeling, in their own way.
- Create Moments of Comfort, Connection, Expression

  It's not enough merely to evoke emotions in exhibitions; it's also important to support visitors in processing those emotions through design.
- Seek Out Opportunities for Empathy

  Look for opportunities to nurture empathetic responses in visitors, because it fuels not only social connection (both bridging and bonding) but also social change.
- Lean into the Hard Emotions

  Don't avoid some emotions just because they are hard. The hardest work is often the most important work.
- Evaluate for Emotions (pp. 103–108)

  Move beyond solely knowledge-based outcomes and integrate emotion with other project outcomes. This can be just as powerful—and just as valid—in terms of the service museums provide to their public audiences.

> the "transformation" that appears in so many organizations' mission statements. And this sense of "feeling like crying" may be one of the few explicit indicators that this progression is happening. And, Pelowski points out, though it is probably not on many visitor surveys. "answering in the affirmative to 'did you feel like crying' may indeed be a salient indicator of outcome in art or other perceptual experience" (p. 21).

All nine are important, and several of them (like empathy and "hard" emotions) will come up later in this chapter, but I want to focus here on "Consider the Objects" and "Make an Emotional Map" because they are, in my estimation, the most potentially disruptive of Norris' and Tisdale's tools, requiring as they do, a reformulation of how we conceive museum experiences from the very beginning. Norris and Tisdale encourage us to think about emotional potential as a prime criterion for the selection of what objects (broadly speaking) we include in an experience, and that we further take the idea of our experience and try to map the emotional landscape, not in a proscriptive way,

> but rather to consider the storytelling arc of an exhibition and how a variety of responses might be engaged throughout the space. You might ask questions such as: What is the emotional progression for visitors and where is its high point?
>
> (p. 104)

This has clear resonances to Zak's work I referred to in Chapter 2, only without the troubling overt manipulation. This is very different to more traditional forms of museum experience design where a collection of objects is decided upon first, and then layers of design and interpretation are added to that list. You will also notice that emotion and storytelling are deeply entangled here. This pairing of storytelling as a vehicle to deliver emotional experiences is something we'll see more of in the next chapter.

Another example is EMOTIVE, an EU-funded research project on emotional storytelling, cultural heritage, and blending physical and digital experiences. The project's premise was that "cultural sites are, in fact, highly emotional places. That regardless of age, location, or state of preservation, they are seedbeds not just of knowledge, but of emotional resonance and human connection" (EMOTIVE 2018). The project prototyped a number of storytelling (and game-like) approaches to heritage interpretation and produced the following recommendations for engaging visitors emotionally:

- Adopt a story-based rather than an object-based approach, supporting interaction between (virtual) characters as well as real visitors, as well as engagement with the objects.
- Blend the online with the on-site experience.
- Seamlessly integrate the pre-, during, and post-visit activities, and the intangible with the tangible.
- Cater to the dominant visiting patterns of museums and cultural heritage sites, which primarily see groups of visitors participating in social experiences with varying—sometimes conflicting—individual motivations.
- Integrate exploration of hybrid 2D/3D spaces in meaningful ways which support the storytelling and the social and emotionally engaging experience of the visit.

> (Perry et al. 2017, p. 2).

EMOTIVE's projects started with an emotionally resonant story, and then objects were selected for their ability to support it. Which is not to say they are unimportant, indeed in most cases they're vital, but our goal shouldn't be just displaying the objects, but rather creating the opportunities for visitors to explore the important information and stories that invisibly surround these objects.

Tell Personal Stories

Telling stories as a way to evoke emotions is widespread, but what kinds of stories have the most impact? Not surprisingly, most people enjoy learning about people more than abstract ideas or litanies of facts. Framing experiences around persons, be they real, composite, or fictional, allows visitors to insert themselves into the vantage point of the people being presented. Philipp Schorch et al. (2015) conducted a lengthy study of Australian visitors to an exhibition on identity and found that the use of personal stories was key to creating the kind of multi-sensory, embodied experiences that facilitate the development of empathy, reflexivity, and critique in visitors, often over periods of time measured in months instead of minutes (p. 238).

This encounter with personal narratives seems to be essential to visitors achieving what Roppola (2012) calls "affective and discursive broadening" which can only occur within "a dialectical space between heart and mind, emotion and reason" (p. 249). Mind and reason alone aren't enough. Even though she's using the language of the old dialectic, she's advocating for creating experiences that encompass both.

Embrace the Difficult Emotions

Engaging with emotional complexity and unpleasant emotions is not something most cultural heritage sites have been good with historically. I've worked on many projects over the years where key content was cut because of its difficulty and objects removed from checklists because they had troubling associations. However, research suggests that wrestling with that complexity and ambiguity is key to visitors making new attachments and senses of affiliation.

Margaret Wetherell et al. (2018) argue that wrestling with difficult emotions is where visitors make new associations and attachments. Though they are fraught, "it is in the complexities and ambiguities of emotional responses to heritage that new and socially productive analysis may be had" (p. 21). This sentiment is shared by Norris and Tisdale (2017) who make "Lean into the Hard Emotions" one of the tools in their toolkit. They rightly point out that visitors

> need us to help them dig into the hard emotions, even if it's scary. It's the only way we will grow and improve, together. And it's even more crucial when race, class, gender, politics, and social views create emotional polarization, where one group's emotional reaction is favored over another's.
>
> (p. 108)

Laurajane Smith (2010) studied the responses of visitors to a British exhibition commemorating the bicentennial of the abolition of the slave trade in the UK and found that many white visitors employed strategies to disengage emotionally from the content of the exhibition to avoid feeling uncomfortable about their country's past. One strategy that had promise to circumvent this was the use of personalized content, in the sense of the content being delivered in the context of a particular person's experience, not personalized in the sense of tailored to the individual visitor. Telling the story of an individual had the ability to help some visitors negotiate difficult feelings better than a broader, more clinical discussion of the topic (p. 202).

> Exhibition strategies and interpretative materials may need to provide the resources and skills for visitors to navigate the emotions that visitors may bring to, or that are triggered by, their visits. Negative emotions, such as guilt and shame, were controversial and difficult issues for a significant set of those interviewed for this study. Although they were emotions that were not intended to be generated by the exhibitions, the point here is that these emotions should not have been ignored by curatorial staff. Rather it is important to recognise that such emotional issues exist and to develop the tools or opportunities within an exhibition to help visitors constructively mediate them.
>
> (p. 209)

Andrea Witcomb (2013) explored the use of affect in history museums in Australia to articulate how emotional evocation can help visitors reflect more critically on the past, the present, and their place in history. In a world full of troubled histories of imperialism, colonialism, domination, and conflict, there is a lot work to do. Witcomb, referencing Walter Benjamin, states,

> Affective forms of knowledge are crucial to enabling this. As Benjamin argues, texts that only present information, such as newspapers, or, in our case, narrative based exhibitions, cannot connect with experience because information renders the critical faculty inactive. This is so because the presentation of information does not encourage deep attention. For Benjamin only art can do that precisely because it engages affective forms of response.
>
> (p. 15)

One of the key ways to provoke an affective response is through surprise. For Witcomb, the subversion of the past visitors thought they knew proved to be an effective way to bring the past into radical tension with the present and promote deep engagement with difficult histories. The vehicle for this productive kind of unsettlement turns out to be narrative. Witcomb finds that "[e]ssential to all of them is the ability to not close off narrative, the requirement that visitors engage imaginatively in the space between themselves and the object or the spatial and esthetic structure of the displays" (p. 13).

Visitors are going to bring their whole selves to our experiences and ignoring "the bad stuff" because it might be upsetting does a disservice to our visitors, because they will still have emotional responses, they'll just have them without any support from the museum. Engaging with the difficult material forthrightly helps us all.

Prompt Visitors to Reflect on Their Emotional State

We've talked at length about the ways that museums can handle emotionally evocative content, but there is also another path to creating emotionally resonant experiences, which is to prompt visitors to both actively reflect on and share their emotions as part of an experience.

Sharing the emotions of others triggers the same brain responses in us as experiencing those emotions ourselves. When you talk with others about someone feeling sad, your brain activates the same structures it does when you yourself feel sad and this effect is largely automatic. You don't have to try to feel it, it just happens (Singer and Lamm 2009, p. 81). Having the opportunity to reflect on the emotions raised by an experience has been shown to be important to the development of historical empathy in history museums (Savenije and de Bruijn 2017). Asking visitors to notice their emotional state also tends to increase their ability to make meaningful connections to that experience, "In general, findings suggest that when given the task of providing emotional responses to artefacts, visitors are motivated to find meaningful and personal connections without relying heavily on curators, exhibit labels, and arrangement of objects" (Alelis et al. 2013, p. 431). Art museum educators have known this for a long time.

Asking visitors how a particular work makes them feel can open up a whole world of associations that a more rational prompt might not elicit. However, asking visitors questions without demonstrating you're listening is disrespectful. This is one arena in which digital technologies excel. They can be a fast, low-impact way to ask visitors questions *and* to demonstrate that we hear them. During the trip to MONA I described in Chapter 1, my lovely and talented wife who has put up with countless museum "side trips" during our vacations together had her own experience with the "O" mobile guide. After about an hour of looking at art and reflecting on how she felt about specific pieces, she loudly exclaimed "Alright! I get it!" in one gallery, took off her headphones, and proceeded to spend the rest of her visit looking at the art and thinking about how it made her feel.

Infect the Experience with Joy

We've covered how hard or negative emotions can be harnessed appropriately. The same applies to positive ones. Kiersten Latham has spent years looking at how visitors process museum visits. In addition to developing a framework she calls Positive Museology, she has also been interested in numinous experiences, those "aha" moments visitors (and museum workers) sometimes experience that are "characterized by deep engagement or transcendence, empathy, and awe or reverence, confirming such aspects as losing a sense of time, time-travel experience, empathic conjuring, strongly affective response, and a sense of spiritual communion" (Latham 2013, pp. 16–17). We encountered her work on visitor-object relationships in Chapter 1, but her more recent focus (2022) has been on the power of positive experiences to infect museum visits with joy.

Latham proposes that creating positive affective experiences are central to museums' ability to promote human flourishing. She builds on the broaden-and-build theory of positive emotions (Fredrickson 2001), which posits that experiences of positive emotions broaden people's repertoire of ways of responding to stimuli, which, in turn, serves to build their enduring physical, intellectual, social, and psychological resources. Latham states that "experiencing positive emotions broadens one's awareness and attention, thereby encouraging more varied, novel, and exploratory actions and/or thoughts" (Latham 2022, p. 618). In a museum setting, this state of mind is obviously a useful one. What I find the most intriguing part of her research has to do with *positive contagion*, the phenomenon of how positive behaviors in social settings can spread from person to person and "infect" others with positivity (p. 617). To operationalize these findings, Latham offers seven ways to infect museums with joy:

1 Be Open
    Rid yourself of expectations and judgments that cloud one's ability to be truly receptive.
2 Create High-Quality Connections
    Create connections that foster mutual appreciation and encourage being or doing things together will recharge visitors' energy and vitality and bring real physiological changes.
3 Cultivate Kindness
    Make kindness (to visitors and staff) part of the institution's reflective learning values and practices.
4 Learn and Apply Your Strengths
    Rather than working from problem-oriented approach to facing the world ("What do we need to fix?"), focus on identifying your strengths and virtues ("What are we good at?") to help visitors and staff flourish, to grow, and stay motivated.
5 Ritualize Gratitude
    Make opportunities to express gratitude a regular practice, in both the exhibition development process and also the exhibition itself.
6 Savor Positivity
    Create opportunities that elongate good moments in which we actively attempt to fully feel, enjoy positive experiences.
7 Visualize Your Future
    Help guide visitors toward positively visualizing the future by purposefully and intentionally designing around positive dreaming and hope.

(Latham 2022, pp. 620–628)

Latham provides museum examples for all seven ways, but I want to draw attention to two that I have witnessed in my own work. The first is to ritualize gratitude. If you've worked in museums for any time you may have noted the tradition of not identifying most of the workers who create the exhibitions and programs and websites we make. Sometimes a big exhibition might have a welcome statement from the director, and curatorial museums often have curators' remarks at the entrance to exhibitions, but the vast majority of the people who work on those projects go unnamed The Peabody Essex Museum (PEM) instituted a practice of identifying the teams that worked on their temporary exhibitions, complete with department photographs, so visitors could see who was responsible for the show they'd just seen. These labels were not well liked by staff. They were labor intensive; the photoshoots were hard to schedule, and the end product often looked almost-identical to the credit panel from the previous exhibition since the museum staff was not that large. I was myself not sold on their merit until the first one was installed and I routinely saw visitors stopped in front of it, reading the names and strange job titles, and saying things like "I didn't know it took this many people!" Thenceforward, they were regularly among the most-read labels in PEM's exhibitions.

The other way to infect museums with joy that I want to call out is to visualize your future. Latham states that by spending time imagining a positive future, visitors can savor it and reap the physiological and mental rewards of spending time using positive emotions. The more time spent in consideration of such things, the higher potential for action on it (p. 629). In Mumbai, a unique children's museum, The Museum of Solutions (MuSo) embodies that idea in a museum where "children become responsible, conscious, caring, and mindful citizens of the world" (MuSo 2023). The vision of Tanvi Jindal Shete, the founder of the museum has been to create a place where children are actively inspired to see themselves as the people who will solve India's (and the world's) problems, empowering them to engage with their world in ways that can lead to positive change. What might our institutions look like if we applied the same philosophy not only to visitors but also to museum workers, for too many of whom joy is in short supply? (Van Damme 2015).

Encourage Empathy

Even a cursory scan of the literature will reveal that empathy is the emotion most commonly referenced by museum professionals. Emotion researchers generally define empathy as the ability to sense other people's emotions, coupled with the ability to imagine what someone else might be thinking or feeling. Elizabeth Segal, social policy analyst and author of *Social Empathy* defines empathy thus,

> Empathy is not imagining how you might feel in the place of another. It is imagining and trying to understand what the other person feels. The difference between thinking about yourself in another's situation and thinking about the other person in that situation is simple but profound, requiring well-developed, differentiated mental abilities. Empathy is other-focused, not self-focused.
>
> (Segal 2019)

Cognitive empathy, sometimes called "perspective taking," refers to our ability to identify and understand other people's emotions.

Gail Anderson, in her book *Reinventing the Museum* (2004), states that civic engagement and social responsibility should be institutional values of the museum (p. 3). Anderson summarizes this trend as "the general movement of dismantling the museum as an ivory tower of exclusivity and toward the construction of a more socially responsive cultural institution in service to the public" (p. 1). Central to this is a call for museums to employ empathy in their work. "To be effective and emotional, the museum must be empathetic, connecting with its audiences. It must invest in a strategic approach of audience development/engagement to increase and diversify audiences, placing people at the centre of museums of the future" (Mazzanti 2021, p. 8). There are book-length investigations on the relationship between empathy and museums such as Arnold de Simine (2013) and Gokcigdem (2016 and 2019). Empathy is seen by Arnold-de Simine as central to the paradigm shift the museum field is witnessing, "Instead of predominantly housing collections, they have become places of recollection, not so much driven by objects but by narratives and performances" (p. 2). Note also the entanglement of emotion and storytelling. Elif Gokcigdem (2019) positions museums as

> a readily available platform for cross-pollination of ideas and the exploration of empathy. They are natural storytellers that can show and tell us how all things are interconnected, and let us feel the wisdom inherited in ancient narratives about our oneness, while discovering new ones through science and exploration.
>
> (p. xvii)

Norris and Tisdale (2017) go even further, centering empathy as the "Holy Grail" of visitor emotions "because it fuels not only social connection (both bridging and bonding) but also social change" (p. 106), an opinion shared by the U.K.-based Empathy Museum, which "explores how empathy can not only transform our personal relationships, but also help tackle global challenges such as prejudice, conflict and inequality" (Empathy Museum 2021).

The VR "Empathy Machine"

In terms of digital technologies' utility to designers, no other example is more often quoted than VR's capacity to be an "empathy machine." This concept comes from the title of filmmaker Chris Milk's 2015 TED Talk "How Virtual Reality Can Create the Ultimate Empathy Machine" and its impact on popular and academic discourse on the subject has been profound. In this short talk, Milk describes a 360-degree video he produced called *Clouds Over Sidra* (United Nations VR 2014) which placed viewers in the company of a young Syrian girl in a refugee camp in Jordan. That experience led him to predict that VR will be a radically transformative technology

> "I think we just start to scratch the surface of the true power of virtual reality. It's not a video game peripheral. It connects humans to other humans in a

profound way that I've never seen before in any other form of media. And it can change people's perception of each other. And that's how I think virtual reality has the potential to actually change the world. So, it's a machine, but through this machine we become more compassionate, we become more empathetic, and we become more connected. And ultimately, we become more human."

(Milk 2015)

Heady stuff, indeed. There is some disambiguation necessary though to understand the context of Milk's assertions, starting with the "_________ as an empathy machine" notion. The first appearance of this idea comes from a 2005 speech by the film critic Robert Ebert, who said,

For me, the movies are like a machine that generates empathy. If it's a great movie, it lets you understand a little bit more about what it's like to be a different gender, a different race, a different age… It helps us to identify with the people who are sharing this journey with us. And that, to me, is the most noble thing that good movies can do and it's a reason to encourage them and to support them and to go to them.

(Ebert 2005)

Note Ebert's assessment of film's potential, letting viewers understand "a little bit more" about other people, places, and times. So, for Milk and others, 360 video-based VR are empathy machines like movies, only much more so.

The scientific evidence thus far, is mixed. Schutte and Stilinović (2017) found that viewers of Milk's *Clouds Over Sidra* in VR had higher levels of empathetic response than viewers who watched a 2D version. Bujić et al. (2020) found that viewers of immersive computer technologies like VR had higher levels of attitudinal change than viewers of 2D analogs. They acknowledge that both novelty and embodiment may be pertinent factors at work, particularly the extent to which the viewer feels able to navigate the virtual space. Herrera (2018) found higher levels of prosocial behaviors like petition signing and donating among views of a VR experience on homelessness, but results otherwise are decidedly mixed. Any kind of perspective-taking experience (placing viewers in the perspective of a homeless person), regardless of level of immersion, tended to increase reports of empathy over similar attempts to transmit the same content without perspective-taking.

Immersion, VR, and empathy are deeply entangled, but as we have seen Chapter 2, immersion is not something unique to VR. Neither is empathy. *Etiquette of the Undercaste,* a 1992 exhibition at the Smithsonian Experimental Gallery, introduced visitors to homelessness by having them lay on a morgue slab and be pushed through a wall so they could be "reborn" on the other side as homeless people which had a profound impact on visitors and their appreciation of homelessness (Molotsky 1992). Rueda (2020) found two reasons to be wary of VR empathy claims: the lack of evidence that VR created empathy more effectively than other media, and the ethical concerns around emotionally manipulating viewers (pp. 6–7). Martingano et al. (2021) conducted a meta-analysis of 43 VR studies with 5,644 participants to evaluate whether Milk's assertion held up. The results were decidedly more mixed. VR experiences *can* certainly increase empathy. Their analysis revealed that while VR could arouse emotional empathy, an immediate compassionate feeling, it did not appear to encourage the kind of cognitive empathy that inspires viewers to actively imagine other peoples' perspectives. They further propose that there are two different brain mechanisms behind emotional and cognitive empathy; an automatic response to emotionally evocative stimuli like watching a child struggle to lift a burden that is too heavy, and a more intensive engagement requiring the viewer to use their imagination to construct others' experiences (p. 1). In a similar vein, Murray (2016) notes Milk's conflation of platform and content, and asserts that VR alone is not enough. To generate empathy, an experience requires "well-chosen and highly specific stories, insightful interpretation, and strong compositional skills within a mature medium of communication." Here we see three of our concepts coming together, emotion, immersion, and storytelling.

It is difficult in the literature to discern how much the active variable in the "VR empathy machine" debate is the immersion versus the VR. Many of the authors above cite the novelty of the medium as requiring further exploration. For us, the potential of virtual reality as a medium lies in discovering its unique affordances, and marrying those with expressive content, what Murray calls "the beauty and truth" of what you want to share that could not be expressed in any other medium (Murray 2016). Despite decades of experimentation, VR is not yet a mature medium. It has hovered maddeningly on the "maybe in the next year or two" horizon for over 15 years. The tremendous investments made in VR by tech corporations like Meta and Microsoft will doubtless accelerate research and experimentation, but for now VR is still, as Murray (2016) puts it "only a platform, and an unstable and uncomfortable one at that."

So what are VR's unique affordances? For Beharry (2016), echoing Murray (2019) and others, the narrative building blocks of VR are navigable space and first-person perspective. Another point he makes that is almost entirely overlooked is the physical masking of the sensorium that almost all VR headsets provide. Vision and hearing are totally restricted to the content provided by the designers. He writes,

> Another channel of emotional arousal specific to VR is its hold on our attention. The more of our sensory bandwidth a medium uses, the more it will consume our attention automatically. VR surrounds us in audiovisual information, which results in a faster ramp up to immersion in an experience that is harder to be distracted from.

And this regard, VR hearkens all the way back to Gilman's (1918) idea of the *skiascope*, a handheld vision shield that restricted the user's field of view and binocular vision, in order to allow them to focus on a single artwork more easily (pp. 238–248).

Understand the Limits of Empathy

Like any tool, empathy is not a panacea for all situations. Richards et al. (2021) found that found that classroom lectures on ancient Greece were significantly superior in terms of the acquisition of factual knowledge, while an immersive VR environment generated an empathic response to the lived experiences of those people. Laurajane Smith (2016) points out that deep emotional engagement doesn't necessarily promote critical thinking. In fact, when presented with emotionally evocative stimuli, many visitors will practice a form of emotional avoidance to deal with potentially disruptive feelings. Mithlo and Sherman (2020) noted that American visitors' preconceptions about Native Americans were difficult to change through perspective-taking exhibits, even those that provoked strong emotional responses. Schlembach and Clewer (2021) problematize the emphasis on empathetic identification which they see as a threat to the kind of critical engagement necessary to generate positive behavioral change. Ramirez et al. (2021) argue that VR experiences designed to induce empathy will almost always be unethical to develop or deploy, due to the manipulation necessary to place viewers in others' place. They recommend instead aiming to make viewers "engaged witnesses" and generate sympathy instead. Linscott (2019), focusing on a subset of empathy experiences geared toward racial awareness, argues that the whole empathy-inducing premise of VR immersive replications of "Blackness" as an experiential category may themselves be another manifestation of the white gaze,

> the purported empathic effects of such simulations may persist after departure from the virtual world, but Blackness itself cannot not be transposed. Blackness can neither be slipped on nor be peeled away from the surface of the white body because it was never there to begin with.

Bollmer (2017) argues the concept of empathy itself is problematic and needs to be placed with "radical compassion." He retraces the intellectual history of empathy to point out that while today we imagine empathy to be a form of relation that acknowledges another's experience, it originally described how one relates to and absorbs objects into one's *own* experience. He argues

> It is not in 'understanding' the other fully through which I come to care for them, but through acknowledging the limits and the infinite inability to grasp another's experience completely. In this, they remain Other, and never part of the same. In this acknowledgment of distance, in the fostering of radical compassion rather than empathy, we can make a world together. 'Liberating' the affective by recognizing and feeling our intertwining is not intrinsically progressive – in fact, it too easily drifts toward the literal subsuming of the Other into the same, doing violence to them, all in the name of understanding.

(p. 74)

Develop Institutional Empathy

One distinct difference between empathy and other emotions as it relates to museums is the extent to which empathy is perceived as a tool of both outward-facing visitor engagement *and* inward-facing organizational change. Empathy is situated at the center of the movement to change museum practice and indeed their role in society. It's no coincidence that Norris and Tisdale's toolkit for using emotions in museums starts its exploration of using emotion with "Start with the Team." In other words, developing visitor-facing products that encourage empathy in visitors must start with museum staff themselves learning and practicing empathy with each other. The museum professionals behind the Empathetic Museum project argue that

> the qualities of the 21st century museum are impossible without an inner core of institutional empathy: the intention of the museum to be, and be perceived as, deeply connected with its community. The time has come to disrupt the persistent lack of institutional empathy in museums.
>
> (Jennings et al. 2019, p. 505)

Similarly, Gilbert (2106) sees tremendous parallels between philosopher Mariana Ortega's (2006) articulation of the "loving, knowing ignorance" of white feminists toward women of color and museums' traditional aloofness to their audiences. Gilbert summarizes current museum practice as,

> an epistemological stance that claims to be based in love but betrays a failure to abandon arrogance; one that claims to possess truth but relies only on partial understandings; one that claims to produce knowledge but in fact creates ignorance.
>
> (p. 130)

Promoting genuine empathy is seen as a way of combating the implicit arrogance that exemplifies much of contemporary museum practice, where traditional assumptions about how and why subject matter gets discussed tend to reinforce the inequities present in Western society. These examples of well-meaning condescension are problematic

> not because they pose public relations problems, but because they represent a failure of the museum's mission. This is a kind of moral leadership that helps both institutions and individuals grow towards fulfilling the museum's proper educational role in a diverse and democratic society.
>
> (Gilbert 2016, p. 138)

To create experiences that are based on "loving, knowing perception," developing the ability to feel empathy become a necessity for museums. This dual emphasis is best summed up by Ariese (2022) who describes the challenge thus,

> Although becoming more empathic is a personal process and challenge, museums can certainly play a role – on the one hand, by leading by

example with their internal communication, policies, and interactions; on the other hand, by supporting and encouraging empathy within and between visitors.

(p. 70)

The Perils of Designing for Emotional Evocation

Though this chapter has hopefully established the importance of emotion in experience design, I want to reiterate an important distinction. There is a difference between designing experiences that allow room for visitors to engage emotionally with them, and ones that are scripted to provoke a specific response. The line between the two can be extremely fine. The hesitation that many practitioners have with evoking emotion is that our experiences become manipulative and prescribed, reducing visitor agency and making them passive receivers of both cognitive and emotional messages from us to an extent that feels unnatural (Bedigan 2016, p. 89). This concern is valid. It is now possible to get extremely instrumentalist in prompting emotional responses in visitors. Jelinčić et al. (2021) list among their findings for prompting emotional responses,

> for the best results, it is recommended to induce joy using aural cues (major key, metre 4/4, ascending melody, no pitch variations, middle C range, stable timbre, no contrast, moderate loudness and moderately fast tempo) and sadness using visual cues (predominantly dark colours, irregular forms, smoother vs harsher sections for texture, moderate contrast and little lightness).

(p. 15)

Clearly, a designer can go too far, and out in the world, many do. Our challenge is therefore to encourage without being manipulative and avoid attempting to dominate visitors, but give them room to engage emotionally, reflect on their emotional response, and form new understandings, rather than become passive consumers (Gadsby 2011, p. 11).

The other peril to bear in mind about creating emotionally resonant experiences is that they are more taxing on visitors since they are experienced more richly. The more mentally expensive the experience, the faster the visitor depletes their reserve of mental energy. In a free-choice environment like a museum or heritage site, this means the more likely they are to disengage and leave. It is a different kind of museum fatigue than the ergonomic one Gilman (1918) first described, but is fatigue, nonetheless.

I photographed this poor fellow in Figure 3.1 at The Tuol Sleng Genocide Museum in Phnom Penh, which is one of the most powerful visitor experiences I've had. After walking through the displays of inmate photographs, recollections of former prisoners, and the stark reality of rooms left the way they were found when the Khmer Rouge fled, I, too needed to just sit down somewhere quiet and process my emotions. Engagement can be exhausting unless you design it to fit

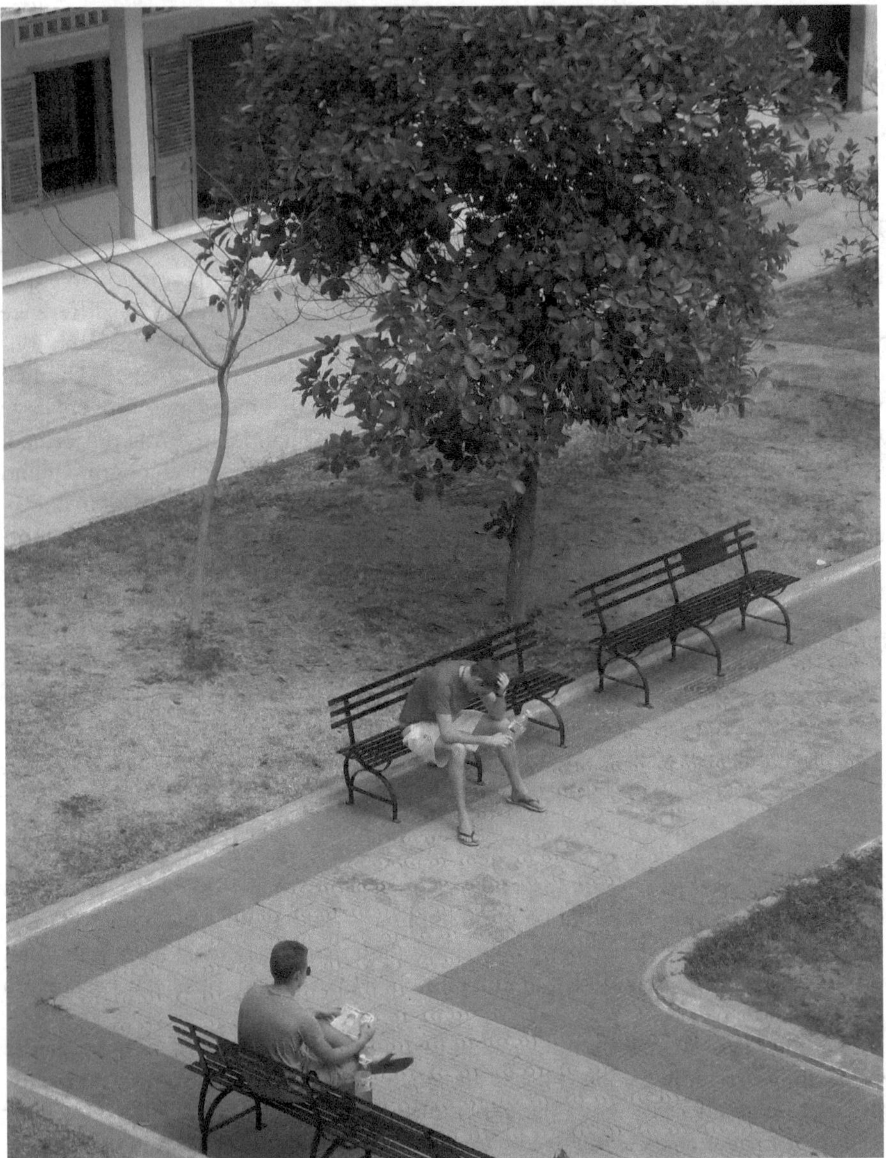

Figure 3.1 Tuol Sleng Genocide Museum, Phnom Penh, Cambodia

within a larger context that provides respite. Norris' and Tisdale's (2017) emotional map of experiences can be a vital tool to help against this overload. One of the most hospitable acts you can perform as a designer is to provide visitors with an experience that not only provides moments of feeling, but also moments of peace. Providing hospitality, according to Owen (2021) may be the most important part of emotional planning that museums can do, because from that sense of feeling hosted as in "feeling looked after" all the other kinds of interactions flow. In the hierarchy of visitor needs, feeling safe is foundational.

Emotional Museum Experiences

The Museum of Broken Relationships, Zagreb, Croatia

The Museum of Broken Relationships, which started as an art project by two artists who were ending their romantic relationship and decided to document their experience, has become a global franchise that bases its entire interpretation around the sharing of emotionally evocative objects and stories of loss.

EMOTIVE Çatalhöyük, Turkey

The EU-funded EMOTIVE project prototyped a number of digital experiences in Scotland, Greece, and the Neolithic Age archaeological site of Çatalhöyük, Turkey that all aimed to change how people experience heritage sites. One of the prototypes employed a chatbot that challenged visitors to examine (and re-examine) their beliefs while discussing those of the inhabitants of Çatalhöyük through questions like "Would you bury someone you cared about under your bed like they did in Çatalhöyük?" Explicitly designing for emotional responses was used to generate feelings of togetherness, cohesion, connection to the site, and empathy for the peoples who lived there.

The Museum of Old and New Art, Hobart Australia

The interpretive delivery system at the Museum of Old and New Art in Hobart, Australia, "The O," is a handheld device which contains all the interpretation about the collection. There are no wall texts, everything is on the device, one of the primary functions of which is to prompt visitors to choose how every object they inquire about makes them feel. Visitors are given a simple Love/Hate choice, and prompted throughout their visit attend to their emotional response to the objects before anything else.

Conclusion

Designing for emotional evocation doesn't mean trying to prescribe how visitors should feel, or at least it shouldn't in my opinion. It is essential, though, that we consider how integral emotion is to our way of being in the world, and what opportunities emotional evocation presents the experience designer.

Before even engaging in what you've created for them, giving visitors explicit permission to have an emotional response is a key scaffold to help them bring their whole selves to that experience. Calls to reflect on how an experience makes you feel, and opportunities to share that with others are powerful tools to encourage deeper engagement. We relate emotionally to other people, not populations or abstract ideas, so wherever possible, find ways to introduce personal stories. Encourage visitors to empathize with other people's lived experiences, while realizing empathy's limitations. Recognize that difficult emotions are not something to be avoided at all cost, but to be acknowledged and embraced. Our institutions strive to be welcoming, inclusive spaces, and part of that welcome should be helping our audiences work through difficult topics and arrive at deeper understandings. That can't happen if we only deal with the pleasant subjects and insist that visitors bottle up their emotions. And above all, remember that we are all emotional beings, all the time.

Reflection

In Practice: Emotion and Play

*By Linda Norris, International Coalition
of Sites of Conscience (ICSC)*

The array of emotions is enormous: jubilant and thrilled, heartbroken and downcast, horrified and shaken, awestruck and impressed to name a few. In different cultures, these emotions also express themselves in very different ways. But play also has many different manifestations: rough and tumble, social play, fantasy play, games with rules, and much more. And, of course, different cultures manifest both emotions and kinds of play in different ways. What's a designer to do?

Members of the International Coalition of Sites of Conscience (ICSC) approach this dilemma in many ways. Founded in 1999, ICSC is the only worldwide network of Sites of Conscience, with over 370 members in more than 65 countries. These members remember a variety of histories and come from a wide range of settings—including long-standing democracies, countries struggling with legacies of violence, as well as post-conflict contexts beginning to address their transitional justice needs. They are all united by their common commitment to use the lessons of the past to find innovative solutions to related social justice issues today. ICSC members creating exhibits range from large state-run institutions to scrappy all-volunteer organizations. Whether your museum is large or small, teams need to bring an understanding of individual emotions into the design process. It's key to understand that there is no possibility that you will be able to ensure that all visitors feel the same emotion through any part of the exhibition.

As I reflected on Rainey and my toolkit on emotions referenced by Ed in this chapter, I would expand upon the idea about human connections by being explicit about the need for community collaborators, ensuring that a multiplicity of voices and emotions are heard, felt and embraced throughout the exhibition development process, not just by visitors at the end of the project. A few examples from ICSC may illustrate how play can be used to facilitate engagement with challenging histories.

Cultural Heritage with Borders Albania has designed a whole series of board games, puzzles, and more to help young people learn about cultural heritage in a country where authoritarian regimes controlled approaches to heritage. Large floor size outdoor board games create joy and solidarity through collaborative play. The Red Star Line Museum in Antwerp, Belgium, has created family games to move through their permanent exhibition—for the youngest visitors, Help Gup the Gull

Move Home, brings forth all of the emotions of a move to a new place through a playful finding and activity game.

The War Childhood Museum in Sarajevo, Bosnia and Herzegovina considers play in two ways—first, as a topic for collection and exhibition, and second, for ongoing programmatic activities. Founded by survivors of the Balkan conflict, every object in the collection comes with a personal story. These objects and stories now expand out from the Balkans and have included stories from both Ukraine and Palestine. A children's workshop is based on the story of a single object from the collection, a toy ragdoll made for a young girl by her mother after they become refugees. In the workshop, participants learn about ways that toys and play can support young people during difficult times and make their own toys from recycled materials.

Three Sites of Conscience (War Childhood Museum, Gulag.cz in the Czech Republic and Le Bois du Cazier in Belgium) are partnered with game developers in an innovative project, Mementos to

> develop games that allow users to inhabit the perspectives of different groups involved in these events, emphasizing the experiences of regular people. Ultimately, the games will encourage players to develop empathy for marginalised groups and learn about the past while drawing connections to similar issues unfolding today.

Artists bring new ideas and energy to integrating play and emotions. As an exhibit developer, they may push what you think of as an exhibition, but the opportunities for new thinking are extensive. The National Public Housing Museum's (Chicago, IL) Artist as Instigator program has included a project by artist Marisa Jahn and architect Rafi Sagal, HOOPcycle, a mobile art installation that brings together basketball's history, its Meso American roots, and a deep sense of playful fun.

At Constitution Hill in South Africa, the Basha Uhuru Freedom Festival commemorates the Soweto Youth Uprising of 1976, with an enormous variety of creative energies—music, dance, visual arts, and more. By engaging community members, particularly young people in the creative, playful expression of rights and the legacies of activists, it moves beyond text-laden exhibitions. Serious ideas can be expressed in a multitude of playful ways.

To return to the question, what's a designer to do? Here are just a few lessons from Sites of Conscience projects:

- Don't go it alone—community partners are vital.
- Consider your own emotions and biases before you begin and continue to check them throughout the project. Create space for team members to support each other in continuing to transparently address emotions and biases.
- Be brave—play can be a powerful tool for addressing emotions.
- Prototype, revise, prototype again. Consider whether you create something that will never be finished, that the emotions and playfulness of visitors can help determine outcomes that may change over time.

References

Alelis, Genevieve, Bobrowicz, Ania, and Ang, Chee Siang. 2013. Exhibiting Emotion: Capturing Visitors' Emotional Responses to Museum Artefacts. *Lecture Notes in Computer Science (Including Subseries Lecture Notes in Artificial Intelligence and Lecture Notes in Bioinformatics)*, vol. 8014 LNCS, no. Part 3.

Anderson, Gail. 2004. Introduction: Reinventing the Museum. In Gail. Anderson (Ed.), *Reinventing the Museum: Historical and Contemporary Perspectives on the Paradigm Shift*. AltaMira Press, p. 1.

Ariese, Csilla E., and Wróblewska, Magdalena. 2022. *Practicing Decoloniality in Museums Book: A Guide with Global Examples*. Amsterdam University Press, p. 70.

Arnold de Simine, Silke. 2013. *Mediating Memory in the Museum: Trauma, Empathy, Nostalgia*. Palgrave Macmillan UK.

Asher, Vidette. 2018. pem.org | Our Goals & Approach for PEM's Neuroscience Initiative.

Bacon, Francis. 1620. Novum Organum, sive Indicia Vera de Interpretatione Naturae. John Bill.

Barrett, Lisa F. 2016. Navigating the Science of Emotion. In H.L. Meiselman (Ed.), *Emotion Measurement*. Woodhead Publishing, pp. 31–63. https://doi.org/10.1016/B978-0-08-100508-8.00002-3

Bedigan, Kirsten M. 2016. Developing Emotions: Perceptions of Emotional Responses in Museum Visitors. *Mediterranean Archaeology and Archaeometry*, vol. 16, no. 5 Special Issue, 2016, p. 89.

Beharry, Clint. 2016. VR: Going Beyond the Empathy Machine | by Harmony Labs | Medium. *Medium*. https://harmonylabs.medium.com/vr-going-beyond-the-empathy-machine-d6245146765c#.qzyfz1m3u

Bohn, Annette, and Berntsen, Dorthe. 2007. Pleasantness Bias in Flashbulb Memories: Positive and Negative Flashbulb Memories of the Fall of the Berlin Wall among East and West Germans. *Memory & Cognition*, vol. 35, no. 3, 2007, pp. 500–575.

Bollmer, Grant. 2017. Empathy Machines. *Media International Australia*, vol. 165, no. 1, 2017, pp. 63–76.

Brosch, Tobias, Klaus R. Scherer, Didier Grandjean, and David Sander. 2013. The Impact of Emotion on Perception, Attention, Memory, and Decision-Making. *Swiss Medical Weekly*, vol. 143, May 2013, pp. 1–10.

Bujić, Mila, Mikko Salminen, Joseph Macey and Juho Hamari. 2020. 'Empathy Machine': How Virtual Reality Affects Human Rights Attitudes. *Internet Research*, vol. 30, no. 5, 2020, pp. 1407–1425.

Csikszentmihalyi, Mihaly, and Hermanson, Kim. 1995. Intrinsic Motivation in Museums: Why Does One Wants to Learn? *Public Institutions for Personal Learning, Establishing a Research Agenda*.

Cuseum. 2020. Neurological Perceptions of Art through Augmented & Virtual Reality. https://www.researchgate.net/publication/341293320_Neurological_Perceptions_of_Art_through_Augmented_Virtual_Reality. (accessed 3.3.2021).

Descartes, Rene. 1644. *Renati descartes principia philosophiæ [Principia philosophiæ. Passions de l'âme. Renati Descartes Specimina philosophiæ, seu, Dissertatio de methodo.]* Ludwig & Daniel Elzevir.

Desmet, P.M.A., Vastenburg, M.H., and Romero, N. 2016. Mood Measurement with Pick-A-Mood: Review of Current Methods and Design of a Pictorial Self-Report Scale. *JDR*, vol. 14, 2016, pp. 241–279.

Dickinson, G., Blair, C., and Ott, B.L. (Eds.). 2010. *Places of Public Memory: The Rhetoric of Museums and Memorials, Rhetoric, Culture, and Social Critique*. Univ. of Alabama Press.

Ebert, Roger. 2005. Roger Ebert on Empathy | Roger Ebert. https://www.rogerebert.com/empathy/video-roger-ebert-on-empathy (accessed 2.5.22).

Emotive. 2018. Emotive - Storytelling for Cultural Heritage. https://emotiveproject.eu/pages/about/background/ (accessed 3.20.24).

Empathy Museum. 2021. https://www.empathymuseum.com/ (accessed 12.30.21).

Falk, John H. 2021. The Role of Emotions in Museum-Going. In The Learning Museum Working Group. (Ed.), *Emotions and Learning in Museums*. NEMO – The Network of European Museum Organisations, pp. 55–61.

Falk, John H., and Dierking, Lynn D. 2000. *Learning from Museums: Visitor Experiences and the Making of Meaning*. AltaMira Press.

Falk, John H., and Gillespie, Katie L. 2009. Investigating the Role of Emotion in Science Center Visitor Learning. *Visitor Studies*, vol. 12, no. 2, 2009, p. 126.

Fredrickson, B.L. 2001. The Role of Positive Emotions in Positive Psychology. *American Psychologist*, vol. 56, 2001, pp. 218–226.

Gadsby, Jenniefer. 2011. The Effect of Encouraging Emotional Value in Museum Experiences. *Museological Review*, vol. 15, no. 1, pp. 1–13.

Gilbert, Lisa. 2016. 'Loving, Knowing Ignorance': A Problem for the Educational Mission of Museums. *Curator: The Museum Journal*, vol. 59, no. 2, 2016, pp. 125–140, 130.

Gilman, Benjamin I. 1918. *Museum Ideals of Purpose and Method*. Riverside Press, 1918.

Gokcigdem, Elif M. 2016. *Fostering Empathy through Museums*. Rowman & Littlefield Publishers.

Gokcigdem, Elif M. 2019. *Designing for Empathy: Perspectives on the Museum Experience*. Rowman & Littlefield.

Haviland-Jones, Jeannette M., Barrett, L.F., and Lewis, M. (Eds.). (2010). Handbook of Emotions, 3rd edn. Guilford Publications.

Herrera, Fernanda, Jeremy Bailenson, Erika Weisz, Elise Ogle, and Jamil Zaki. 2018. Building Long-Term Empathy: A Large-Scale Comparison of Traditional and Virtual Reality Perspective-Taking. *PLoS ONE*, vol. 13, no. 10, pp. 1–37.

Hohenstein, J., and Moussouri, T. 2018. *Museum Learning: Theory and Research as Tools for Enhancing Practice*. Routledge, ISBN: 9781138901124. quoted in Bimbo, Alberto Del. Emotions in Digital. In The Learning Museum Working Group (Ed.), *Emotions and Learning in Museums*.

James, William. 1890. *The Principles of Psychology*. Dover. quoted in Brosch, Tobias, Klaus R. Scherer, Didier Grandjean, and David Sander. 2013. The Impact of Emotion on Perception, Attention, Memory, and Decision-Making. *Swiss Medical Weekly*, vol. 143, May 2013, p. 2.

Jelinčić, Daniela A., Marta Šveb, and Alan E. Stewart. 2021. Designing Sensory Museum Experiences for Visitors' Emotional Responses. *Museum Management and Curatorship*, vol. 37, no. 5, pp. 513–30.

Jennings, Gretchen, Jim Cullen, Janeen Bryant, Kayleigh Bryant-Greenwell, Stacey Mann, Charlette Hove, and Nayeli Zepeda. 2019. The Empathetic Museum: A New Institutional Identity. *Curator*, vol. 62, no. 4, 2019, p. 505.

Kensinger, Elizabeth, Rachel Garoff-Eaton, and Daniel Schacter. 2007. How Negative Emotion Enhances the Visual Specificity of a Memory. *Journal of Cognitive Neuroscience*, vol. 19, no. 11, 2007, p. 1885.

Lane, H. Chad. 2015. Enhancing Informal Learning Experiences with Affect-Aware Technologies. In Calvo, Rafael, Sidney K. D'Mello, Jonathan Gratch, and Arvid Kappas (Eds.), The Oxford Handbook of Affective Computing, Oxford Library of Psychology, pp. 435–436.

LaPlaca Cohen, and Kelton Global (2017). Culture Track '17. p. 32.

LaPlaca Cohen, and Slover Linett (2021). CULTURE + COMMUNITY IN A TIME OF CRISIS: Key Findings from Wave 2. p 23.

Latham, K.F. 2013. Numinous Experiences with Museum Objects. *Visitor Studies*, vol. 16, 2013, pp. 16–17.

Latham, K.F. 2022. Infecting Museums with Joy: Seven Ways. *Library Trends*, vol. 70, 2022, pp. 616–634.

Linscott, Charles P. 2019. Virtually and Actually Black: On VR and Racial Empathy. *ASAP/ Journal*, vol. 4, no. 2, 2019, p. 306.

Martingano, Alison J., Fernanda Hererra, and Sara Konrath. 2021. Supplemental Material for Virtual Reality Improves Emotional but Not Cognitive Empathy: A Meta-Analysis. *Technology, Mind, and Behavior*, vol. 2, no. 1, 2021. p. 1.

Mazzanti, Paolo. 2021. Emotions Inside/Out Museums. In The Learning Museum Working Group. (Ed.), *Emotions and Learning in Museums*. NEMO, Network of European museum organisations, p. 8.

McGaugh, James L. 2000. Memory - A Century of Consideration. *Science*, vol, 287, 2000, pp. 248–251.

McGaugh, James L. 2013. Making Lasting Memories: Remembering the Significant. *Proceedings of the National Academy of Sciences of the United States of America*, vol. 110, no. SUPPL2, 2013, p. 10404.

Merriam-Webster. 2021. Emotion Definition & Meaning. https://www.merriam-webster. com/dictionary/emotion (accessed 12.19.21).

Milk, Chris. 2015. How Virtual Reality Can Create the Ultimate Empathy Machine. *TED2015*, https://www.ted.com/talks/chris_milk_how_virtual_reality_can_create_the_ultimate_ empathy_machine

Mithlo, Nancy M., and Sherman, Aleksandra. 2020. Perspective-Taking Can Lead to Increased Bias: A Call for 'Less Certain' Positions in American Indian Contexts. *Curator*, vol. 63, no. 3, 2020, pp. 353–369.

Molotsky, Irvin. 1992. Washington Journal; In a Museum, a Taste of Homelessness. *New York Times*, 4 Feb. 1992, p. A–10.

Murray, Janet H. 2016. Not a Film and Not an Empathy Machine. *Immerse*, https://immerse. news/not-a-film-and-not-an-empathy-machine-48b63b0eda93

Murray, Janet H. 2019. Hamlet on the *Holodeck*: The *Future* of *Narrative* in Cyberspace. MIT Press.

MuSo. 2023. https://www.museumofsolutions.in/#/about (accessed 3.24.24).

Nahum-Shani, Inbal, Steven D. Shaw, Stephanie M. Carpenter, Susan A. Murphy, and Carolyn Yoon. 2022. Engagement in Digital Interventions. *American Psychologist*, vol. 77, no. 7, p 828.

Niven, Karen. 2013. Affect. In: Gellman, Marc. D., Turner, J. Rick. (Eds.), Encyclopedia of Behavioral Medicine. Springer, pp. 49–50.

Norris, Linda, and Tisdale, Rainey. 2017. Developing a Toolkit for Emotion in Museums. *Exhibition*, Spring 2017. pp. 100–108.

Ochsner, Kevin N. 2000. Are Affective Events Richly Recollected or Simply Familiar? The Experience and Process of Recognizing Feelings Past. *Journal of Experimental Psychology: General*, vol. 129, no. 2, 2000, pp. 242–261.

Ortega, M. 2006. Being Lovingly, Knowingly Ignorant: White Feminism and Women of Color. *Hypatia*, vol. 21, 2006, pp. 56–74.

Owen, Tom. 2021. Planning for Emotions in Museums. *Emotions and Learning in Museums*.

Pelowski, Matthew, and Akiba, Fuminori. 2011. A Model of Art Perception, Evaluation and Emotion in Transformative Aesthetic Experience. *New Ideas in Psychology*, vol. 29, no. 2, Aug. 2011, p. 84.

Pelowski, Matthew. 2015. Tears and Transformation: Feeling like Crying as an Indicator of Insightful or 'Aesthetic' Experience with Art. *Frontiers in Psychology*, vol. 6, July 2015, pp. 1664–1078.

Peng, Jingyu. 2019. How Does This Exhibition Make You Feel? Measuring Sensory and Emotional Experience of In-Gallery Digital Technology with GSR Devices. MuseWeb 2019.

Perry, Sara, Maria Roussou, Maria Economou, Hilary Young, and Laia Pujol. 2017. Moving beyond the Virtual Museum: Engaging Visitors Emotionally. *Proceedings of the 2017 23rd International Conference on Virtual Systems and Multimedia (VSMM)*.

Ramirez, Erick J., Miles Elliott, and Per-Erik Milam. 2021. What It's like to Be a _____: Why It's (Often) Unethical to Use VR as an Empathy Nudging Tool. *Ethics and Information Technology*, vol. 23, no. 3, 2021, pp. 527–542.

Richards, Deborah, Susan Lupack, Ayse Bilgin, Bronwyn, Neil, and Meredith Porte. 2021. Learning with the Heart or with the Mind: Using Virtual Reality to Bring Historical Experiences to Life and Arouse Empathy. Behaviour *and* Information Technology, 42 (1), pp. 1–24.

Roppola, Tiina. 2012. *Designing for the Museum Visitor Experience*. Routledge. p. 249.

Rueda, Jon, and Lara, Francisco. 2020. Virtual Reality and Empathy Enhancement: Ethical Aspects. *Frontiers in Robotics and AI*, vol. 7, no. November, 2020, pp. 6–7.

Savenije, Geerte M., and de Bruijn, Pieter. 2017. Historical Empathy in a Museum: Uniting Contextualisation and Emotional Engagement. *International Journal of Heritage Studies*, vol. 23, no. 9, 2017, pp. 832–845.

Schlembach, Raphael, and Clewer, Nicola. 2021. 'Forced Empathy': Manipulation, Trauma and Affect in Virtual Reality Film. *International Journal of Cultural Studies*, vol. 24, no. 5, 2021, pp. 827–843.

Schorch, Philipp, Jessica Walton, Naomi Priest and Yin Paradies. 2015. Encountering the 'Other': Interpreting Student Experiences of a Multi-Sensory Museum Exhibition. *Journal of Intercultural Studies*, vol. 36, no. 2, 2015, p. 238.

Schutte, Nicola S., and Stilinović, Emma J. 2017. Facilitating Empathy through Virtual Reality. *Motivation and Emotion*, vol. 41, no. 6, Dec. 2017, pp. 708–712. https://doi.org/10.1007/s11031-017-9641-7

Segal, Elizabeth. 2019. A Sophisticate's Primer on Empathy – and Its Limits. Aeon Essays.

Simmonds, E., and Royal, M. 2023. *Pleasure, Connection and Purpose: How Museums Can Leverage Emotions to Build Greater Public Support*. Association of Independent Museums.

Singer, Tania, and Lamm, Claus. 2009. The Social Neuroscience of Empathy. *Annals of the New York Academy of Sciences*, vol. 1156, 2009, p. 81.

Smith, L., and Campbell, G. 2015. The Elephant in the Room: Heritage, Affect, and Emotion. In W. Logan, M.N. Craith, and U. Kockel (Eds.), *A Companion to Heritage Studies*. Wiley, pp. 443–460.

Smith, Laurajane. 2010. 'Man's Inhumanity to Man' and Other Platitudes of Avoidance and Misrecognition: An Analysis of Visitor Responses to Exhibitions Marking the 1807 Bicentenary. *Museum and Society*, vol. 8, no. 3, 2010, pp. 193–214.

Smith, Laurajane. 2016. Changing Views? Emotional Intelligence, Registers of Engagement and the Museum Visit. In V. Gosselin and P. Livingstone (Eds.), *Museums and the Past. Constructing Historical Consciousness*. UBC Press, pp. 101–121.

Sutherland, Matthew R., and Mather, Mara. 2017. Arousal (But Not Valence) Amplifies the Impact of Salience. *Cognition and Emotion*, vol. 9931, no. June, 2017, pp. 1–17.

United Nations VR. 2014. Syrian Refugee Crisis – UN Virtual Reality. Retrieved September 15, 2024, from https://unvr.sdgactioncampaign.org/cloudsoversidra/

Van Damme, Marieke. 2015. Joyful Museums: Together We Can Make Work Better. *Joyful Museums*. http://www.joyfulmuseums.com/resources/joyful-museums-together-we-can-make-work-better/ (accessed 7.21.21).

Wetherell, Margaret, Laurajane Smith, and Gary Campbell. 2018. Introduction: Affective Heritage Practices. In Wetherell, Margaret, Laurajane Smith, and Gary Campbell (Eds.), *Emotion, Affective Practices, and the Past in the Present*. Routledge, pp 1–21.

Witcomb, Andrea. 2013. Understanding the Role of Affect in Producing a Critical Pedagogy for History Museums. *Museum Management and Curatorship*, vol. 28, no. 3, Aug. 2013, pp. 255–271.

4　Narrative Transportation

Storytelling in a Digital Age

Our next topic, narrative transportation, though intricately entwined with the other concepts mentioned in this book, is different in one important way. Unlike sensory immersion, emotional evocation, and gameful participation, narrative transportation through storytelling is already a core technique that museums rely upon to engage visitors. A Bing search on the text string "museum tells the story of" returned over six million hits in April 2024.[1] Leslie Bedford (2001) goes so far as call storytelling "the real work of museums." As Orhan Pamuk (2016) says, "In museums we have History, but what we need is stories." Yet at the same time, storytelling is routinely offered up in museum conferences and workshops as a novel technique to add your practitioner's tool kit. Museums are both full of stories and not.

The question of how storytelling has (or hasn't) changed as a result of the advent of digital technologies is a live one. Yilmaz and Ciğerci (2019) provide a variety of examples of different definitions of digital storytelling that are current. But as museum experience designers, we're interested in visitors and how to engage them, and from the visitors' perspective, the desire to be transported by a compelling story remains constant, however the storytelling is delivered. Storytelling is a vital tool, Barbara Hardy writes, because

> …we dream in narrative, day dream in narrative, remember, anticipate, hope, despair, believe, doubt, plan, revise, criticize, construct, gossip, learn, hate, and love by narrative. In order really to live, we make up stories about ourselves and others, about the personal as well as the social past and future.
>
> (Hardy 1968, p. 5)

For museums and their missions to improve visitors' lives, storytelling is essential because,

> Stories are the most fundamental way we learn. They have a beginning, a middle, and an end. They teach without preaching, encouraging both personal

DOI: 10.4324/9781032638690-4

reflection and public discussion. Stories inspire wonder and awe; they allow a listener to imagine another time and place, to find the universal in the particular, and to feel empathy for others. They preserve individual and collective memory and speak to both the adult and the child.

(Bedford 2001, p. 33)

In this chapter, I will explore the third of four concepts for creating playful engagement: narrative transportation, discuss how evolution and storytelling are linked and consider how compelling museum storytelling engages more of the mind and body, improves our ability to remember details, and makes us feel more generous, charitable, and compassionate. I will explore some of the complications and opportunities digital technologies have added to the mix, and highlight examples of museum storytelling that really deliver.

The Long History of Storytelling

Storytelling is a human universal and is presumed to have been a substantial factor in human evolution. Stories are in fact one of our oldest technologies, like using fire. Stories cannot be found in the paleontological record since they don't fossilize, but it's most likely that storytelling is even older than our species. After the invention of language itself, storytelling might be the most important tool we use. As Brian Boyd notes, storytelling

> impacted our development, our individual and social behavior, cognition, and emotion… and presumably our genes. It made us more dependent on learning from experiences not our own… Fiction in turn arose from our particularly strong hominin and human predisposition for play, itself adaptive for our social existence, as a learning, a bonding, and a corrective mechanism…

Boyd (2017) goes so far as to adapt linguist Daniel Dor's dictum "First we invented language. Then language changed us" (Dor 2015, p. 4) to assert "First we invented stories, then they [stories] changed us." Stories have literally changed who we are, as a species, as societies and as individuals.

Two of the evolutionary changes that occurred to make us storytellers and story consumers were what Garcia-Pelegrin, et al. (2021) call Mental Time Travel and a Theory of Mind. Mental Time Travel is the ability to imagine other times and places, past, present and future, and insert ourselves into them. The Theory of Mind is the ability to infer and attribute mental states to others. Together, these brain mechanisms allow us to receive a story and infer how the characters in the story might have felt. In other words, Janet Murray's "Active Creation of Belief" which we encountered in Chapter Two, has a very, very long prehistory. The act of mentally inserting yourself into a narrative and creating in your mind an imagined world where you participate in the action is deeply rooted in us.

Stories Give Objects Meaning

The centrality of storytelling to the human experience is hopefully clear to you. It is one of the variables that distinguish us from all other animals. We are storytellers, and until artificial intelligence evolves more, storytelling is a uniquely human ability. I'm reiterating this point because I have often encountered colleagues in the field who express sentiments (usually in opposition to interpretation) that we should "let the objects speak for themselves." As Christopher Wilk et al. (2004) writes,

> While some of us possess the visual sensitivity, historical knowledge or imaginative skills that would make standing in front of a museum object free of interpretive support a pleasurable and meaningful experience, many museum visitors desire some form of guidance in learning how to approach museum objects.

This misplacement of agency is insidious and easy to fall into. But it can blind us to what is really happening and where it is (or isn't) happening, which is in the visitors' mind. Here's a little thought experiment to illustrate it.

Imagine that the sword in Figure 4.1 is in a museum in Iceland. It is said to be the very sword that Erik the Red used to kill the sons of Thorgest, which led to his exile from Iceland and his founding of the first European settlement on Greenland. It is a direct link to the Viking sagas and the earliest days of Iceland. This sword is a national treasure.

Now let's imagine that I am a comic book supervillain of the Lex Luthor variety; incredibly intelligent, with vast resources, and prone to overly complicated plots. I have taken a dislike to the country of Iceland for some reason and concoct a scheme to deprive them of a piece of their heritage. I develop a sophisticated computer virus that can infect every computer on Earth and on one particular night, I send this virus out to destroy every digital reference to the sword. At the same time, my agents have been stealing or destroying every book, photograph, or picture of the sword. I design a memory-erasing device that I unleash on the inhabitants of Planet Earth that destroys any memories of the sword. Lastly, one of my minions sneaks into the museum that same night, opens the case, removes the label, and slips off into the night, cackling evilly. At no time do I or my accomplices touch the sword itself (Figure 4.2).

So, what is this sword now? Stylistic analysis might allow an expert to see similarities with weapons made in Norway during the 10th and 11th centuries. A metallurgical analysis of the sword could indicate where the metal might have been sourced. Further tests might also uncover other facts about the item. But no amount of scientific scrutiny or close observation will ever find a trace of Erik or Thorgest's sons. Even if you could examine every single atom of the weapon, it would never reveal that information. Without the stories, this sword is just a sword. And the stories do not reside in that object. They hover around it like a swarm of invisible bees. If the stories are going to be told, we need to tell them and not just hope that visitors will "get it."

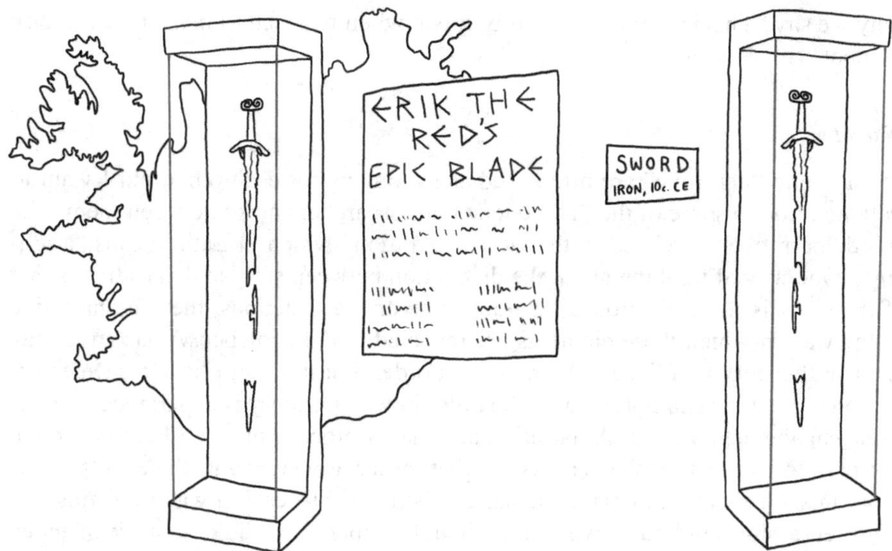

Figure 4.1 Erik the Red's sword. Image by Phoebe Rogue

Figure 4.2 A sword. Image by Phoebe Rogue

The Hallmarks of Narrative Transportation

So much for storytelling in general and its long history. What is the outcome of storytelling that makes it desirable? The audiences for stories do more than willingly suspend disbelief in the obvious fiction of a story; they project themselves *into* the worlds of the stories, Murray's "the active creation of belief" we encountered in Chapter 2. The characters and settings in these stories become as real as people and places we've known personally, and the evolutionarily older parts of our brains simulate the emotions we imagine the characters might feel; the phenomenon called "narrative transportation." Before we look at that, though, let's take a moment and talk about terms.

Story

According to the Cambridge Dictionary, a story is "a description, either true or imagined, of a connected series of events." Stories contain some common elements, like characters, events, and a time sequence. The characters possess motivations and agency; they act, and their actions impact the story. The story is told by a narrator, either present or omnipresent. The events consist of actions carried out by characters who have reasons for the things they do. There is some kind of conflict involved that reaches a resolution by the end of the story. "How does the story end?" reflects our assumption that stories have to resolve to be satisfying. Stories are also linked with the idea of subjectivity (Wong 2016) and unseriousness. Saying that something is "only a story" implies both fictionality and lack of importance. Stories are not by default thought to be a factual recitation, that's why we say "This is a true story" in English, when we need to make that veracity evident.

Narrative

"Story" and "narrative" are often used as synonyms for each other, but I want to call attention to some of the distinctions that researchers make between them. The word "narrative" is related to the word "narration" which in Latin means "a telling." One way of thinking about the distinction between story and narrative is that if the story is the collection of characters, events and actions, then the narrative is the way in which these elements are revealed to the audience. A narrative may present the story in a linear, chronological order, but it doesn't have to. Detective fiction is a classic example of how the order in which a story is experienced affects your engagement with it. A narrative also has a higher purpose, there is a point the narrator wants to make. This is the plot. A narrative recounts the events of the story in such a way as to make the narrator's point. The easiest way to distinguish between a story and narrative is this thought experiment: Take a stack of index cards and write down the sequence of events you want to share. That's your story. As the storyteller, you might want to arrange those cards in a particular sequence to more strongly make your point. That's your narrative.

Narrative is a powerful tool for teaching and learning for many reasons. Szurmak and Thuna (2013) posit that storytelling is powerful because it employs the same strategies our brains already use to learn. They call out three elements as being particularly important, namely that narratives take abstract concepts and make them concrete, narratives provide a context for the audience to place new knowledge into which improves their retention and understanding, and that narratives create immediate emotional experiences that the audience can relate to and remember (pp. 550–551).

Storytelling

The act of transmitting those constructed narratives is storytelling. I will use Sibierska's (2017) definition of storytelling as "the process of composing narratives, i.e. translating the conceptual into the material [or digital] via a given medium" (p. 48). In the museum context, Jane Nielsen (2017) proposes that, "Storytelling can be viewed as the concept that combines the articulation of understandings that defines museum communication and the engaging narrative that forms the story" (p. 445). In its earliest forms of verbal and non-verbal usage, storytelling was always a performance; the story occurs only in the act of it being told. Since the advent of written language, and especially since the advent of digital forms of recording, we are able to capture the act of storytelling and create a product that preserves it and makes it infinitely replicable. At its heart, though, it still an act we perform. Storytelling also requires the storyteller to take on the role of "the narrator." As we read at the beginning of the chapter, this role is one of the most ancient ones and the relationship between storyteller and audience one of the most primal. If you agree with Bedford (and me) that storytelling is the real business of museums, then steorytelling should be a primary job competency for museum professionals.

Narrative Transportation

It is a well-established fact that the narrative transportation effect—that state of "getting lost in a good story"—elicits powerful affective and cognitive responses in story receivers, and can alter personal beliefs, attitudes, and intentions as a result of being swept away by a story and transported into a narrative world that modifies their perception of their world of origin (Van Laer, Feiereisen, and Visconti 2019, p. 135). It shares similarities with both immersion and flow. But what is narrative transportation and how can we best employ it to further our goals of creating memorable, transformative museum experiences? The psychologist Richard Gerrig (1993) defines narrative transportation as a process where someone ("the traveler") is transported, by some means of transportation ("the story"), as a result of performing certain actions (listening, reading, watching, etc.). The traveler goes some distance from his or her world of origin, which makes some aspects of the world of origin inaccessible. The traveler returns to the world of origin, somewhat changed by the journey (pp. 10–11).

If we parse this definition closely, we can see how narrative transportation has interesting parallels with playful engagement and the other concepts we've discussed thus far. *Someone is transported* speaks to the intrinsic motivation humans have to seek out these kinds of experiences. We are transported because we *want* to be transported: it is a self-satisfying or *autotelic* experience. Gerrig takes care to point out that "being transported" makes the traveler seem like a passive subject when in fact "readers perform narratives" in their minds. *By some means of transportation* refers to the products we create. They are the websites, virtual worlds, exhibitions, and stories that we seek to create. *Performing certain actions* is a form of Murray's Active Creation of Belief from Chapter 2. We have to work to achieve this state, through attending to the storyteller, be it a label, person, or media piece. *The traveler goes some distance* speaks to our human propensity to project our reality into whatever narrative world we construct in our minds. Unless otherwise explicitly stated, we will assume that the world functions like ours. The more different the narrative world, the more the differences must be explained. The mental balancing act we perform as travelers makes *some aspects of the world of origin inaccessible*. To partake in the pleasure of narrative transportation, we give up some of our ability to be in our default worlds. That's why we gasp at sudden shocks in a movie, even though we know we are safely seated and unable to be affected by the narrative. And why a visit to a museum is seen as a break from the default worlds of visitors. And last, but certainly not least, the idea that the traveler *returns to the world of origin, somewhat changed* has everything to do with creating memorable experiences and museums' missions to transform visitors' lives.

As an intrinsically motivated activity, travelers need to both receive and interpret the story to achieve a state of narrative transportation. They do this in two main ways. They deploy their empathy try to understand the experience of the characters, and they create vivid mental imagery of the story, so they feel as though they are experiencing the events themselves (Van Laer et al. 2014, p. 799). Narrative transportation is a result of emotional evocation and can't happen unless the traveler cares enough to participate and engage. Narrative transportation is similar to other constructs, such as Csikszentmihalyi's concept of flow (1991), and immersion. There are important distinctions, though. Flow is a general construct and doesn't require empathy or mental imagery. Immersion is primarily an experiential response to aesthetic and visual elements of images, whereas narrative transportation relies on a story with plot and characters (Van Laer et al. 2014, p. 800).

Storytelling is a Play Activity

Along with the evolution of language, Lauer (2022) proposes that the concept of childhood and the performance of the fireside chat (another magic circle) were critical to the development of storytelling. In childhood, particularly its status as a lengthy time period when we learn how to behave through play, we see a reflection of Huizinga and his argument about the centrality of play in society, and in the fireside chat—a special time and place where "an act apart," in this case, storytelling, is performed—we see the original magic circle, where audience (visitor), storyteller (object) and fireside (interaction alibi) first come together.

While in modern societies storytelling is often understood to exclusively involve words, either written or spoken, and storytelling is viewed as a primarily literary endeavor, this never been the only way to tell stories. Historically, storytelling was a much broader phenomenon, not confined to language, and probably traces its origins back to non- or pre-linguistic activities (Sibierska 2017). Language is a powerful tool, but it is by no means the only one the storyteller possesses. "Stories can be choreographed, mimed, and re-enacted without engaging in language, think for example of ballet and contemporary dance, in which complex concepts are often transmitted only through movement" (Garcia-Pelegrin et al. 2021, p. 6).

We Tell Stories to Collectively Make Sense of the World

How did the ability to tell and receive stories change us? For Bietti et al. (2019) storytelling was a key factor in the development of human culture itself. Evolutionarily speaking, it served three main functions, "(a) manipulating the behavior of the audience to enhance the fitness of the narrator, (b) transmitting survival-relevant information while avoiding the costs involved in the first-hand acquisition of that information, and (c) maintaining social bonds or group-level cooperation" (p. 710). In other words, storytelling created "the storyteller" as a valuable skill, helped our ancestors make sense of novel situations thus allowing groups to benefit from individual knowledge, and built a sense of collective identity. Storytelling became intrinsically linked to the survival and development of our species (Garcia-Pelegrin et al. 2021, pp. 2–3). It is tempting to draw a parallel between the storytellers' and museums' perceived status as valuable to society. To the extent that museums tell the stories that are important ("Who are we?," "Where did we come from?," "What do we value?," "What do we need to know to survive?"), they are enacting the storyteller's prime function. And while much of this theorizing has no direct physical evidence to support it, studies of isolated modern societies show similar patterns. In their study of a modern Filipino hunter-gatherer population, Smith et al. (2017) found that the presence of good storytellers was associated with increased cooperation in their communities, indicating that at least one use of storytelling among our hunter gatherer ancestors may have been to organize and promote cooperation.

Visitors create stories as they experience their lives, and as they experience our work, even if we haven't explicitly created a narrative for them. This is for me one of the most compelling arguments for why we should be creating narratives in our products, because visitors are going to make up narratives anyway. This was ably demonstrated in 1944 by two psychologists, Fritz Heider and Marianne Simmel. They constructed a 2 1/2-minute-long animation of a series of geometric shapes which changed position over the course of the animation. This was shown to groups of college students who were then asked to describe what they had seen. Without fail, the subjects constructed narratives to describe what they'd seen. The shapes became characters, and their movements were the result of the characters' motivations. The story varied from subject to subject, but the creation of a narrative was near-universal (Heider and Simmel 1944).

This effect was also noticed in the early 20th century by the Soviet filmmaker Lev Kuleshov. He created three short film montages featuring two identical clips of a famous Russian actor looking blankly at the screen with another scene in between, a bowl of soup, a dead girl in a coffin, and woman reclining on a couch. When Kuleshov showed audiences these three films, viewers created narratives complete with imagined emotional states for the blank-looking actor. For the actor-soup-actor montage, he was obviously hungry. In the actor-dead girl-actor montage, he was grieving. And for the actor-woman-actor montage, he was lusting after the woman. Later scientific experiments have both confirmed the Kuleshov Effect (Mobbs et al. 2006) and found that the addition of music to the same experiment significantly increased viewers' perception of the emotional state of an actor (Baranowski and Hecht 2017).

We Tell Stories to Define (and Redefine) Ourselves

Stories are not just product for externally sharing knowledge. We employ stories with ourselves to make sense of life and our place in the world as we grow and change. Psychologists call this "narrative identity" which can be thought of as, "a person's internalized and evolving story of how he or she has become the person he or she is becoming" (McAdams 2019, p. 2). We use narrative identities to create an autobiography of our past and point us toward some imagined future that anchors us in time and provides us with a feeling of purpose. In doing so, we are both narrator and audience. But we do not create our self-narratives out of thin air.

In constructing narrative identity, human beings plagiarize shamelessly from their respective cultures, borrowing and appropriating master narratives, common images and metaphors, and prevailing plotlines… Narrative identity, therefore, is a joint production, an invention of the storytelling person and the culture within which the person's story finds its meanings and significance. Other people in the author's life, along with groups and institutions, may also exert an authorial force. Therefore, the autobiographical author is, in reality, a co-author.

(McAdams 2019, p. 14).

Museums have the ability to "exert an authorial force" on visitors. This is part of our potential to transform visitors' lives, and I would argue is a necessary precursor to behavior change. A person can, through narrative transportation, change from being someone who doesn't take action on a subject to someone who does, and from being indifferent to something to finding an empathic connection to people, places, and events far removed from their everyday lives. This transformation is more likely to occur if we are willing to tell them carefully crafted stories.

Stories Improve our Ability to Remember

As we've seen thus far, we are awash in stories all the time. Stories are how we make sense of the world and ourselves, and how we connect to others. Stories can influence us to change our thinking and behavior, all things that make them essential to a museum experience. But on top of that, we remember information better if it is part of a narrative. Brain studies have shown that events are better remembered if they form a coherent narrative (Cohn-Sheehy et al. 2022). Psychologists have found that subjects given a list of words to recall who constructed a narrative around them were six to seven times better able to recall the words than subjects told to merely memorize the list (Bower and Clark 1969).

While it's possible to tell a story that's not emotionally compelling, it is very difficult to make such a story memorable, because we seek out emotional evocation as a criterion for what we remember and what gets forgotten. Telling emotionally compelling stories can increase our engagement with them and recall of them, even in topics that might not seem particularly "emotional," like paleontology (Callanan et al. 2021). These stories "can draw visitors… into a 'circle of belonging' created by the sharing of a story and its values of reference. Stories encourage our empathy and lead us to engage in emotional relationships with others" (Silvaggi 2021, p. 42). As we saw in Chapter 3, emotions in general, and empathy in particular, is a tool is integral to both memory and learning, and storytelling is a natural vehicle in which to embed them.

Emilie Sitzia (2016) compared multiple theories of narrative and her distillation makes four important points that neatly sum up what we've been talking about here: First, that human beings think in narratives and through narratives; Second, that human beings remember in narratives; Third, that human beings use narrative to construct our identity (or identities) as well as our reality; and Fourth, that visitors perceive museum exhibitions (and all museum experiences I would argue), as narratives (pp. 5–7).

"Digital" Storytelling?

Into this million-year-old pattern of storytelling and story consuming, digital technologies have landed with tremendous impact. Digital technologies add the potential to tell these stories in new places, allow for non-linear exploration of narrative and opportunities for visitors to participate in the storytelling act as never before. But to what extent does their digitality represent a departure from the past, versus an evolution or continuation? By and large, I agree with Amelia Wong (2015) who finds the term "digital storytelling" unproductive, since it is a technologically determinist concept that leads not to digital stories but to stories that happen to be digital. As experience designers looking for tools fit for task, it becomes vitally important to heed Janet Murray's admonition about working with emerging technologies and the lure of the shiny new thing. "The technical adventurism and grubby glamour of working in emerging technologies can make it hard to figure out what is good or bad from what is just new" (Murray 2016).

Digital Storytelling and Immersion

The intersection of immersion and narrative in the digital era is broad and complicated. Though we met first Janet Murray's work in the chapter on immersion, she was actually interested in narrative and its affordances

Sidebar

In 2016, I attended a workshop at the Lower East Side Tenement Museum in New York that aimed to explore digital storytelling in museums with the goal of trying to understand what, if anything, was unique about "digital" storytelling in museums and to understand its attributes. After three intense days of lectures, discussion, and visits to area museums, the clearest insight we had was to shift our framing and think about "digital age storytelling" rather than "digital storytelling," because we felt that centering storytelling rather than digitality allowed us to discuss formats and affordances of digital tools without losing sight of the goal of communicating stories. Digital storytelling is not a particular way to tell stories, but refers to this cultural moment in which diverse experiments are trying to understand the impact of digital media on narrative (Wong 2016). As I wrote in the workshop,

Storytelling that takes advantage of the affordances of the digital realm is 'digital storytelling,' but it first has to be 'storytelling.' Storytelling is a and contours in the emergent digital era. And she was far from alone. At the beginning of this century, literary theorist Marie-Laure Ryan was calling for the emancipation of digital narrative from older models, while acknowledging that narrative as a structure transcends medium (2002). For Ryan, digital narrative's main distinction from other forms is its interactivity. The ability for the user to choose their path through a text is novel. For Ryan, digital narrative's unique contribution would be "as a movie that creates a heightened sense of presence by opening its world to the body of the spectator and by letting this body watch the action from various perspectives" (p. 604). Long

way into the world. I think the most important thing "digital" storytelling has to offer that other media forms don't is its ability to gracefully allow nonlinearity to coexist within the framework of 'the story.' Digital storytelling, done well, is a scaffold to allow really deep exploration of a subject.

(quoted in Haley Goldman 2016).

before the current vogue for storyworlds, Ryan situates that and the idea of embodiment as central to digital storytelling. This interactivity, though, does not make it easy to tell stories since a narrative is a sequential organization of events, and the ability to create any possible sequence does not mean that it will be a coherent narrative. Ryan believes these conflicting statements need to meet somewhere in the middle (p. 607). To further complicate matters, digital storytelling and immersion also includes games (Bell et al. 2018) as we'll see in Chapter 5.

Museums and Transmedia

Henry Jenkins defines "transmedia storytelling," a term he popularized, as

> a process where integral elements of a fiction get dispersed systematically across multiple delivery channels for the purpose of creating a unified and coordinated entertainment experience. Ideally, each medium makes its own unique contribution to the unfolding of the story.
>
> (Jenkins 2007)

This is not limited to fiction obviously. Transmedia storytelling is a process of world building: "Most often, transmedia stories are based not on individual characters or specific plots but rather complex fictional worlds which can sustain multiple interrelated characters and their stories." Because weaving together various narrative threads to convey a sense of this larger world—a "storyworld"—requires Herculean coordination, the most successful examples tend to be created by a single artist or team or through the collaboration enabled by media conglomerates that own film studios, publishing imprints, etc. (Jenkins 2007). I would add many museum product teams to this list as well.

Though much of the writing about transmedia has focused on the realm of text and speech, museum exhibitions can also be viewed as transmedia storytelling experiences. Dan Spock has called the museum exhibition "the medium of media" in that it can gracefully accommodate almost any medium we choose to include in them (quoted in Dillenburg 2011). Objects real and virtual, texts, sounds, moving images, interactive devices, scent. You name it, somebody has tried including it in an exhibition that visitors are free to explore in a self-directed manner and sequence. In essence, museums have been producing nonlinear transmedia narratives for a very long time, though you won't see them referenced in the histories of hypertext or transmedia storytelling. So, while much of the discourse around digital storytelling comes from contexts that are unfamiliar to museum professionals, transmedia storytelling and world building are not dissimilar to the work we do. So, what are some tools we might employ to tell better stories?

Tools for Museum Storytelling

There are already excellent resources available to practitioners who want to improve their writing. Beverly Serrell's work blending rigorous evaluation and interpretation has given rise to two important books, "Exhibit Labels" (2015) and "The Big Idea" (2019) that I have relied upon for years in my own work and which I recommend to anyone trying to communicate with museum visitors. Given storytelling's centrality to how human beings communicate, learn, and remember, what are some of the tools we can employ in our work to tell more stories and tell them better?

Look at Archetypal Structures

In the Western tradition best exemplified by Shakespeare's plays, a sequence which has come to be known as "Freytag's pyramid" has become a literary standard. This sequence expresses the dramatic arc in five phases: exposition, rising action, climax, falling action, and dénouement (Freytag 1900). On a larger scale, the search for universal story forms has been undertaken by numerous scholars. Joseph Campbell's *The Hero with a Thousand Faces* (1973) introduced the concept of the monomyth, the idea that a universal story form underlies many mythological traditions. His idea of the hero's journey has influenced countless writers since then and found a warm reception in places as diverse as Star Wars and Disney movies (Moyers 1988).

Others have attempted to define even larger structures. The novelist Kurt Vonnegut considered his best piece of work to be his rejected Master of Anthropology thesis for the University of Chicago where he discerned eight major story arcs in Western literature (Vonnegut 1963, pp. 312–316). In 2012, then Pixar story artist Emma Coats tweeted a series of 22 "story basics" over the course of a month and a half that represented the fundamentals of storytelling she had distilled from her colleagues (Coats 2012). Reagan et al. (2016) enumerated a half dozen attempts to classify universal story shapes whose authors propose anywhere from 3 to 36 different primal shapes. They then go on propose six emotional arcs in all stories, based on a computer-aided textual analysis of 1,737 English narratives of a certain minimum size and complexity found in Project Gutenberg. They are: Rags to riches (rise), Tragedy, or Riches to rags (fall), Man in a hole (fall->rise), Icarus (rise->fall), Cinderella (rise->fall->rise), and Oedipus (fall->rise->fall).

This is not to say that any one of these schema is the answer to your problem. It is however worth considering at the outset of your project and how it might reflect these widely understood narrative forms and how these forms might already exist in the stories you're trying to tell.

Fiction Can Be Your Friend

This is likely to get me in more trouble than any other statement in this book, so let me preface things by saying that I do not advocate abandoning museums' commitment to being places that are trustworthy sources of accurate information. I *do* advocate we be less timid in our storytelling and exercising authorial power. I think museums have a conflicted relationship with storytelling partly because of the connotation between stories and fiction. Museums are places to find the real and authentic, they exist to exhibit what was and is, so the idea of fiction is understandably troubling to many practitioners. But I think we often fail to appreciate the role that storytelling, even the fictional, plays in our lives. Consider that our most intimate story—our personal narrative—is a fiction, an assignment of value to a collection of events, and a culling of facts to produce a coherent narrative. As the psychoanalyst James Hollis (2003) says, "To find our truths we must travel consciously, by way of our fictions" (p. 85).

Be Clear Who's Telling the Story

Narrative perspective—whose perspective is the story being told from—is one of the most important features of any story. The magic circle of the ancient fireside talk requires a storyteller. Museums have traditionally shied away from attributing authorship to their stories. "The Museum Voice" an impersonal, allegedly neutral institutional voice was the norm throughout the 19th and 20th centuries and continues today, despite a growing chorus of voices decrying "neutrality" as tacit support for all the problems that afflict us in the 21st century. If museums are not neutral (Murawski 2017), then how do we understand and articulate a narrative that allows us to tell more authentic stories?

One way is to acknowledge our subjectivity explicitly. Beverly Serrell (2019) argues that having a point of view is a prerequisite to articulating what she calls "The Big Idea" of a project (p. 10), a method I have practiced for many years and heartily endorse. Jeanne Goswami (2018) takes the literary concept of the unreliable narrator and reframes it as an essential quality for museums to pursue in their storytelling. For Goswami, acknowledging our inherent unreliability could actually help museums craft more authentic narratives by foregrounding the perspectives, assumptions and biases of the storytellers, and allow visitors the agency to evaluate both the story and the storyteller as they evaluate the narratives we present to them. To that end, she presents three questions museum interested in storytelling should consider:

- Have you alerted your audience to your implication in the narrative, to the role you and your institution played in constructing our understanding of this object or collection?
- Have you adopted a forceful point of view that makes your relationship to your subject(s) explicit and reveals your subjectivity?
- Have you communicated your message in a way that remains true to your desired outcome but invites your visitors to extrapolate their own truths?

(p. 10)

Another way is to be clear about perspective. Studies have shown that first-person narratives create a more immediate sense of closeness and familiarity with the protagonist and thus more likely to generate empathy for that character than third-person narratives (Kaufman and Libby 2012). In their study of narrative perspective, Shalom and Gross found that participants identified with a character more when the narrative was told from that character's perspective and resulted in a higher identification with the character, leading to a greater persuasiveness of the narrative (Shalom and Gross 2022, pp. 2–3). Other studies found that for some difficult topics, visitors exhibited a tendency to withdraw emotionally from first-person narratives that they found painful and that thus third-person narratives might be a more effective way to handle those topics (Mithlo and Sherman 2020). Regardless of topic, being clear about your perspective and acknowledging can help us tell better, more authentic stories.

Tell Multiple Stories, Not Just One

Being clear about identifying authorship is important, and related to that is the decision about whether you want to create a single discrete narrative or a structure where several narratives can coexist: the concept of a storyworld. Chimamanda Ngoni Adichie (2009) famously problematized the idea of the overly simplistic and generalized "single story" and particularly its role in marginalizing people and rendering them two-dimensional. "[W]hen we reject the single story, when we realize that there is never a single story about any place, we regain a kind of paradise." As we have seen in this chapter, narratives are how we structure the world in our minds, so relying on a single story comes with risks. As Rebecca Solnit wrote in The Guardian (2023),

> Every crisis is in part a storytelling crisis. This is as true of climate chaos as anything else. We are hemmed in by stories that prevent us from seeing, or believing in, or acting on the possibilities for change. Some are habits of mind, some are industry propaganda. Sometimes, the situation has changed but the stories haven't, and people follow the old versions, like outdated maps, into dead ends.

(Solnit 2023)

So how can we as experience designers create narratives that do not trap visitors in "single stories"? One way would be to consider developing storyworlds where visitors can encounter multiple narratives.

What is a storyworld? There are two different uses of the term, so let's be clear about which one I'm going to discuss. For narratologists, the term is used to describe the world we create in our heads as we're consuming a narrative, visualizing places and events, relating them to other places and events in the story as part of our processing of the narrative (Herman 2000; Ryan 2022). The second definition, the one which I'm interested in, comes from fantasy literature. A storyworld is the sum total of all the content of a real or fictional world within which multiple narratives can be told.

> the whole of the "narrative universe" that a story and or stories emerge from. It contains the characters, settings, the time periods (backstories and future stories), props, and events and actions that take place in the storyworld. A story world can contain a "canon" which defines the "rules" of the story-world universe as well.
>
> (Morie and McCallum 2019, p. 483)

One of the earliest and best-known examples is J.R.R. Tolkien's Middle Earth, from which came *The Hobbit, The Lord of the Rings*, and numerous other stories through a process Tolkien called "secondary world creation" (Tolkien 2006). Storyworld building is an integral part of fantasy and science fiction literature, video and computer games, television and film.

How does thinking of storyworld building rather than just telling a good story help us design museum experiences? The differences between crafting a story and crafting a world in which stories play out are significant. World building is immersive by nature. World building accommodates multiple pathways through the storyworld. There are strong resonances between non-linear museum exhibitions and open world "sandbox" video games where players are free to chart their own course across a landscape and encounter multiple characters, events, and tasks. Storyworlds as an organizing principle also make room for different narratives to co-exist more gracefully. In a field where social justice (Huhn and Anderson 2021) and racial representation (Griem and Allen 2022) are often found to be wanting, storyworlds present an opportunity to build more inclusive and diverse products.

Narrative versus *Immersive, or Narrative* and *Immersive?*

As we discussed in Chapter 2, immersion has a great deal of overlap with narrative, and in some of the theories of immersion, narrative transportation itself is formulated as a kind of immersion, in this case in a narrative. But as we have seen, stories, narratives, and the act of performing a narrative for an audience have many unique characteristics and are in many ways integral to our experience of the world. So as an experience designer, you might be tempted to try to choose one tool to the exclusion of the other. And for concepts as interrelated as narrative and immersion, that would be inadvisable.

Sitzia (2016) lays out some of the ways that immersive and discursive types of exhibitions have very different kinds of impacts on visitors, the most salient one being that engaging with an openly identified narrative allows the visitors to maintain a critical distance to the experience. They experience it as a performance, and can respond accordingly. An immersive experience, though becomes part of *our* narrative; it integrates with our story and therefore it is harder for us to look at it critically or analytically. Despite these differences though, the ways human beings learn in narrative-based and immersive-based experiences complement each other and resonate in ways that are mutually reinforcing. For Sitzia,

> immersive and discursive modes of exhibition seem rather equivalent or complementary in the way they promote learning, and we can already quite confidently say that a hybrid exhibition environment with some immersive parts and discursive parts seems to be an ideal museum learning environment… To achieve an optimum visitor learning experience, it is then the role of the museum to create environments and support material that allow visitors to move between the discursive and the immersive.
>
> (p. 11)

The Dark Side of Storytelling

Stories can be used to inform, to share, to educate, to engage. They can also be used to deceive, to mislead, to conceal, and to manipulate. Coen (2019) argues that a key factor in the development of human intelligence was a storytelling arms race between true and false stories and our need to establish a balance between trust and doubt in the stories we share and receive (p. 67). We cannot accept everything we are told at face value, nor can we simply reject everything out of hand and remain functioning members of society. Skepticism is a good thing, but it can also be made to serve nefarious purposes. Chesney and Citron (2019) coined the phrase "The Liar's Dividend" to describe how those interested in telling false stories can weaponize skepticism to get audiences to doubt authentic stories. To make matters worse, "this dividend flows, perversely, in proportion to success in educating the public about the dangers of deep fakes. The liar's dividend would run with the grain of larger trends involving truth skepticism" (p. 1785). The more we aim to equip our visitors to employ healthy skepticism, the more potent a tool it becomes to those seeking to decide.

So how do we take stories and ascertain their veracity? Schwarz et al. (2016) identified two strategies people can use to process statements: an effortful analytic strategy or a less effortful intuitive strategy not unlike Kahneman's Attention Systems 2 and 1. They also found five criteria people employ as they evaluate the truth of a statement:

• General acceptance by others
• Amount of supporting evidence
• Compatibility with their beliefs
• General coherence of the statement
• The credibility of the source of the information

"Authenticity"

At the heart of the museum visit is a paradox; a celebration of "authenticity" in a thoroughly decontextualized space. Penrose (2020) studied visitors to the Anne Frank House in Amsterdam where some of the spaces where the Frank family hid are mostly empty and the density of authentic objects is low. Despite this, the spaces are felt to be "authentic" because of their connection to the story of Anne and her family and this can, in turn, lead to visitors feeling a personal identification with that story and that they have had an "authentic" experience. His findings

> affirm the idea that <u>principles</u> of authenticity matter, as do those of its counterparts 'truth', 'fact' and 'integrity'. While the meaning of these and other similar words will never be uncontested, the conviction that they have value is worth upholding.
>
> (p. 1264)

Narrative Museum Experiences

Amgueddfa Cymru—National Museum Wales, **With New Eyes I See** *(2014)*

This site-specific interactive documentary explored how documentary storytelling can become an experience or a journey beyond a flat screen. Using specially modified miniprojectors that looked like flashlights, visitors were led around Cardiff to learn about the staff of Amgueddfa Cymru—National Museum Wales who went off to World War I.

Australian Centre for the Moving Image (ACMI) **Wonderland** *(2018)*

This travelling exhibition married a number of transmedia storytelling layers with moments of deep immersion to explore the 150+ year history of Lewis Carroll's story *Alice in Wonderland* and the history of special effects through its more than 30 film and television adaptations. Wonderland explored how this precocious heroine inspired revolutionary filmmaking, from groundbreaking special effects and animation to evocative storytelling and technological development. The world's first physical survey of Alice on screen, it uses the 30+ film and TV adaptations of the classic story to showcase the history of special effects.

Peabody Essex Museum, **Story Pods** *(2019)*

As part of the museum's expansion and reinstallation of its maritime collections, the team created storytelling moment for three "difficult" objects: objects with complicated narratives and little of the traditional visual appeal that draws visitors to an object. Designed as enclosed, intimate spaces, the "story pods" each hold a single object and a small group of visitors in enough isolation to allow visitors to focus in an otherwise crowded gallery space. Through audio, video, and text, a narrator tells a fairly lengthy, coherent narrative which held visitors' attention for long periods (up to six minutes per object) and were successful in encouraging close looking at those objects.

Museum of Jewish Heritage, Survivor Stories: An Interactive Dialog (2024)

This installation makes use of artificial intelligences and hours of interviews conducted with Holocaust survivors to create a collective storytelling project that puts museum visitors in direct conversation with avatars of these survivors. Visitors can ask questions, and the AI will assemble an answer based on the recorded testimonies and display that survivor responding.

Conclusion

The concept of narrative transportation, the sense of "getting lost in a good story" relies on the ancient technology of storytelling, which is, as we've seen, possibly older than our species. I bring this up to highlight the fact that regardless of the new ways we discover to tell stories, the fundamental act remains remarkably constant. Storytelling in the digital era still requires us to tell compelling stories with clear points of view and a larger purpose. Visitors are going to turn our experiences into stories, whether or not we explicitly create narratives for them. This should be a powerful incentive to design for narrative transportation.

Reflection

The Liminal Stage

by Sean Stewart

When it came to museums, I was a disappointment to my father.

He was an archaeologist. To be in a room with a coin or vase was enough to connect him to Roman Britain. I was a reader, addicted to what Ed calls narrative transport. To me, the objects were inert. My way of accessing Roman Britain was sitting on a bench reading *The Lantern Bearers,* oblivious to the exhibits, until my Dad was ready to go.

In traditional narrative art, the audience is asked to ignore their present world and imagine themselves in another one. In a cinema, we literally sit still, turn off the lights and silence our cell phones so that nothing about our current world intrudes on the fiction. (And if we don't, the ushers will kick us out!)

But immersing yourself in another world—what Janet Murray calls "the active creation of belief"—is much harder if you are also walking around, googling things, chatting with friends or minding your kids, as is frequently the case in IRL-based immersive experiences such as LARPS, theme parks, and museums. It's easy to get caught in an uncanny valley: neither wholly in your own life, nor in Roman Britain, but loitering in the airport lounge between the two.

Immersive storytelling, from murder-mystery dinner theater to *Sleep No More,* is the attempt to have your cake and eat it, too; to create a liminal stage where your audience lives and acts in their default world and your story world at the same time.

An Alternate Reality

I grew up to be a novelist—but I was also an early adopter of interactive fiction. I was playing D&D five years before the kids in *Stranger Things* and put myself through college running LARPs. Today I am best known as the writer on the team that created the Alternate Reality Game (ARG) genre. Ironically, the creator of the format, Jordan Weisman, first pitched it to me as being like archaeology: What if we took a story, he said, and broke it into a thousand parts like an ancient vase, and then let people on the internet find all the bits and work together to reassemble them?

By reimagining a linear story as a collection of microtexts to be pieced together like a jigsaw puzzle, Jordan brilliantly solved for the profound tension between games and stories. While stories are crafted for emotional impact, games must focus on what the players do. Jordan's solution was to craft the story, then hide the pieces and coax the audience into reassembling it—their absolutely essential game play participation. It was collective, social exploration and play; basically the "game loop" of Science in the age of the Royal Society, but hotwired as an entertainment platform.

The Magic Circle

The first ARG, now known as The Beast, debuted in the spring of 2001, as a teaser for Steven Spielberg's film ***A.I.: Artificial Intelligence***. Set in the year 2142, The Beast played out across hundreds of websites and emails, with clues hidden in newspapers, TV ads, faxes (remember faxes?) phone calls, and even live meetups

One of the most interesting things about the story is the ease with which players understood their relationship to the game. When they spoke to one another, it was 2001. When they spoke to characters in the game, it was 2142. You might read a newspaper dated 2001, but if there was a clue from the game in it, THAT part was happening in the future. They were Schrödinger's audience, living in two timelines at once. "I'm playing a character exactly like me in every way," as one player said, "except she thinks it's real."

What Do I Do?

In a traditional narrative, the action is driven by the protagonist's motivation. When you move the audience into a more active role, they need their own. If back when my Dad dragged me to the museum I'd had a treasure to find or a child to save, I would have been wildly excited. Without that, there was nothing to activate the exhibits for me. They were just objects under glass.

When Characters Claim You as Their Own

Primed with a mission to solve a mystery, players plunged into the world of 2142. As they did, the characters reached out to them *as if they were part of that world.* They asked for advice, wheedled or flirted or threatened according to their own goals. They explicitly gave the players a role to play in 2142—and established real emotional relationships with them.

I didn't understand how powerful these relationships were until the death of the grandmother who had raised Laia, our main character. Then next morning I woke to find hundreds of condolence emails in Laia's inbox, ranging from "I'm sorry for your loss," to "I was raised by my grandmother, too. I know the grief you are feeling," to "My grandfather died last week. I'm writing to you the night of his funeral."

I had published several award-winning novels by this time, but this… this kind of response was wholly new and different.

You can see a variation of this practice in the Holocaust Museum in D.C. or the National WWII museum in New Orleans where visitors draw a slip of paper with a name and short biography on it, then pass through the exhibit, and find out what happened to "their" person by the end of the war. I think there is a great deal more to be explored here, to let visitors bring something of themselves to that choosing. If a visitor were to be confronted by different hobbies or outfits or pieces of music, and in choosing their favorite they were connected to a certain character, then they would have put a piece of themselves into forging bond, like a lock of hair or a drop of blood used in a wizard's spell.

The Liminal Stage

A museum makes a lousy cinema. It's a physical space that must be navigated. The crowds and noise, even the very presence of helpful docents all resist letting the visitor erase their own real life in favor of imaginative submersion in another world. But might a museum be better understood not as a cinema, but something more theatrical—a liminal stage, one that straddles the line between the user's default world and the world the story evokes?

That real user actions can drive story events is rapidly becoming our default expectation for the simple reason that today's entertainment is increasingly delivered to phones and computers. Unlike books or cinemas, these new entertainment platforms are explicitly built to take user input: we speak, we swipe, we click, and we share. We are the audience, but we are actors, too, strutting and fretting across Schrödinger's stage—real and fictional at the same time.

For this new hybrid form of storytelling, one that lies at the intersection of Hadrian's Wall and our everyday life, "she's exactly like me, except she thinks it's real" might just be the perfect actor, and a museum the perfect stage.

Note

1 Museum tells the story of. (n.d.). Bing. Retrieved April 7, 2024, from https://www.bing. com/search?q="museum+tells+the+story+of"&form=QBLH&sp=-1&lq=0&pq="mus eum+tells+the+story+of".

References

Adichie, Chimamanda N. 2009. Adichie: The danger of a single story | TED Talk. https://www.ted.com/talks/chimamanda_ngozi_adichie_the_danger_of_a_single_story/transcript?language=en. (accessed 3.16.2022).

Baranowski, Andreas M., and Hecht, H. 2017. The Auditory Kuleshov Effect: Multisensory Integration in Movie Editing. *Perception*, vol. 46, 2017, pp. 624–631.

Bedford, Leslie. 2001. Storytelling: The Real Work of Museums. *Curator*, vol. 44, 2001. pp. 27–34.

Bell, Alice, Astrid Ensslin, Isabelle van der Bom, and Jen Smith. 2018. Immersion in Digital Fiction: A Cognitive, Empirical Approach. *International Journal of Literary Linguistics*, vol. 7, 2018, pp. 1–22.

Bietti, Lucas M., Tilston, Ottilie, and Bangerter, Adrian. 2019. Storytelling as Adaptive Collective Sensemaking. *Topics in Cognitive Science*, vol. 11, 2019, pp. 710–732.

Bower, Gordon H., and Clark, Michal C. 1969. Narrative Stories as Mediators for SerialL. *Psychonomic Science*, vol. 14, no. 4, 1969, pp. 181–182.

Boyd, Brian. 2017. The Evolution of Stories: From Mimesis to Language, from Fact to Fiction. *Wiley Interdisciplinary Reviews: Cognitive Science*, vol. 9, no. 1, 2017, pp. 1–16.

Callanan, Maureen A., Claudia L. Castañeda, Graciela Solis, Megan R. Luce, Mathew Diep, Sam R. McHugh, Jennifer L. Martin, Judy Scotchmoor, and Sara DeAngelis. 2021. "He Fell in and That's How He Became a Fossil!": Engagement with a Storytelling Exhibit Predicts Families' Explanatory Science Talk During a Museum Visit. *Frontiers in Psychology*, vol. 12, 2021, pp. 1–10.

Cambridge Dictionary. 2024. Story. April 10. https://dictionary.cambridge.org/us/dictionary/english/story

Campbell, Joseph. 1973. *The Hero with a Thousand Faces*. Princeton University Press.

Chesney, Robert, and Citron, Danielle K. 2018. Deep Fakes: A Looming Challenge for Privacy, Democracy, and National Security. California Law Review, Vol. 107, No. 6 (2019), pp. 1753–1820.

Coats, Emma. 2012. #storybasics 1: You Admire a Character for Trying More than for Their Successes. [Tweet]. *Twitter*. https://twitter.com/lawnrocket/status/200673877972615168

Coen, Enrico. 2019. The Storytelling Arms Race: Origin of Human Intelligence and the Scientific Mind. *Heredity*, vol. 123, no. 1, 2019, p. 67.

Cohn-Sheehy, Brendan I. Angelique I. Delarazan, Jordan E. Crivelli-Decker, Zachariah M. Reagh, Nidhi S. Mundada, Andrew P. Yonelinas, Jeffrey M. Zacks and Charan Ranganath. 2022. Narratives Bridge the Divide between Distant Events in Episodic Memory. *Memory & Cognition*, vol. 50, no. 3, 2022, pp. 478–494.

Csikszentmihalyi, Mihalyi. 1991. *Flow: The psychology of optimal experience*. HarperPerennial.

Dillenburg, Eugene. 2011. What, If Anything, Is a Museum? *Exhibitionist, Spring '11*, pp. 8–13.

Dor, Daniel. 2015. *The Instruction of Imagination: Language as a Social Communication Technology*. Oxford University Press.

Freytag, Gustav. 1900. *Freytag's Technique of the Drama: An Exposition of Dramatic Composition and Art* (E.J. MacEwan, Trans.). Scott, Foresman.

Garcia-Pelegrin, Elias, Wilkins, Clive, and Clayton, Nicola S. 2021. The Ape That Lived to Tell the Tale. The Evolution of the Art of Storytelling and Its Relationship to Mental Time Travel and Theory of Mind. *Frontiers in Psychology*, vol. 12, 2021, pp. 1–15.

Gerrig, Richard J. 1993. *Experiencing Narrative Worlds: On the Psychological Activities of Reading*. Yale Univ. Press.

Goswami, Jeanne. 2018. The Museum as Unreliable Narrator: What We Can Learn from Nick Carraway. *The International Journal of the Inclusive Museum*, vol. 11, no. 1, 2018, pp. 1–11.

Griem, Madeline, and Allen, Douglas L. 2022. Challenging Whiteness and Storytelling in Museums: An Examination of Racial Representation in Kansas City Heritage Institutions. *Southeastern Geographer*, vol. 62, 2022, p. 22.

Haley Goldman, Kate. 2016. *Digital Storytelling Workshop Synthesis*. Supported by the National Endowment of the Humanities and the Lower East Side Tenement Museum.

Hardy, Barbara. 1968. Towards a Poetics of Fiction: An Approach through Narrative. *NOVEL: A Forum on Fiction*, vol. 2, no. 5, 1968, pp. 5–14.

Heider, Fritz, and Simmel, Marianne. 1944. An Experimental Study of Apparent Behavior. *The American Journal of Psychology*, vol. 57, no. 2, 1944, p. 244.

Herman, David 2000, September 18. Narratology as a Cognitive Science. *Image [&] Narrative*, vol. 1 no. 1, 2000. https://www.imageandnarrative.be/inarchive/narratology/davidherman.htm. (accessed 3.28.2020)

Hollis, James. 2003. *On this Journey We Call Our Life: Living the Questions*. Inner City Books.

Huhn, Arianna, and Anderson, Annika. 2021. Promoting Social Justice through Storytelling in Museums. *Museum and Society*, vol. 19, 2021, pp. 351–368.

Jenkins, Henry. 2007, March 21. *Transmedia Storytelling 101—Pop Junctions*. Henry Jenkins.

Lauer, Gerhard. 2022. Language, Childhood, and Fire: How We Learned to Love Sharing Stories. *Frontiers in Psychology*, vol. 12. pp. 1–8.

Kaufman, Geoff F., and Libby, Lisa K. 2012. Changing Beliefs and Behavior through Experience-Taking. *Journal of Personality and Social Psychology*, vol. 103, no. 1, 2012, pp. 1–19. https://doi.org/10.1037/a0027525

McAdams, Dan P. 2019. "First We Invented Stories, Then They Changed Us": The Evolution of Narrative Identity. *Evolutionary Studies in Imaginative Culture*, vol. 3, 2019, pp. 1–18.

Mithlo, Nancy Marie, and Sherman, Aleksandra 2020. Perspective-Taking Can Lead to Increased Bias: A Call for 'Less Certain' Positions in American Indian Contexts. *Curator: The Museum Journal*, vol. 63, no. 3, 2020, pp. 353–369. https://doi.org/10.1111/cura.12373

Mobbs, Dean, Nikolaus Weiskopf, Hakwan C. Lau, Eric Featherstone, Ray J. Dolan, and Chris D. Frith. 2016. The Kuleshov Effect: The Influence of Contextual Framing on Emotional Attributions. *Social Cognitive and Affective Neuroscience*, vol. 1, no. 2, Aug. 2006, p. 100.

McCallum, Kate. 2019. Immersive Experience: Convergence, Storyworlds, and the Power for Social Impact. In Morie, Jacquelyn Ford, and Kate McCallum (Eds.), *Handbook of Research on the Global Impacts and Roles of Immersive Media*. IGI Global, pp. 453–484.

Moyers, Bill. 1988. Joseph Campbell and the Power of Myth – "The Hero's Adventure." *BillMoyers.Com*. https://billmoyers.com/content/ep-1-joseph-campbell-and-the-power-of-myth-the-hero's-adventure-audio/

Murawski, Mike. 2017, August 31. Museums Are Not Neutral. *Art Museum Teaching*. https://artmuseumteaching.com/2017/08/31/museums-are-not-neutral/

Murray, Janet H. 2016. "Not a Film and Not an Empathy Machine." *Immerse*, https://immerse.news/not-a-film-and-not-an-empathy-machine-48b63b0eda93.

Museum tells the story of. (n.d.). Bing. Retrieved April 7, 2024, from https://www.bing.com/search?q="museum+tells+the+story+of"&form=QBLH&sp=-1&lq=0&pq="museum+tells+the+story+of"

Nielsen, Jane K. 2017. Museum Communication and Storytelling: Articulating Understandings within the Museum Structure. *Museum Management and Curatorship*, vol. 32, no. 5, 2017, pp. 440–455.

Pamuk, Orhan. 2016. Orhan Pamuk's manifesto for museums [News]. *The Art Newspaper - International Art News and Events*, 2016, July 5.

Penrose, Jan. 2020. Authenticity, Authentication and Experiential Authenticity: Telling Stories in Museums. *Social and Cultural Geography*, vol. 21, 2020, p. 1247.

Reagan, Andrew J, Lewis Mitchell, Dilan Kiley, Christopher M. Danforth, and Peter Sheridan Dodds. 2016. The Emotional Arcs of Stories are Dominated by Six Basic Shapes. *EPJ Data Science*, vol. 5, no. 1, 2016. pp. 1–8.

Ryan, Marie.-Laure. 2002. Beyond Myth and Metaphor: Narrative in Digital Media. *Poetics Today*, vol. 23, no. 4, 2002, pp. 581–609.

Ryan, Marie.-Laure. 2022. *A New Anatomy of Storyworlds: What Is, What If, As If*. The Ohio State University Press.

Schwarz, Norbert, Newman, Eryn, and Leach, William. 2016. Making the Truth Stick & the Myths Fade: Lessons from Cognitive Psychology. *Behavioral Science & Policy*, vol. 2, 2016, pp. 85–95.

Shalom, Maya, and Gross, Zehavit. 2022. The Link between Memory, Narrative and Empathy in Teaching Difficult Knowledge in Holocaust Education. *Frontiers in Education*, vol. 7, no. 866457, 2022, pp. 2–3.

Serrell, Beverly. 2015. *Exhibit Labels: An Interpretive Approach*, 2nd edn. Rowman & Littlefield.

Serrell, Beverly. 2019. *The Big Idea: Getting to an Exhibition's Big Idea*. Beverly Serrell & Associates.

Sibierska, Marta. 2017. Storytelling Without Telling: The Non-Linguistic Nature of Narratives from Evolutionary and Narratological Perspectives. *Language and Communication*, vol. 54, 2017, pp. 47–55.

Silvaggi, Antonia. 2021. Emotions, Stories and Storytelling for Audience Engagement Strategies. In Mazzanti, Paolo, and Margherita Sani (Eds.), *Emotions and Learning in Museums*, 2021, NEMO (The Network of European Museum Organisations). p. 42.

Sitzia, Emilie. 2016. Narrative Theories and Learning in Contemporary Art Museums: A Theoretical Exploration. *Stedelijk Studies*, vol. 1, 2016, pp. 1–15.

Smith, Daniel, Philip Schlaepfer, Katie Major, Mark Dyble, Abigail E. Page, James Thompson,

Nikhil Chaudhary, Gul Deniz Salali, Ruth Mace, Leonora Astete, Marilyn Ngales, Lucio Vinicius, and Andrea Bamberg Migliano. 2017. Cooperation and the Evolution of Hunter-Gatherer Storytelling. *Nature Communications*, vol. 8, 2017. pp. 1–9.

Solnit, Rebecca 2023. 'If You Win the Popular Imagination, You Change the Game': Why We Need New Stories on Climate. *The Guardian*.

Szurmak, Joanna, and Thuna, Mindy 2013. *Tell Me a Story: The Use of Narrative as a Tool for Instruction*. ACRL, pp. 546–552.

Tolkien, John Ronald Reuel 2006. On Fairy Stories. In Christopher Tolkien (Ed.), *The Monsters and The Critics and Other Essays* (Paperback ed). HarperCollins.

Van Laer, Tom, De Ruyter, Ko, Visconti, Luca M., and Wetzels, Martin 2014. The Extended Transportation-Imagery Model: A Meta-Analysis of the Antecedents and Consequences of Consumers' Narrative Transportation. *Journal of Consumer Research*, vol. 40, no. 5, 2014, pp. 797–817.

Van Laer, Tom, Feiereisen, Stephanie, and Visconti, Luca M. 2019. Storytelling in the Digital Era: A Meta-Analysis of Relevant Moderators of the Narrative Transportation Effect. *Journal of Business Research*, vol. 96, 2019, pp. 135–146.

Vonnegut, Kurt. 1963. *Cat's Cradle*. Delacorte Press.

Wilk, Christopher, Nick Humphrey, and Laboratorio Museotecnico. (Eds.). 2004. *Creating the British Galleries at the V & A: A Study in Museology*. V & A Publications; Distributed in North America by Harry N. Abrams. p. 22.

Wong, Amelia. 2015. The whole story, and then some: 'digital storytelling' in evolving museum practice. In *Museums and the Web 2015: Proceedings*. https://mw2015. museumsandtheweb.com/paper/the-whole-story-and-then-some-digital-storytelling-in-evolving-museum-practice/ (accessed 10.19.2021).

Wong, Amelia. 2016. Beyond Questions of Definition to Questions of Practice – DigitalStory. https://web.archive.org/web/20211019022402/https://digitalstory.lestm.org/index.php/2016/06/30/beyond-questions-of-definition-to-questions-of-practice/. (accessed 10.19.2021)

Yilmaz, Recep, and Fatih Mehmet Ciğerci. A Brief History of Storytelling:From Primitive Dance to Digital Narration In Yılmaz, Recep., M. Nur Erdem, and Filiz Resuloglu. (Eds.). 2019. *Handbook of Research on Transmedia Storytelling and Narrative Strategies: Advances in Media, Entertainment, and the Arts*. IGI Global.

5 Gameful Participation

Encouraging Playfulness

Many years ago, I worked on an exhibition on aging. As part of that show, I developed a computer interactive where visitors could "interview" well-known elders, like Maya Angelou, Julia Child, and others. One of those interviewees was the Canadian American economist and diplomat John Kenneth Galbraith who at that time was already in his 90s. When asked what the hardest part was of getting older, he said that his doctor had told him he had to give up downhill skiing, saying, "I had been an enthusiastic, if not very skillful, skier" and the pleasure he derived from this play activity (sport being a kind of play) stemmed not from becoming the best skier or beating his friends, but in enjoying the ability he did have and improving. This distinction between "winning" and savoring mastery has stayed with me ever since.

In this chapter, I will explore the last of our four concepts for creating playful engagement: *gameful participation*, namely, creating the circumstances (the interaction alibi) that allows visitors to engage using approaches from game design. Gameful design in this sense is "a framework for learning and teaching through "game developer thinking" rather than concentrating on game mechanics" (Dichev et al. 2015, p. 91). Play is the act of mastering a challenge mentally and/or physically. Effort being rewarded with increased mastery (not necessarily victory) is a powerful incentive to learn, and thus something we should pay attention to as experience designers. Games are a subset of play, and their advantage over other forms of play is that rules lower the barrier to entry. If you know what's expected of you, your more likely to be able to engage safely.

I've saved it for last because it's also possibly the messiest of the four concepts, for several reasons. First, it requires us to distinguish between the intersections of play, games, gamification, and gameful design. Second, as you have already hopefully seen in the previous chapters, the other three concepts will all make multiple appearances, so be prepared for even more narrative, emotion, and immersion. Lastly, both museum experience design and game design are what game theorists Katie Salen Tekinbaş and Eric Zimmerman (2003) call second-order design problems. The thing we supposedly create, the museum experience, is actually something the visitor creates with their mind and body. We create the circumstance and situations that allow visitors to have an experience,

DOI: 10.4324/9781032638690-5

but the visitor is the one doing the hard work. Read their description of game design,

> The goal of successful game design is meaningful play, but play is something that emerges from the functioning of the rules. As a game designer, you can never directly design play. You can only design the rules that give rise to it. Game designers create experience, but only indirectly.
>
> (2003, p. 168)

The same applies to museum experience design. This recognition that experience can only be indirectly designed for is just one important learning that cultural institutions can embrace.

In this chapter, we'll explore a bit of the history of play and how we employ play throughout our lives to learn and practice. We'll explore how play and games get conflated and try to untangle them, explore some of the complications and opportunities digital games provide to museums, and highlight some examples of gameful museum experiences that provoke playful engagement. Let's turn our attention to play and games and how they relate to, and differ from one another

The Hallmarks of Gameful Participation

As usual, let's start with definitions. To understand gameful participation, we will need to start with the root activity of play and its accompanying mindset, playfulness. From there, we will look at the subset of play that are games. From there, we will explore how various mechanics of gameplay have been appropriated through gamification, and finally to gameful design.

Play and Playfulness

Play is a universal experience, something all humans do. It is a deeply rooted part of our being and our capacity for play has been key to the evolution of the human species. Archaeological evidence of play and play materials has been found in excavations all over the world, and theorists posit that the development of play even predates language in humans (Sutton-Smith 1997; Stenros 2015). It is a truly ancient feature of our humanity.[1]

Bernard de Koven describes (2013) play as "the enactment of anything that is not for real. Play is intended to be without consequence." This lack of consequence is important. The only outcome of play is having played. You can't play a test, or a work assignment, because those have outcomes with real world consequences. For Huizinga, play has three main characteristics: it is voluntary, it is not "ordinary" or "real", and it is limited in time and space. Play begins, and then at a certain moment it is "over," and we return to our default life (Huizinga 1949). Play is an activity that is satisfying in and of itself, in other words, another autotelic or self-satisfying experience. For the vast majority of visitors, a museum visit is a play experience.

Frank Oppenheimer, the founding director of the Exploratorium acknowledged this when he said, "No one ever flunked a museum." Much though museums may privilege education and appreciation as their reasons for existence, the reason visitors come is to have a satisfying time.

Play is an activity, and what causes play is a baked-in mindset we possess, namely playfulness. Stenros (2015) states,

> At the core of play and games is the mindset of **playfulness**. The impetus to play is older than language, culture, even mankind… Indeed, it is biological in nature. As this playfulness is shared, it becomes socially framed, **play** emerges, and as these shared forms are codified, we call them **games**.
>
> (p. 201)

As a mindset, playfulness can be applied to any situation. As Masek and Stenros (2021) found in their survey on understandings of playfulness,

> Playfulness [is]… neither a 'what' or a 'why' but rather a 'how.' … any activity, motivation, or affordance can be playful based upon how it is structured or organized. If a person (intentionally or unintentionally) chooses engagement over reality, they are choosing playfully. If an object is designed to generate engagement more than a relevant consequence, it is playful in its design.
>
> (p. 23)

With our model of playful engagement, we are attempting to tap into a mindset that is deep seated and powerfully connected to our experience of being human.

Playfulness is also inherently social. Play is a way we connect with each other. It is a unique method of becoming involved with others instead of creating distance (Masek and Stenros 2021, p. 15). I have long objected to techniques like gamification as it was practiced in the 2010s primarily because it did not foster social connection. Gamification focused on game mechanics to essentially fool people into thinking they were playing when they weren't. Stenros points to the risk of this shallowness,

> If the importance of a playful mindset is not understood, then enacting the forms of play or inhabiting the arenas of games run the risk of being hollow. The very ingredient that is at the heart of play is missing.
>
> (Stenros 2015, p. 204)

People can tell the difference between playing and *being* played, and will usually react negatively to the latter.

While play may be something we all do, adults and children play differently. Children play almost without conscious effort. If you've ever observed a child turn a fork into a spaceship, or suddenly declare, "I'm a tiger! Grrr!" you know how easily children slip into and out of play. They step into and out of the magic circle with ease. For adults in Western societies, the motivation for play—consequence-free enjoyment—also sits in direct tension with norms about adult identity. Adults are serious, play is childish. This is why adults in particular require alibis as we discussed in Chapter 1 if they are to feel safe entering the magic circles we make for them.

In the current century, the old distinction between play and serious adult behavior has been powerfully challenged. Adults in the 21st century play many more games than adults did 50 years ago. Digital technologies have thrust games into our workplaces and pockets and the growth of the entertainment industries presents adults with opportunities to play everywhere they go. I believe we are living through a generational shift where the role of play will likely continue to expand (or reassert itself) into all aspects of our lives, including museumgoing. Our particular challenge as museum experience designers then is to design opportunities for meaningful play, not just for children, but for everyone.

Historically, play experiences in museums have most commonly manifested in carefully demarcated play spaces, aimed at younger children. The exploding presence and prevalence of play and games in society are affecting how we live, learn, and work to such an extent that Eric Zimmerman sees the current century as "The Ludic Century" and places play and games at the center, "Being playful is the engine of innovation and creativity: as we play, we think about thinking and we learn to act in new ways. As a cultural form, games have a particularly direct connection with play" (Zimmerman 2015, p. 21). Games are particularly well-suited tools for fostering creativity, critical thinking, and problem-solving. For us, they are an opportunity to engage visitors of all ages, not just children, and help play to escape the play space.

Games

As a subset of the larger category of play, games have distinct qualities and it is important to distinguish between them. The French sociologist Roger Caillois (1961) used the Greek word *paidia* to describe the experiential and behavioral qualities of playing, and the Latin word *ludus* to denote the qualities of gaming. We already encountered *ludus* in Chapter 1 in the form of Huizinga's book titled *Homo Ludens*. I have endeavored throughout this book to avoid jargon wherever possible, but Caillois' use of *paidia* and *ludus* has been widely adopted by scholars.[2] *Ludus*[3] in particular is widely used. There is "ludology", the study of games which is practiced by "ludologists", and "ludic" meaning "having to do with games". I will use the words play and games throughout, but you should be aware of these specialist terms.

So, what distinguishes games from the larger realm of play?

Whereas paidia (or "playing") denotes a more freeform, expressive, improvisational, even "tumultuous" recombination of behaviors and meanings, ludus (or "gaming") captures playing structured by rules and competitive strife toward goals. Along those lines, classic definitions in game studies state that gaming and games – in contrast to playing and toys – are characterized by explicit rule systems and the competition or strife.

(Deterding et al. 2011, p. 11)

Clark Abt, the father of Serious Games, defined a game as, "an activity among two or more independent decision-makers seeking to achieve their objectives in some limiting context" (Abt 1970, pp. 6–7), where that limiting context is rules. In their foundational book on game design, Katie Salen Tekinbaş and Eric Zimmerman define a game as, "a system in which players engage in an artificial conflict, defined by rules, that results in a quantifiable outcome" (Tekinbaş and Zimmerman 2003, p. 80). Jesper Juul (2003) surveyed a number of influential definitions of games to arrive at his own which I have found useful in my own work and will use throughout this book,

> A game is a rule-based formal system with a variable and quantifiable outcome, where different outcomes are assigned different values, the player exerts effort in order to influence the outcome, the player feels attached to the outcome, and the consequences of the activity are optional and negotiable.

(p. 10)

Broadly speaking then, games are a specific kind of play activity which have defined beginnings and endings, explicit guidelines that direct the players in how to play, and clear outcomes. For me, one of the clearest distinctions between the experience of playing a game and that of visiting a museum is that you know that with a games there are rules, and you know what the objectives are. With museums, the rules are largely unwritten and unspoken (aside from prohibitions like "no photography" "no touching", etc.) and the objectives are also implied. How does a novice visitor know they've done it "right"? This may seem obvious to you if you're an experienced museum goer, but if museums are going to better engage their potential audiences, they will need to be more explicit and prescriptive. How do know when you've "won" a museum visit or beaten your personal best museum visit? How do you know when you've "finished" a museum visit other than through exhaustion? Games give us as designers the opportunity to build experiences that support visitor engagement more effectively.

This is where interaction alibis can play a vital role. Here's an example. The first time I went to the immersive art space MeowWolf, we were waiting in line with a crowd of other visitors who were waiting to go in. A MeowWolf staff person was working the line, checking tickets, answering questions, and welcoming visitors. At one point she started a brief "before you go in" talk and ended it with, "If you get about halfway through and you feel like you're completely lost and don't know what's going on, you probably doing it right." She quickly added that we should feel free to talk to any staff we encountered if we felt we needed help. That little acknowledgement of the overwhelmingness of the experience, and the reassurance that that was alright made a big difference in our visit.

Serious (?) Games

The idea of harnessing the obvious power of games to attract and hold player's attention has led many developers to try to make games that serve an educational purpose. Before gamification or gameful design, there were serious games. It sounds like an oxymoron, since almost all the definitions of games position them in opposition to serious endeavors. What makes a "serious" game serious? Clark Abt, who coined the phrase "serious games" described them as games that,

> have an explicit and carefully thought-out educational purpose and are not intended to be played primarily for amusement. This does not mean that serious games are not, or should not be, entertaining. We reject the somewhat Calvinistic notion that serious and virtuous activities cannot be "fun."
>
> (Abt 1970, p. 9)

In this sense, serious games encompass both of the meanings of "ludus" which can mean both a game and a school. One might argue that serious games are the original form of gamification, where the engagement that players feel while playing is harnessed to fulfill a separate, serious goal, in this case learning or training. A good example of this would be wargames, originally board games popularized by the Prussian military in the early 19th century as training aids for young officers which became successful in both serious and non-serious contexts (Schuurman 2017).

This interlinking of games as both diversion and teaching aide can be particularly seen in how serious games and computing have co-evolved over the past century (Djaouti et al. 2011). This connection of digital technologies and gaming has also given rise to game-based learning (GBL), which differs from serious games in that it centers the making and playing of games as a learning context (Becker 2021, p. 3). The study by Morard et al. (2023) of serious games in museum contexts found evidence that games do have the potential to create more active learners and critical thinkers (p. 131). They further go on to recommend open-ended games and collaborative gameplay as key to successful game-based learning. They also recommend that the problems to be solved in the game be ones that are not frequently encountered (p. 148) which echoes Espen Aarseth's contention that "The actual world is not a good playground" (Aarseth 2019, p. 139). This admonition harkens back to our discussion of immersion and the need for the immersive environment to differ noticeably from the environment we are leaving. In games, the same need for appreciable transition applies.

Gamification vs Gameful Design

Like the larger category of play, the idea of games sits uneasily in the landscape of serious cultural and heritage organizations whose lofty purposes are to better humanity through their work. In the early 2000s, though, a potential solution appeared that promised to provide the benefits of game playing without the need to engage in playing actual games. This was called "gamification." It is described by

Gabe Zicherman, an early proponent, as, "using some elements of game systems in the cause of a business objective. … The presence of key game mechanics, such as points, badges, levels, challenges, leaderboards, rewards, and onboarding, are signals that a game is taking place" (Zichermann 2011). The theory is that by creating non-games with game mechanics built into them, the positive associations people feel for games are transferred to the non-game. The satisfying feeling of increased mastery is coopted to achieve a non-game business goal. Gamification quickly became a phenomenon in the early social media days of the 2010s, and is still with us today. I've been conflicted about gamification for a long time (Rodley 2011, 2018) because of the way it exploits our desire to play without actually giving us a real game experience.

Gamification is not just a con that targets users. Game designer Margaret Robertson warned of gamification's lure for designers, "It tricks people into believing that there's a simple way to imbue their thing (bank, gym, job, government, genital health outreach program, etc.) with the psychological, emotional and social power of a great game" (Robertson 2010). The idea that simply applying some of the trappings of a game can make whatever you're designing more attractive and popular to users is appealing and led to countless gamified experiences. Chances are, if you've earned "points" on a credit card, or an airline loyalty account "rewards" you with perks when you reach a certain level, you've been gamified. The creators of these experiences hope that by gamifying their products, you will use them more often, but this extrinsic motivation runs completely counter to the intrinsic motivation to play. Stenros (2015) points out

> a central paradox of gamification and other applications of playful activities for external goals: the mindset that gives rise to playing and games is deeply connected to being performed for its own sake… Playfulness is not located in a system or an artifact, but in the participant.
>
> (p. 203)

Like it or not, gamification works, up to a point. In Hamari et al.'s (2014) study they found that "gamification provides positive effects, however, the effects are greatly dependent on the context in which the gamification is being implemented, as well as on the users using it" (Hamari et al. 2014). Sailer et al. (2017) found that "… badges, leaderboards, and performance graphs positively affect competence need satisfaction, as well as perceived task meaningfulness, while avatars, meaningful stories, and teammates affect experiences of social relatedness. Perceived decision freedom, however, could not be affected as intended." Their conclusion in part stated that "gamification is not effective per se, but that specific game design elements have specific psychological effects" (p. 379). Mitchell et al. (2017) question the very assumption that gamification works because people are intrinsically motivated to play games and suggest that "the mechanics of gamification may involve different factors beyond the production of intrinsic motivation through gameplay" (p. 18).

So much for gamification.

Gameful Design

While I may have reservations about applying gamification to museum experiences, it is undeniable that many of the qualities that players feel while playing games are like the ones we seek to instill in visitors. Another way to think about applying game design theory and techniques to non-game applications is gameful design, which focuses on intrinsic motivations like positive affect, mastery, and meaning making (Dichev et al. 2015, pp. 91–92), what Deterding calls "the experiential qualities characteristic for gameplay" (Deterding 2015b, p. 297). In their study of creating gamefully designed museum experiences, De Angeli and O'Neill (2020) describe the benefit of gameful design thus: "Gameful experiences provide the same emotional and psychological experiences as games while benefitting players. Rather than exploiting players, they enhance their overall value creation using game affordances (e.g. achievements, challenges and stories), stimulating participation, creativity, curiosity and engagement" (p. 39).

Landers et al. (2019) unpack the idea of gamefulness by proposing that it be replaced with three more specific constructs: *gameful design*, which is the design process used to create *gameful systems*, which are ones that create in their users a *gameful experience* (p. 4). As designers, we may be most interested in gameful design, but it is important to remember the reason it's useful is that it helps create a gameful experience in the minds of the people using the thing. Gameful experience is a state of mind with three psychological characteristics:

- Players need to perceive presented goals to be non-trivial and achievable (the goals will require some player effort to achieve,)
- Players need to be motivated to pursue those goals under arbitrary externally imposed constraints (they require a compelling interaction alibi,) and,
- Players need to believe their actions within these constraints are volitional (they need to feel intrinsically motivated) (p. 3).

I find gamefulness to be a valuable concept because rather than relying on using the trappings of a game, it focuses on recreating the experiential quality of playing a game, and gets us thinking about how the tools and mindsets that game designers use to create the framework for that to happen can be applied to the museum visit. "In short, gameful design attempts to design systems that serve specific functions and uses and facilitate both through motivating, enjoyable experiences" (Deterding 2015b, p. 301). Whereas gamification coopts the mechanics of gameplay, gameful design seeks to instill a sense of playfulness in its products. It becomes a useful lens to view museum experience design through because it focuses on the experience from the visitor's perspective, that cybernetic system of visitor, object, and alibi.

Gameful Participation

That was a lot of definitions to wade through, but it is important to disambiguate terms, and given the messy Venn diagram of these concepts, being clear about what we're talking about is crucial.

Now that we've teased apart gamefulness from its parent ideas, we can talk about gameful participation. Gameful participation is the act of engaging in a motivating, gamefully designed activity that provides visitors with the experiential qualities of game play.

Encouraging Playfulness

Encouraging play as an activity and playfulness as a mindset might seem completely uncontroversial to you, but the museum sector as a whole is still in the process of shedding the mindset that play is not an appropriate tool for the serious business of museums. Holdgaard and Olesen (2023) surveyed 137 recently published studies on play in museums and found that almost all kinds of museums have explored play as a tool. Play also seems to predominantly mean digitally mediated play aimed primarily at children. There has been significantly less work on play with young adults and adults. As we've seen in other examples in this book, even though play might be referenced in the title of a study, half of the papers in Holdgaard and Oleson's survey had no definition of play. Museums are employing play, but there's room for growth, both in understanding what it means, and using it well.

An important and obvious exception to this trend is children's museums. Because children are their primary audience, these museums have long employed play as a central part of the experience. The Association of Children's Museums (ACM), a professional association representing more than 400 children's museums across the US, has stated that "Play is learning, and it is critical to the healthy social, emotional, and cognitive development of children" (ACM 2024). Despite this, even children's museums seem to be unclear about what exactly play means to them. Jessica Luke et al. (2021) studied how children's museums conceptualize play specifically, and how they position themselves and their work relative to play. They found that the role of play in the mission of children's museums is central, even if the word "play" doesn't appear. Almost three quarters of the museums they surveyed didn't have a definition of play even though over three quarters think play and learning are closely related. Only a quarter measure play at their museum though two thirds described social and cognitive development as clear benefits of play and over half cited emotional development as a benefit. Luke et al. conclude with,

> These findings suggest to us that while children's museums are laying claim
> to play as a significant aspect of their mission, they do not seem to have
> shared understandings of what play is, what it looks like, or how it manifests
> within their museum. Without clear definitions, it is difficult to discuss play
> within the museum or with stakeholders.
>
> (p. 71)

They go on to pose the question, "[A]re children's museums strategically avoiding the construct of play because it isn't seen as an essential element of learning by policy makers, funders and consumers?" (p. 71).

If even children's museums are conflicted about the appropriateness of play as an explicit construct in their work, it is understandable that the rest of the field may be ambivalent. There is reason to believe that play will be more fully embraced as policy and funding will catch up to the research. But we need not wait. Let's look at a few of the ways museums can encourage playfulness and participation.

Games Have Rules and Those Rules are Explicit

Perhaps the biggest distinction between games and all other sorts of play is that games are governed by rules while play is unstructured. "What we find there, at the very heart of games, is the space of games RULES, framed as formal systems" (Tekinbaş and Zimmerman 2003, p. 98). The rules set out the boundaries of the game's play and make explicit what can and cannot be done within the context of the game. To intentionally not follow the rules is to cheat and that is socially unacceptable.

A key feature of rules is that they need to be accessible to potential players and unambiguous enough to allow gameplay to occur. In computer games, the rules are baked into the software that creates the gameplay so that facet is not present, but in every type of gameplay, adjudicating the rules is an inherent part of playing,

> The rules of games have to be sufficiently well defined… that you do not have to argue about them every time you play. In fact, the playing of a non-electronic game is an activity that in itself involves trying to remove any unclearness in the game rules: If there is disagreement about the rules of the game, the game is stopped until the disagreement has been solved.
>
> (Juul 2003, p. 10).

Gameplay Can Lead to Flow

We've mentioned psychologist Mihaly Csikszentmihalyi's concept of *flow* several times already. His 1990 book, "Flow: The Psychology of Optimal Experience" laid out a framework for understanding how we experience moments of supremely satisfying engagement, what Csikszentmihalyi termed *flow* experiences. In a flow experience, our intrinsic motivation leads us to engage with whatever the task at hand is both mentally and emotionally. We feel challenged by the task, but not overwhelmed. We believe it's possible to succeed and that we must devote effort to the task. When this comes to pass, we can experience high levels of satisfaction and enjoyment regardless of any external reward for success. Our engagement with the task is so intense that it makes us lose track of the outside world. If you recall the definition of playful engagement I proposed in Chapter 1, you'll recognize it shares many of the same elements: focused attention, intrinsic motivation, and satisfying emotional outcome.

Flow experiences can happen anywhere, but gameplay can be a particularly hospitable venue for flow to occur. It already relies on many of the same preconditions that Csikszentmihalyi proposed for flow experiences. Achieving flow has been proposed as a prime criterion for measuring how enjoyable games are (Sweetser and Wyeth 2005; Takatalo et al. 2010). When a player is totally immersed (there's that word again) in gameplay, that flow experience can also lead to the player developing both skills and understandings, two things most if not all museums aspire to instill in visitors. The end goal of designing for playful engagement in a museum setting is to create the opportunity for visitors to have the kind of optimally enjoyable and satisfying experience that museums are already well-positioned to provide (Taheri and Jafari 2012). Sarah Brin's reflection in this chapter will present a contrary view on flow and its utility.

Gameplay Can Create Fiero

Getting lost in a moment of flow is not the only thing gameplay can create in players. The sense of increasing mastery is also a powerful incentive to continue playing. Nicole Lazzaro (2004) has appropriated the Italian word *fiero* "triumph" to describe this feeling of personal triumph and associates it with Seymour Papert's notion of "hard fun," the idea that part of what we enjoy about games is that they are not too easy (Papert 1998). Jane McGonigal, who popularized the term (2009), describes fiero as the thrill of triumph we get when we accomplish something really hard. Fiero is not synonymous with winning, it is rather an internal sense of increasing one's mastery. In this sense, it is not dissimilar to Friedrich Nietzsche's description of happiness as "The feeling that power increases—that a resistance is overcome" (Nietzsche 1990, p. 125). The example I began the chapter with of J.K. Galbraith reflecting on skiing was really him describing the appeal of fiero, of that progression from, "Can I do it? I don't know if I can. I think I can do it. I'm doing it! I did it!"

Games excel at giving us the feeling of triumph over circumstance and the associated chemical rewards of dopamine release that literally make us feel better. Advocates of game-based learning like McGonigal argue that museums' potential to inspire fiero could be harnessed through gameful experiences that transform the visitor experience from being a spectator sport to one where visitors take that feeling of fiero home and have a memorable, active experience (McGonigal 2009, p. 8).

Tools for Creating Gameful Museums

Now that we have made sense of the intertwined concepts of play, games, playfulness, and gamefulness, hopefully the potential benefits of gamefully designed experiences are clear. The important question then becomes how we apply these to our work. If we are going to build museum experiences that are more than traditional displays with a layer of gamified elements add to them,

Here are some of the tools that can encourage gameful participation in any kind of museum setting be it online or in-person.

Have Clear Rules

Museums are *very* good at telling visitors what *not* to do. Do not touch, Do not sit, No photography, No backpacks, No running, No baby carriages, No food or drink, No loud talking. The list goes on. And while these rules can certainly be important, they are not the complete set of rules, and the important ones are almost always left unsaid. An example: Imagine if you were teaching someone how to play a card game like poker, and you only told them what not to do. How well do you think they would they be able to play the game? Not as well as they would if they had all the rules: what is acceptable, what is encouraged, what is celebrated. Museums are too often like a game where nobody ever tells you how to play. They tell you how not to play, and correct you when you get it wrong. As we discussed in Chapter 1, avoiding embarrassment is a primary inhibiting factor for adult behavior in social settings. The idea of the interaction alibi provides a way to think about concrete scaffolds to support visitors in whatever tasks they engage in, and games, by virtue of their rule-based nature, make them excellent formats to think about providing that alibi.

The rules of a game provide visitors with a concrete understanding of what they can do in order to play the game. Inviting visitors to play a game is basically saying, "Here are the rules. Follow them and you'll be fine." Good rules are the raw materials that create that feeling of safety that allows people to become players. "Rules build on each other, create webs of meaning that serve as building blocks of social worlds and physical activities" (Stenros and Montola 2024, p. 193). As designers, crafting rules and their interactions with humans requires care and attention, because all the learning and social interaction arises out of the functioning of the rules.

This need for clear rules becomes even more challenging in museums because so many of the behavioral norms are unwritten. In their study of two hybrid smartphone-based games at the Museum of Yugoslavia in Belgrade, Løvlie et al. (2021) highlighted the importance of this explicit contract,

> To increase the number of visitors who will feel safe enough to play, social contracts need to be properly established; both between players and other visitors, as well as between players and the museum. This is always challenging when it comes to hybrid experiences, such as pervasive games, where the digital content acts as a hidden layer only accessible to those engaged in it. However, it shows how important it is both to communicate to visitors beforehand what they can expect from the experience, as well as to provide players with the possibility to opt-out at any moment.
>
> (p. 17)

One of my personal favorite artworks at The Museum of Fine Arts, Boston is Jeppe Hein's "PLEASE…", a neon sculpture of a series of words describing actions one might take at a museum, "PLEASE ENJOY RELAX ~~STEAL~~ DANCE TOUCH FLIRT ~~SMOKE~~ WONDER FEEL MUSE ~~EAT~~ SING LISTEN TALK ASK

~~TOUCH NEON~~ LOOK COMMUNICATE TOUCH EACH OTHER USE CAMERA ~~FLASH~~" (MFA Boston 2024). For many years it was placed near the entrance to the museum and was one of the first works visitors encountered. It combines both the dos and the don'ts in a compelling manner that lets visitors imagine what's possible and not just what's forbidden. This kind of alibi is in short supply in too many museums. It would be even better if that permission were coming directly from the museum and not from an artist, or more often cultural critics proclaiming a "right" way to visit a (usually art) museum (Rodley 2014). I am encouraged by the number of museums that have taken concrete steps to give visitors guidance by providing more explicit guidelines for their museum visit.

Creating gameful moments need not be limited to the exhibitions and educational contexts. Kristiansen and Moseley's study of museum lobbies (2018) presents an array of contexts where activities like ticket buying, orientation, or reflecting on a visit while waiting for the rest of one's group could be designed gamefully.

Let Visitors Teach Each Other

It is a rare museum that has enough front of house staff to answer every and all questions visitors might have during a visit. Online, that number drops practically to zero. So, the people most visitors spend their time with are other visitors. Csikszentmihalyi and Hermanson (1995) noted that one strength that physical museum experiences had was their public, inherently social dimension. Even if you visit by yourself, you do so in the presence of others and that shared space is powerful, because sometimes the object in the magic circle is another person. They write,

> We learn about connectedness through rituals such as ceremonies or rock concerts and whenever we are exposed to an event that is shared with others that feeling of connectedness is reaffirmed and strengthened… Perhaps one of the of major underdeveloped functions of museums is to provide opportunities for individually meaningful experiences that also connect with the experiences of others.
>
> (p. 75)

Providing opportunities for gameful participation can serve this social and socializing function of establishing and strengthening social bonds.

Many times in my career I have seen a family group in a museum where a child begins messing about with an exhibit while asking one of the adults in the group, "What do I do?", sending the adult on a quest to find the label or instructions which they read aloud, even when the child is old enough to read the label themselves. In this social interaction, both engagement and connection are enhanced. This phenomenon is already well-known in museums. Evaluators have long studied the impact of labels by how much they get read out loud or repeated. This practice, described by McManus (1989) as "text echo" often happens in (but is by no means restricted to) intergenerational groups. One person reading or paraphrasing written texts can spread that knowledge to visitors who never look at the label. The same occurs with cues around gameplay. Watching someone playing a game provides potential players with a wealth of clues as to whether that game is worth their time or not. Gameful experiences can explicitly invite visitors into the temporary role of "player" and create moments of social teaching and learning where even complete strangers interact fluidly and unselfconsciously.

The first truly large-scale museum game I remember was Epidemik, at le Cité de Sciences et de l'Industrie in Paris. The highlight of the exhibition was a room-sized multiplayer game about the spread of epidemics. As you entered the room, a circle was projected onto the floor around you that showed your health and other variables, and as you walked around the room and your circle came into contact with other visitors you stood a chance of getting "infected." Visitors would often look at each other and adjust their gameplay based on how they saw others playing the game, like keeping to the perimeter of the room. Epidemik encouraged social play in a way that didn't require a lot of explanation.

Visitors also look to each other and employ surreptitious observation as a way of deciding their next steps. The aging exhibition I mentioned at the beginning of the chapter (Silverstein et al. 2001) also featured a video component explaining Tai Chi Chu'an as a helpful form of exercise. Visitors entered a semi-enclosed space and watched a video and were encouraged to follow along with a recording of an instructor demonstrating poses. The prototype did not do well until we added a partial bamboo screen over the entrance. It provided enough cover that visitors could try something many had no experience doing without feeling like they were putting themselves on display. And visitors outside could easily see right through the curtain to ascertain what was going on inside. This combination of official guidance and surreptitious monitoring can create the circumstances for visitors, even complete strangers, to engage with each other, some echoed by Pip Simpson of the Young V & A (formerly the Victoria & Albert Museum of Childhood): "We know from our research that guided play is the most effective… We are setting up parameters to help visitors play and to encourage more collaborative play" (Parry 2020, p. 30).

Allow for Multiple Ways to Play

My family are avid players of the word game Boggle, where you shake up 16 dice printed with letters into a 4 × 4 grid and then try to make as many English words as possible out adjacent letters in a given period of time. My sons have occasionally decided, without telling the rest of us, on their own goals that were different than everyone else's. Once, it involved only making the longest words possible. Once, it involved only making plausible sounding gibberish words, like "glimp" and "crem". In both cases, they didn't "win" the game, but enjoyed themselves immensely. And in the case of the made-up word game, it provided the rest of the players with several minutes of fun trying to imagine what the made-up words might mean.

Obviously, both of these are examples of players deciding to play a different game that could be considered unhelpful or transgressive. But part of the creation of the magic circle of play is a negotiation of the rules and norms, and also their renegotiation. Good gameful experiences can accommodate a certain degree of tinkering. Poorly designed gameful experiences often force you down one path, and one path only. You may have encountered one of these games before. My go-to example is the genre of "quizzes that have been reframed as games but are still really quizzes." If you don't give the right answer to the question, you can't advance, and the only way to win is to answer the questions correctly.

At the Museum of Science, Boston, we built a multistep design interactive where visitors assembled robots out of a variety of parts. They then could test their robot on a variety of surfaces to see how it performed on inclines, rough terrain, etc. (Tisdal 2006, p. 18). I watched a group take their robot out of the interactive and put it on the gallery floor, which seemed odd, so I slunk over and eavesdropped. They had tested their design on all the surfaces we had provided and wondered how it'd do on another kind of surface—a carpeted floor. This was not a scenario we had planned for or encouraged, but it was one that the space accommodated. They created their own challenge and went for it.

One of my favorite examples of making a museum visit a gamefully participatory experience was the iPhone game Tate Trumps, which was commissioned by the Tate Museum in 2010. Tate Trumps didn't attempt to explain the process of looking at art. It privileged procedural learning to "provide clues and methods for learning how to solve a task rather than teach what is right or wrong, or what are true or false" (Champion 2011, p. 84). Using the idea of collecting cards representing artworks visitors had looked at, Tate Trumps provided three different games visitors could play. In Battle Mode, players would try to answer a prompt like "which artwork would win in a fight?" Mood Mode gave players an emotional mood, like "absurd" and then the players would find artworks that they felt captured that mood. In Collector Mode they were challenged to find art they might want to have in their home. In each of these modes, players would practice their observational and interpretive skills and spend prolonged periods of time looking at artworks (Economou and Meintani 2011, p. 16; Brin 2015, p. 16). You can also see how Tate Trumps gave visitors multiple ways to play, straightforward rules, and an alibi for how a pair of visitors could visit together and have a satisfying social experience. Just by making the game, Tate was saying "Having and looking at art is OK."

Design the Game to Match the Museum

One issue that has plagued museum games and has only intensified in the wake of the hype around gamification has been games that are ill-matched to their setting. I still have vivid memories of a museum game that alleged to teach me about disease and the human immune system, but was really just a pinball game where the balls were called white blood cells, and the "goal" of the game was to hit the bad cells (the targets and spinners) to get a high score. There is an underlying equation behind many museum games that leads to lots of these kinds of mismatched visitor experiences. It goes something like this:

My thing ≠ fun enough
Games = fun
My thing, gamified = more funner!

The reality is a little more complicated and requires a more thoughtful approach. We have to learn to reject the mindset that simply adding fancy trappings improves the experience.

Our design work is subtle and complex. To enter the magic circle of a museum game, visitors have to decide to be *both* players and museum visitors. The gameful experience we design, therefore, has to satisfy both desires. Just playing a game is not in itself enough for an engaging museum experience. Good gameful museum experiences have to make sense in both their content and context. If that balance isn't struck, then it becomes harder for visitors to enter and maintain a state of playfulness. In their study of an audio-based mobile game, Wakkary and Hatala (2007) found that,

> learning effectiveness and functionality can be balanced productively with playful interaction… if designers balance the engagement between play and awareness of the environment, and balance the richness of ambiguity with the richness of information that links the audio content to the artifacts.
>
> (pp. 189–190)

The clearest guidance I have seen to date comes from Løvlie et al.'s (2021) description the design process for two hybrid games at the Museum of Yugoslavia. They posed three guiding questions for their design process:

- How would the digital experience be linked to the physical exhibits, technically?
- How would the digital interaction (the game) be connected with the physical exhibits, conceptually?
- How would the game facilitate play—and in particular, critical play?"

(p. 8).

To go back to the Tate example, it addresses all three questions. The game required the museum context in order to work, visitors needed to think and feel things about the objects to play the game, and the discussing of why players chose the objects they did stimulated reflection. When the gameful experience and the museum experience are in harmony, then magic can happen.

Don't Let Fear of Mischief Stop You

In my years as an exhibit developer in a science museum, trying to make exhibits as "foolproof" as possible meant spending a lot of time watching visitors and trying to remove anything that got in the way of them doing what we wanted them to do, which was learn about whatever science, technology, engineering, and mathematics (STEM)-related topic we were creating. The idea that we might build in some way that visitors could express their own agency outside of the limits we imposed was unheard-of to me. If visitors tried to use an exhibit to do something we hadn't planned, that was considered negative behavior. This need for control of the content and the context what Adorno (1981) called "the authoritarian gesture" (p. 176) describes the whole struggle museums face in the 21st century. Museums want visitors to come in, to appreciate what is on offer, to bring their whole selves and more and more commonly, find how the content of the museum speaks to them on a personal level. At the same time, the traditional museum model is an authoritarian one, where control is made manifest by the presence of guards, the ubiquity of signage that tells one what not to do, and interpretation that often provides only a singular viewpoint.

This fear of ceding control of the experience to the people having the experience manifests in many ways, but is most commonly found in the reluctance to give visitors the ability to be creative. This tendency to restrict visitor agency has developed in order to reduce the possibility of them making mischief, what Staffan Björk coined "The Generalized Mischief Metric" $t(p)$, where (t) is amount of time that elapses before a penis (p) appears in your user generated content (quoted in Deterding 2011, p. 117). To forestall this inevitability, museums will frequently censor themselves dramatically because time and energy are limited, and content moderation and restocking consumables are time-consuming jobs.

But mischief is not necessarily an unalloyed negative. Mischief is an attitude of playfulness that manifests as transgressing the expected norms of a playful experience. For Stenros (2015) and others, mischief "is an important part in negotiating social contracts online [and onsite!], forging societies through experimentation; as a tool for performative actions, serendipitous creation, and appropriation" (p. 182). A playful experience that can allow mischief to an extent and still work can be powerful. Ryding (2020) studied a mobile web app called *Never Let Me Go*, a two-player game, at the National Gallery of Denmark, where visitors created impromptu experiences in-situ for a companion, in the role of either Controller who directed their companion to perform actions like look at a work of art or answer questions, or Avatar, who acted out the Controllers suggestions. Their finding was that

Allowing for play means losing a certain amount of control over visitors. 'Never let me go' gave participants an alibi to do things they wouldn't normally do when visiting an art museum… encouraging playful behaviour is not putting the museum at risk (in terms of inappropriate behaviour, vandalism etc.). Instead, it enables visitors to find new, more embodied, perhaps unexpected, ways to encounter the art.

(p. 7)

SIDEBAR: Games as Objects

Unlike the other concepts we've looked at thus far, computer and video games have not only been thought of as tools for museums to employ, but as subject matter for display. Major art museums like the Smithsonian, The Museum of

Digital Games

Digital games, which include video games and computer games, have an even more complicated history, combining as they do the urge to maximize the capabilities of new technologies and employ games as an engagement tool. This dynamic has marked the development of computer games from the dawn of digital computing. In 1961, The Hingham Institute Study Group on Space Warfare at MIT proposed a Theory of Computer Toys that stated that a good computer demonstration program ought to satisfy three criteria:

- It should *demonstrate*, that is, it should show off as many of the computer's resources as possible, and tax those resources to the limit.
- Within a consistent framework, it should be *interesting*, which means every run should be different.
- It should involve the onlooker in a *pleasurable* and active way—in short, it should be a game.

> (Hingham Institute, 1961
> quoted in Graetz, 1981)

Their demonstration of this theory was the two-player game *Spacewar!* the first video game solely designed for entertainment and the progenitor of countless other games that created the magic circle of a game situated in between two (or more) people (Graetz 1981; Djaouti et al. 2011, p. 5). It is worth noting that the first criterion in the theory above is to tax the computer's power and the game criterion comes last. More than half a century later this dynamic can still be seen in the veritable arms race between

Modern Art (MoMA), the Tate, and many others have mounted exhibitions on computer and video games as subjects worthy of attention due to their technological sophistication, ubiquity in modern societies, and artistry. I am interested in using games as ways to engage visitors, not as already-created products to be described and contextualized, but I think it is important to provide at least a sketch of how museums have attempted to treat games like other topics they choose to exhibit and how amenable they are to this treatment.

Brin (2015) covers several of these milestone moments. In 2012, the Museum of Modern Art (MoMA) in New York City announced that they would begin acquiring computer games as design artifacts. Their initial list of 40 games to be accessioned reads like the beginning of a canon of "important" computer and videogames, and many were playable in some form in the museum. In 2012, the Smithsonian Institution also mounted a major exhibition on the art of videogames. In both cases, game artifacts take center stage for obvious reasons like audience throughput. These are just two examples of a phenomenon that is widespread. The final example I will cite here major game developers and computer hardware makers. This phenomenon is neatly summed up by Rick Sayre, Visual Effects (VFX) Supervisor & Senior Scientist at Pixar Animation Studios who said: "*Artistic appetite always outstrips technical capacity.*" to explain why, despite 25 years of advances in computing hardware and software, it still took Pixar roughly the same amount of time to make a film (Sayre, personal conversation, 2009). Where this affects us in designing museum experiences is that the "latest and greatest" technologies are also often untested and potentially troublesome ones. This may not be an issue to a dedicated gamer wrestling with a wonky graphics card, but to a museum visitor just trying to enjoy their visit, be it in-person or online, that kind of needless friction will usually end their visit, and possibly prejudice them against ever returning.

Museum Games

In the beginning of the 21st century, the explosive growth of Web 2.0 and social media also marked the beginning of a mini-Renaissance of museum computer game projects. Institutions all over the world tried to find ways to engage online audiences, both inside and outside their walls, and produced some exceptional game experiences. Some notable examples include:

Epidemik, Cité de Sciences et de l'Industrie, 2007–2009

"Epidemik", produced by La Cité des Sciences in Paris and Virtuél, explored past and future epidemics to help visitors understand the health, social,

is the Victoria and Albert Museum's Videogames! exhibition in 2018. The exhibition does not differ substantially from other previous efforts described above, with one important exception. The V&A's project was also the location for Michael McMaster's PhD research. McMaster, a veteran game designer and developer of the popular "The Untitled Goose Game" among others, came to the work with deep understanding of the subject of computer game design, but not museology and spent six months observing the process by which the V&A developed the exhibition. The resulting ethnographic study, "Videogames and the Public Museum: Six Months Behind the Scenes" (2023) is a fascinating read on large art museum culture in the early 21st century and how uneasily topics like video games fit in the traditional models for how things get turned into exhibitions.

Games are tools for indulging our playfulness, and as such, they challenge traditional museological approaches to display. Looking at concept art from a game, or interviews with game designers, or examples of the hardware that run the game do not allow visitors to have the experience of playing the game. Imagine an exhibition economic, and political issues raised by epidemic crises and the role that everyone can play a role in preventing and fighting against these diseases. The centerpiece of the exhibition was a massive multiplayer game that used computer vision and projection mapping to engage groups of visitors in epidemic scenarios.

Launchball, The Science Museum, London, 2007–present

The Science Museum hired Preloaded to develop a level-based game where players could develop an understanding of kinematics and Newton's laws while trying to progress through a series of levels, and even design their own levels. The wildly successful game has been recoded from Adobe Flash to HTML 5 in 2016 and is still available (Science Museum 2023).

Ghosts of a Chance, Smithsonian American Art Museum, 2008–2010

Ghosts of a Chance was an alternative reality game (ARG) developed by the Smithsonian American Art Museum and CityMystery between 2008 and 2010. It employed a variety of digital and analogue channels that enlisted players to help two fictional curators being haunted by ghosts.

Tate Trumps, Tate Museum, 2009

Tate Trumps was a free iPhone game commissioned by the Tate Museum and developed by Hide & Seek. Players would use their phones to select

on chocolate where you were able to learn all about chocolate, but never taste it. That is what most game exhibitions provide visitors. As McMaster observed, "the making of Videogames was business-as-usual for the V&A. Gradually, though, I became aware of a distinct feeling of incompatibility or mistranslation… the V&A's 'business-as-usual'— its conventional methods of exhibition-making—seemed ill-equipped to engage videogames as an exhibitionary subject" (McMaster 2023, p. 7).

In essential ways, games are different, and if we want to employ them, we need to think carefully about how we can provide visitors with the important thing, the playing, and not satisfy ourselves with merely displaying the props that allow gameplay to happen. Frank Lantz sums up the dilemma we face when we choose to use games in our work, "Making a game combines everything that's hard about building a bridge with everything that's hard about composing an opera. Games are operas made out of bridges" (Lantz 2014 quoted in McMaster 2023, p. 69).

artworks within the Tate's permanent collection to answer amusing prompts like "which artwork would win in a fight?" Along the way, players would practice their observational and interpretive skills.

Murder at the Met, the Metropolitan Museum of Art, 2012

As part of the reopening of its American Wing, the Metropolitan Museum of Art partnered with Green Door Labs to create a mobile phone-based game that would help younger visitors learn about the Met's collection and orient themselves to the new wing. The game combined both in-person and digital elements as visitors tried to solve a murder mystery (Pletcher 2021).

Send Me SFMOMA, San Fransisco Museum of Modern Art, 2017–2020

Send Me SFMOMA was conceived as a way to bring transparency to the museum's collection and encouraging visitors to explore and discuss SFMOMA's objects. Technically more of a toy than a game, mobile phone users could text the words "send me" followed by a keyword, a color, or even an emoji and receive a related SFMOMA artwork image and caption via text message. Despite its popularity, the museum decided to focus on in-gallery engagements and sunset the service in 2020.

These are but a few of the examples of museums employing games as a tool to engage audiences.

Conclusion

Congratulations! You have made it through the gameful participation chapter! You've just won 10,000 points! Read on to earn more!!

Just kidding…

As you've hopefully seen in our long, winding journey through play and related concepts, Huizinga's idea of the magic circle keeps appearing, alongside the necessary interaction alibis. The importance of creating the conditions for visitors to feel safe enough to step outside themselves is Job #1 for any experience designer, and museum experience designers in particular. If we are to overcome what Elaine Gurian (2005) terms "threshold fear" that hinders visitors from fully participating in museum experiences, then creating gameful experiences can provide the players with clearly bounded opportunities to use their imagination and creativity while developing critical faculties. This idea of effort being rewarded with mastery (not necessarily victory) is a powerful incentive to learn. When people decide to play, they take on the role of player with the hope that they will be challenged, experience pleasure, and master new ideas and skills. And that's a win for them and us!

Reflection
Updating the Playful Museum

by Sarah Brin

Sarah Brin is a strategic advisor for organizations working with immersive experiences, creative technology, and audience engagement. You can learn more about her work at www.sarahbrin.com.

The period between 2010 and 2018 was an exciting time to be working in museums. Many of us felt energized by the possibilities of Web 2.0, the emerging field of creative technology, and the possibility of reaching new audiences.

This included a curiosity around games. As we researched the potentials for games and play, museum professionals across disciplines pushed back against the negative stereotype of the typical gamer (adolescent, male, social outcast) to argue that games and play were meaningful components of culture, and that they could be expressive, educational, and timely touchpoints for connecting with audiences. As we developed the scaffolding to culturally legitimize games, we borrowed theory from psychology, art history, educational theory and other disciplines to convince institutions that there was more to games than *Grand Theft Auto* and *Doom*.

As a museum scholar and consultant, I developed research reports about the validity of games as cultural artifacts, designed public programs, and commissioned work in partnership with museums around the world. This work, and the work of my co-conspirators, was successful. Games received the recognition we had worked for. We saw a boom in games and play-focused research programs, exhibitions, interpretive initiatives and more. But just as any other trend crests and ebbs, many of these initiatives have faded away.

I'm pleased to see a renewed interest in playful museum experiences, and that it's accompanied by an understanding that the term "play" encompasses a broad spectrum of human behaviors and is more than something just for children. But now that games are back in museums, how are we building on the discourse and the learnings from the first time around? What new hypotheses are we testing?

Since we have a second chance to talk about games, play, and museums, I'd like us to introduce some new complexity into the discussion. This essay offers three suggestions for adding some much-needed texture into the discourse concerning museums and games.

The first is to shift focus away from "Games" with a "Capital G" and toward a more nuanced understanding of play. By relieving ourselves of the challenge of designing museum games, we can instead focus on playful experiences that capture and engage audiences. My second suggestion is that Csikszentmihalyi's concept of "flow" as a transcendent experience has served its utility in legitimizing the study and application of games and play in museum contexts. We can now release this idea and consider other types of aspirational play-states that may be more helpful for 21st-century audiences. And finally, I suggest that we develop tools to help us better understand and design for different types of museum publics and play experiences.

Less about Games, More about Play

In my work as both a researcher and as an advisor to museums, I have witnessed many institutions struggle with designing, financing, and maintaining digital games. Many of these games did not turn out to be good, and even fewer of them were actually *fun*. I don't say this to dunk on intelligent and hard-working museum professionals, but instead to acknowledge the anxiety associated with following trends, appealing to changing audiences, and keeping up with emerging technologies. It's hard. Games are very popular and it's exciting to think about creating a blockbuster experience. But in chasing the *form* of games, it's easy to overlook the (arguably more transformative and engaging) *experience* of play.

What is play? Play scholar Miguel Sicart (2014) writes: "Play is contextual… it's a messier network of people, rules, negotiations, and objects. Play happens in a tangled world of people, things, spaces, or cultures" (p. 6). To Sicart, play happens amidst and within different systems and it is not limited exclusively to the magic circle of games. He explains, "…playfulness is an *attitude*… a stance toward an activity – a psychological, physical and emotional perspective we take" (p. 22).

To Sicart and others, true playfulness isn't simply about winning or memorizing rules. It requires an understanding of how systems work (and how they can be navigated, altered, or destroyed). A playful perspective can be applied to a game just as it can be applied to natural history, to software code, a fine artwork, or anything else.

Can a museum be playful? It's no secret that museums are their own tangle of rules, objects, and hierarchies. As Swarupa Anila (2017) writes, museum interpretation exists; to "support visitor meaning making… to identify what dominant narratives emerge and whose stories are being told. It is then crucial to examine who is on another side of those power dynamics" (p. 110). This strikes me as relevant at a moment in which the acceleration of digital technologies continues to influence more of our everyday lives. The far-reaching grasp of tech monopolies, the proliferation of generative AI, and the popularization of livestreaming are all nodes in complex networks of power, culture, and identity. Earlier in the 2000s, many of us were energized by the internet's potential to bring people together and unlock knowledge. We're now at a less optimistic time in technological history. Now, more than ever, stewardship of our audiences means foregrounding critical thinking, and creative visions of what a different world might look like. Institutions may have an integral role in shaping visitors' views of the world, and encouraging individuals to approach these phenomena playfully will be some of the most critical work of the 21st-century museum.

Flow Does Us No Favors

In her 2010 TED talk, author and game designer Jane McGonigal urged her audience:

> If we want to solve problems like hunger, poverty, climate change, global conflict, obesity, I believe that we need to aspire to play games online for at least 21 billion hours a week, by the end of the next decade.

McGonigal (2010) was and is the figurehead for the belief that "games can change the world" because of gamers' ability to collaborate, focus their attention deeply and achieve a flow state that could then be harnessed toward their overcoming societal challenges. This is a wonderful idea. Elsewhere I've cited the amazing outcomes from the game Foldit, an MMO-like game in which players compete with each other to create the best protein folds that contribute to medical research.

However, over a decade after her TED talk, it's worth adding complexity to McGonigal's thesis. Is it really that easy to change the world? Did we?

The terms "game" and "play" still carry unhelpful connotations of being juvenile and trivial. In 2010, few people understood that games can be sophisticated, thought-provoking, or experimental. Theorists and game designers embraced flow because it added legitimacy to their field. "Cziksentmihaly's focus on flow thus helped to bypass cultural stigmas attached to play in a society that values intense productivity," writes play scholar Braxton Soderman (2021 p 21). Through flow, Cziksentmihaly added much needed validation to the then-nascent field of game studies. However, as Soderman notes,

> The actual experience of flow is precarious and difficult to verify… For some players it also can be short-lived or non-existent; the immersion that it offers is only one state in a panoply of cognitive, emotional, social and kinesthetic experiences that arise during gameplay and the political and social ideologies that ground the concept of flow do not always hit their mark.
>
> (p. 18)

I'm concerned that flow is a difficult state for many museumgoers to achieve in gallery contexts, and that it places too much of an emphasis on an end-state rather than a holistic process. In prioritizing flow, we have overlooked other meaningful or transformative aspects of play. Is flow something that most people can attain in a museum space, especially if they are learning new game controls or perceiving others queuing behind them for their turns? And surely in a moment in which we require social cohesion and collaboration to solve the big problems of our world (including phenomena like climate change and income inequality), is it strategic for museum professionals to strive for eliciting the primarily singular, isolated feeling in players? What if instead, we as museum professionals thought about the social, collaborative, non-competitive types of play associated with the New Games Movement of the 1960 and 70s? Especially within today's context of weaponized misinformation and antagonistic social media exchanges, the play modalities described in the New Games Foundation's 1976 *The New Games Book* feels aspirational:

> "Many can be played competitively… Others have no object, really, besides getting people together and enjoying each other…You can change the rules if you don't like them. So long as you all agree on what's fair, you can make the game into whatever you want it to be."
>
> (pp. 1–2)

Another concern I share with Soderman is that in the attempt to distinguish "good" games and play from their negative counterparts, prioritizing flow creates a dichotomy in which play is only positive when it's *useful*. Play is a complex set of behaviors. Parsing out productive play from within the broad spectrum of all its different manifestations is impossible. Further, as Soderman remarks, efforts to engineer and gamify play behaviors is "symptomatic of a broader culture that seeks to capture consumers in streams of profitable consumption" (p 21).

I am inspired by playful projects like Navild Acosta and Sosa's *Black Power Naps*. The project creates spa-like spaces in museums for those who are "undocumented, disabled, or at lower income levels" and are subsequently more likely to experience sleep deprivation, exhaustion and the health issues caused by life stressors. *Black Power Naps* doesn't ask museumgoers to work harder or to engage in productive recreation. But rather, it asks "How can we dream when we don't sleep?" (MoMA 2023) By recognizing the transformative power of rest and relaxation (and ostensibly play), *Black Power Naps* invite audiences to resist the hyper-capitalist status quo.

Designing a Taxonomy

I've spent a significant chunk of my career working as an in-gallery educator, and *Bloom's Taxonomy* is a common tool we use to design and evaluate interpretive programs. For those who are unfamiliar, *Bloom's* is a pyramidal hierarchy that identifies and orders types of learning according to complexity. The bottom (and simplest) tier of the pyramid describes the ability to define and recall concepts. As the hierarchy narrows, it describes increasingly more complex responses, like the ability to draw connections between ideas and to synthesize new ones.

While *Bloom's Taxonomy* may not be perfect, it's useful for defining, developing and measuring museum education initiatives. As such, I'd like to suggest we create a taxonomy for playful museum experiences. We know that play can manifest in many different ways (mimicry, cheating, roleplay, etc.). If we want to continue refining our skills as experience designers and championing the merits of playful museum experiences, we need to be more specific about the types of play we want to elicit from our audiences.

I'm researching this paradigm and it's still a work in progress. But preliminarily, I'd suggest that many of the play behaviors we see in museum games designed for children would go at the bottom of the pyramid. "Spot the difference," arbitrary time limits, and mazes are examples of a few. These activities are appropriate for young children, but they're pretty boring for anyone else.

In the middle sections of what I will cheekily call *Brin's Taxonomy*, we might see play behaviors associated with the ability to understand and follow rules. But perhaps the most valuable (and difficult to elicit) museum play behaviors is *modding*. Modding is a term borrowed from game studies that describes the process in which a user alters a game's source code to change its look, mechanics, or content. Examples of this practice include *Velvet-Strike*, a 2002 mod of the popular multiplayer online videogame *Counter-Strike*, in which artists replaced the game's bullets with anti-war graffiti. *Lose/Lose* by the artist Zach Gage is a mod of the arcade classic *Space Invaders*, but for every alien a player kills, a random file gets deleted from their PC's hard drive.

I position modding as an advanced museum player behavior because it requires audiences to understand rules and objectives and then make decisions about how they want to change them. I'm not suggesting that players literally manipulate digital source code within the gallery (although I like that idea!), but that they can recognize how systems work and successfully alter them, even if it means breaking them. Games excel at communicating complex systems and can be powerful tools for cultivating critical thinking skills — abilities that are crucial in an era of misinformation and AI-generated content.

There are many pervasive systems in our world worth scrutinizing, playing with, or otherwise modding. Take, for example, the hierarchical structure of museums themselves. Do they need to be that way? Or perhaps the proliferation of generative AI models. These models are "black boxes," meaning no one, not even the software developers themselves, fully understands how they work. Is that worth questioning?

Cultivating modding-type play behavior is far from simple. And it's risky. But it's worth doing.

If we seek to rehabilitate museums and address their historical shortcomings, we have an opportunity to revolutionize the way we incorporate games and play into these spaces. By moving our focus to playful design instead of games, adding depth to simplistic notions of flow and embracing a more nuanced taxonomy for play's transformative potential, we can equip visitors with the critical thinking skills and playful perspectives necessary to navigate our complex world. In doing so, we can help ensure that museums remain engaging, vital, and relevant institutions in the 21st century and beyond.

Notes

1 And not just humans. Mammals, birds, reptiles, amphibians, and more, have all been identified by biologists as engaging in play (Miller 2017).
2 Though not without critique, like Aarseth and Günzel (2019).
3 One interesting etymological tidbit that is germane to this discussion is that though ludus currently is used to describe games, to the ancient Romans, it had two meanings; a ludus could be a game, or it could be a school. This acknowledgement of the deep connection between play and learning is something that has been lost in modern Western

society, where "education versus entertainment" is a well-entrenched dialectic that gives birth to horrifying portmanteaus like "edutainment" by practitioners trying to bring both together. We'll talk more about this when we get to serious games later in the chapter.

References

Aarseth, Espen. 2019. Ludoforming: Changing Actual, Historical or Fictional Topographies into Ludic Topologies. In Aarseth, Espen, and Günzel, Stephan (Eds.). *Ludotopia: Spaces, Places and Territories in Computer Games*, 1st edn, vol. 63, p. 139.

Aarseth, Espen, and Günzel, Stephan. (Eds.). 2019. *Ludotopia: Spaces, Places and Territories in Computer Games*, Media Studies vol. 63. transcript Verlag.

Abt, Clark C. 1970. *Serious Games*. Viking Press.

Adorno, Theodor W. 1981. Valéry Proust Museum. In Adorno, Theodor W. *Prisms*, MIT Press. pp. 175–185.

Anila, Swarupa. 2017. Inclusion Requires Fracturing. *Journal of Museum Education*, vol. 42, no. 2, 2017, pp. 108–119.

Association of Children's Museums. 2024. About ACM. Retrieved May 21, 2024, from https://childrensmuseums.org/about/

Becker, Katrin. 2021. What's the Difference between Gamification, Serious Games, Educational Games, and Game-Based Learning? *Academia Letters*, Article 209, 2021, pp. 1–4.

Brin, Sarah. 2015. Games for Museums, Museums for Games: A Report on Arts Engagement for SFMOMA.

Caillois, Roger. 1961. *Man, Play, and Games*. Free Press of Glencoe.

Champion, Erik. 2011. *Playing with the Past*. Springer London.

Csikszentmihalyi, Mihalyi, and Hermanson, Kim. 1995. Intrinsic Motivation in Museums: Why Does One Wants to Learn? *Public Institutions for Personal Learning, Establishing a Research Agenda*, p. 75.

De Angeli, Daniela, and O'Neill, Eamonn. 2020. Towards a Gameful Museum: Empowering Museum Professionals via Playing and Making Games. *The International Journal of the Inclusive Museum*, vol. 13, no. 1, 2020, pp. 37–53.

de Koven, Bernard. 2013. *The Well-Played Game: A Player's Philosophy*. MIT Press.

Deterding, Sebastian. 2011. *Don't Play Games with Me! Promises and Pitfalls of Gameful Design*. Webdirections @media, London, May 27, 2011.

Deterding, Sebastian. 2015b. The Lens of Intrinsic Skill Atoms: A Method for Gameful Design. *Human–Computer Interaction*, vol. 30, nos. 3–4, 2015b, pp. 294–335.

Deterding, Sebastian, Dixon, Dan, Khaled, Rilla, and Nacke, Lennart. 2011. From Game Design Elements to Gamefulness: Defining "Gamification." *Proceedings of the 15th International Academic MindTrek Conference. 15th International Academic MindTrek Conference*.

Dichev, Christo, Dicheva, Darina, Angelova, Galia, and Agre, Gennady. 2015. From Gamification to Gameful Design and Gameful Experience in Learning. *Cybernetics and Information Technologies*, vol. 14, no. 4, 2015, pp. 91–92.

Djaouti, Damien, Alvarez, Julian, Jessel, Jean-Pierre, and Rampnoux, Olivier. 2011. Origins of Serious Games. In Minhua Ma, Andreas Oikonomou, and Lakhmi C. Jain (Eds.), *Serious Games and Edutainment Applications*. Springer London.

Economou, Maria., and Meintani, Elpiniki. 2011, May 26. Promising Beginnings? Evaluating Museum Mobile Phone Apps. *Re-Thinking Technology in Museums: Towards a New Understanding of People's Experience in Museums. Rethinking Technology in Museums 2011*. Limerick, Ireland.

Graetz, J.M. 1981. The Origin of Spacewar. *Creative Computing*, vol. 7, no. 8, 1981, p. 7.

Gurian, Elaine H. 2005. Threshold Fear. In S. MacLeod (Ed.), *Reshaping Museum Spaces: Architecture, Design, Exhibitions*. Routledge.

Hamari, Juho, Koivisto, Jonna, and Sarsa, Harri. 2014. Does Gamification Work? —A Literature Review of Empirical Studies on Gamification. *2014 47th Hawaii International Conference on System Sciences*, pp. 3025–3034.

Hingham Institute Study Group on Space Warfare. 1961. Theory of Computer Toys. quoted in Graetz, J.M. 1981, August. The Origin of Spacewar! *Creative Computing*, vol. 7, no. 8.

Holdgaard, Nanna, and Olesen, Anne R. 2023. Play in Museums: A Scoping Review. *Museum Management and Curatorship*, 2023, 1–24.

Huizinga, Johan. 1949. *Homo Ludens: A Study of the Play-Element in Culture*. Routledge & Kegan Paul Ltd.

Juul, Jesper 2003. The Game, the Player, the World. In M. Copier and Raessens (Eds.), *Level Up: Digital Games Research Conference Proceedings*, p. 10.

Kristiansen, Erik., and Moseley, Alex. 2018. Games in the Lobby: A Playful Approach. In Ross Parry, Ruth Page, Alex Moseley (Eds.), *Museum Thresholds: The Design and Media of Arrival*. Routledge, Taylor & Francis Group. pp. 175–188.

Landers, Richard N., Tondello, Gustavo F., Kappen, Dennis L., Collmus, Andrew B., Mekler, Elisa D., and Nacke, Lennart E. 2019. Defining Gameful Experience as a Psychological State Caused by Gameplay: Replacing the Term 'Gamefulness' with Three Distinct Constructs. *International Journal of Human Computer Studies*, vol. 127, 2019, pp. 81–94.

Lazzaro, Nicole 2004. Why We Play Games: Four Keys to More Emotion Without Story. *Game Developers Conference*.

Løvlie, Anders Sundnes, Karin Ryding, Jocelyn Spence, Paulina Rajkowska, Annika Waern, Tim Wray, Steve Benford, William Preston, and Emily Clare-Thorn .2021. Playing Games with Tito: Designing Hybrid Museum Experiences for Critical Play. *Journal on Computing and Cultural Heritage*, vol. 14, no. 2, 2021, pp. 1–26.

Luke, Jessica J., Nicole R. Rivera, Leonor A. Colbert & Catherine J. Scharon 2021. The Problem of Play in Children's Museums. *International Journal of Play*, vol. 10, no. 1, 2021, pp. 63–74.

Masek, Leland, and Stenros, Jaakko. 2021. The Meaning of Playfulness: A Review of the Contemporary Definitions of the Concept across Disciplines. *Eludamos: Journal for Computer Game Culture*, vol. 12, no. 1, 2021, pp. 13–37.

McGonigal, Jane. 2009, March 1. *Fiero! Museums as Happiness Engineers*. American Alliance of Museums.

McGonigal, Jane. 2010. Games Can Make a Better World. *TED*. https://janemcgonigal. com/2014/01/06/transcript-games-can-make-a-better-world/

McManus, Paulette M. 1989. Oh, Yes, They Do: How Museum Visitors Read Labels and Interact with Exhibit Texts. *Curator: The Museum Journal*, vol. 32, no. 3, 1989, pp. 174–189.

McMaster, Michael. 2023. *Videogames and the Public Museum: Six Months Behind the Scenes [PhD]*. RMIT University.

MFABoston. 2024. PLEASE… (2008). MFABoston. Retrieved August 9, 2024, from https://collections.mfa.org/objects/555077/please;jsessionid=7BA60BA4242C1101167 D27E2C9A232FC

Miller, Lance J. 2017. Creating a Common Terminology for Play Behavior to Increase Cross-Disciplinary Research. *Learning & Behavior*, vol. 45, no. 4, 2017, pp. 330–334.

Mitchell, Robert, Schuster, Lisa, and Drennan, Judy 2017. Understanding How Gamification Influences Behaviour in Social Marketing. *Australasian Marketing Journal*, vol. 25, no. 1, 2017, pp. 12–19.

MoMA. 2023. Black Power Naps La Biblioteca Is Open. *Moma.Org*. https://www.moma.org/calendar/exhibitions/5551

Morard, Simon, Sanchez, Eric, and Bonnat, Catherine 2023. Museum Games and Personal Epistemology: A Study on Students' Critical Thinking with a Mixed Reality Game. *International Journal of Serious Games*, vol. 10, no. 4, 2023, pp. 131–151.

Nietzsche, Friedrich. 1990. *The Twilight of the Idols and the Anti-Christ: Or How to Philosophize with a Hammer* (M. Tanner, Ed.; R.J. Hollingdale, Trans.; Reissue edition). Penguin Classics.

Papert, Seymour. 1998. Does Easy Do It? Children, Games, and Learning. *Game Developer*, June, 1988.

Parry, Caroline. 2020. Play Time. *Museums Journal*, vol. 120, no. 3, 2020, pp. 26–31.

Pletcher, Kellian. 2021. Personal communication, 2021.

Robertson, Margaret. 2010. Can't Play, Won't Play. Hide and Seek. https://www.hideandseek.net/2010/10/06/cant-play-wont-play/

Rodley, Ed. 2011, July 1. Gaming the Museum – Separating Fad from Function – Part Three of? *Thinking about Museums*. https://thinkingaboutmuseums.com/2011/07/01/gaming-the-museum-separating-fad-from-function-part-three-of/

Rodley, Ed. 2014, October 9. How to View Critics Telling You How to View Art in a Museum. *Thinking about Museums*.

Rodley, Ed. 2018, March 5. Peeling the Onion, Part One: Gamification. *Thinking about Museums*. https://thinkingaboutmuseums.com/2018/03/05/peeling-the-onion-of-gamification-part-one/

Ryding, Karin. 2020. The Silent Conversation: Designing for Introspection and Social Play in Art Museums. *Proceedings of the 2020 CHI Conference on Human Factors in Computing Systems*, pp. 1–10.

Sailer, Michael, Hense, Jan Ulrich, Mayr, Sarah K., and Mandl, Heinz. 2017. How Gamification Motivates: An Experimental Study of the Effects of Specific Game Design Elements on Psychological Need Satisfaction. *Computers in Human Behavior*, vol. 69, 2017, pp. 371–380.

Sayre, Richard, (2009). personal communication.

Science Museum (2023). Launchball. https://sciencemuseum.org.uk/launchpad/launchball/

Schuurman, Paul. 2017. Models of War 1770–1830: The Birth of Wargames and the Trade-Off between Realism and Simplicity. *History of European Ideas*, vol. 43, no. 5, 2017, pp. 442–455.

Sicart, Miguel. 2014. Play *Matters*. The MIT Press.

Silverstein, Nina M., Garcia, Conrad, and Landis, Abraham L. 2001. Museums and Aging: Reflections on the Aging Visitor, Volunteer, and Employee. *The Journal of Museum Education*, vol. 26, no. 1, 2001, pp. 3–7.

Soderman, Braxton. 2021. Against *F*low: Video *G*ames and the *F*lowing *S*ubject. The MIT Press.

Stenros, Jaakko 2015. Behind Games: Playful Mindsets and Transformative Practices. In S.P. Walz & S. Deterding (Eds.), *The Gameful World*. The MIT Press, pp. 201–222.

Stenros, Jaakko 2015. *Playfulness, Play, and Games. A Constructionist Ludology Approach*. University of Tampere, p. 182.

Stenros, Jaakko, and Montola, Markus. 2024. *The Rule Book: The Building Blocks of Games*. The MIT Press.

Sutton-Smith, Brian. 1997. *The Ambiguity of Play*. Harvard University Press.

Sweetser, Penelope, and Wyeth, Peta. 2005. GameFlow: A Model for Evaluating Player Enjoyment in Games. *ACM Computers in Entertainment*, vol. 3, no. 3, 2005, pp. 1–24.

Taheri, Babak, and Jafari, Aliakbar. 2012. Museums as Playful Venues in the Leisure Society. In Richard Sharpley & Philip Stone (Eds.), *The Contemporary Tourist Experience: Concepts and Consequences*. Routledge, p. 206.

Takatalo, Jari, Jukka Häkkinen, Jyrki Kaistinen, and Göte Nyman. 2010. Presence, Involvement, and Flow in Digital Games. In R. Bernhaupt (Ed.), *Evaluating User Experience in Games*. Springer Verlag, pp. 23–46.

Tekinbaş, Katie. Salen, and Zimmerman, Eric. 2003. *Rules of Play: Game Design Fundamentals*. MIT Press, p. 688.

Tisdal, Cary. 2006. *Remedial Evaluation of Star Wars: Where Science Meets Imagination* (0307875). Tisdal Consulting.

Wakkary, Ron, and Marek Hatala. 2007. Situated Play in a Tangible Interface and Adaptive Audio Museum Guide. *Personal and Ubiquitous Computing*, 11, 2007, pp. 189–190.

Zichermann, Gabe. 2011. The Purpose of Gamification—O'Reilly Radar. Retrieved June 9, 2024, from https://radar.oreilly.com/2011/04/gamification-purpose-marketing.html

Zimmerman, Eric. 2015. Manifesto for a Ludic Century. In S.P. Walz and S. Deterding (Eds.), *The Gameful World*. The MIT Press, p. 21.

6 Putting Together the Pieces of Playful Engagement

So, here we are, at the conclusion. You are about to step out of the magic circle you conjured up when you decided to read this book, a circle that consisted of you the reader, the object that is the book (in either its physical or digital form), and the interaction alibi of reading a professional book to develop your practice. The fact that you made it this far tells me that your intrinsic motivation was coupled with some focused attention. Hopefully, the reading was pleasurable in its own right, and there were times when the text spoke to your condition or experience and connected with you emotionally. The real test will begin when you put this book down. I hope you will have found ideas and concepts that are worth remembering and including in your practice as you go forth in your work. In short, I hope reading this book has been a playfully engaging experience.

When I started the journey that writing this book turned out to be, I felt convinced that there was something special about sensory immersion, emotional evocation, narrative transportation, and gameful participation. Trying to untangle them, understand them, and look at their intersections turned into a major research project. And as is so often the case, where I thought I was going—an exploration of these four discrete but related topics—turned into something deeper and more foundational: namely, trying to define what I meant by "engagement" and the framework of the magic circle of the museum visit. I wanted to have a way to understand engagement from the visitor's perspective, not my practitioner's one, and to be able to describe the magic of the museum visits I've witnessed and experienced so many times in my own life.

If we take the position that playful engagement is an intrinsically motivated process in which a person directs their conscious, focused attention to a satisfying experience which triggers an emotional response, leads to the creation or reinforcement of a memory, and influences their behavior afterward, then it follows that the concepts of sensory immersion, emotional evocation, narrative transportation, and gameful participation are useful concepts because they help us help visitors achieve this state, and their beneficial effects often synergize.

Sensory immersion, that sense of embodied presence, causes us to pay more attention to our surroundings, and we therefore experience them more richly and are more likely to remember them. Emotional evocation increases the

DOI: 10.4324/9781032638690-6

memorability of experiences by creating emotionally satisfying moments. Narrative transportation leverages our predisposition to make experiences into narratives in order to help us remember things. And finally, gameful participation provides a scaffold to encourage playfulness, our intrinsic motivation to engage in play in order to feel the satisfying sense of personal triumph and increased mastery that comes from challenging ourselves to do something that might be beyond our capabilities.

As you have seen many times in the previous chapters, these four concepts rarely appear in isolation. Instead, they support and amplify each other, and while I hesitate to say that an ideal museum experience should include all four, I do believe that the transformative moments, the really numinous ones that people report having and remembering decades later, usually include at least three. Carne y Arena, though it is described as an "immersive" experience, relies heavily on the three other concepts to achieve its effect on participants. The Museum of Broken Relationships is deeply emotional because of the storytelling around the objects on display. And the list goes on…

So, look around at the organizations you work with or for. If you were able to rebuild them from scratch to create a magic circle of playful engagement, what would you do? What kind of interactions alibis would you develop to give visitors the confidence to do things they didn't even know they could? Knowing what you know now about sensory immersion, how might you build environments that made visitors acutely aware of themselves and the space around them? And having primed them thus, how might you encourage them to deeper levels of absorption, saturation, and even overflow? Understanding the primacy of our emotional responses to stimuli, how might you center emotion in your planning? Knowing how much we rely on narrative to structure our inner and outer worlds, what kinds of stories might you want to tell? And lastly, knowing how essential playfulness is to cultivate and to exercise, particularly as we grow older, what kinds of experiences might you design to let visitors gamefully participate in your work?

In short, it's a great time to be an experience designer because we have learned so much about how human beings operate in their minds and bodies, in the world, and in society. On top of that, there is so much creative foment happening in the world, both in our particular corner, but more importantly out in the wild, in a bewildering variety of space and places. There is growing awareness that audiences for cultural experiences need more than just access to content. They need to be treated as complete people, with intellectual, emotional, and physical needs that can and should be addressed through careful design. So, I will end as I began, with Voltaire. Candide said to his friends, "Allons mes amis, il faut cultiver nos jardins." "Come friends, we must tend to our gardens." I don't take that admonition lightly, but share Adam Gopnik's interpretation of the statement:

By 'garden' Voltaire meant a garden, not a field—not the land and task to which we are chained by nature but the better place we build by love. The force of that last great injunction, "We must cultivate our garden," is that our responsibility is local, and concentrated on immediate action.

(Gopnik 2005)

You have the opportunity to build these better places with love. I look forward to seeing what you make of your gardens!

Reference

Gopnik, Adam. 2005, February 27. *Voltaire's Garden, with Principles*. The New Yorker.

Index